Religion Between Commercialization and Political Trade-offs

The Case of Islam

Raphael Israeli

Strategic Book Publishing
www.sbpra.com

For more information about special discounts for bulk purchasers, please contact Strategic Book Publishing Special Sales at bookorder@ sbpra.net.

ISBN: 978-1-68235-963-1

CONTENTS

Apologia and Acknowledgments

Much writing and many statements by politicians, clerics, merchants and scholars, and no less international gatherings that have been seeking scholarly legitimacy, propaganda gain, political advantage, an innovative pastime or just financial sustenance, have been currently churned out, mostly geared to demonstrate that wide and abusive usage has been made of religion and its symbols, taking advantage of the innocence and ignorance of their rank and file followers, to make material gains; worse, religion has been used to justify or delegitimize commercial deals or political demarches that would otherwise be shunned and disqualified as wrong, illegal, immoral, indecent or repulsive. Most of those episodes have been treated in monetary terms, evaluating their benefits or drawbacks both in material terms and with regard to their misuse of religion to laud or condemn their utility to society, humanity or faith. But the political, social, moral and internationally disruptive effects of those misdeeds have been usually and dismissively sidetracked and relegated to secondary planes of attention and discussion.

It is therefore the intention of this volume not only to point to the nitty gritty real commercialization that exists in all religions, specifically in Islam, but also draw attention to the much wider worldwide significance of "commercialization" of religion, going back to the original meaning of the word as the process of the *quid pro quo* exchange between two or more parties, not only of goods and money, as commerce suggests, but referring to the "trade" synonym of the word, which has generated "to trade", "to trade off" one substance or essence for another, not necessarily from the pecuniary or material world. In other words, not only goods and money can be traded off or commercialized, but also, political interests; for example: one country trading off to another the right to fish in its territorial waters, in return for recognition by that trading partner of its own territorial integrity, historical narrative or its interpretation of some vague idea or principle.

****

In addition to my usual indebtedness to my home base at the Truman Institute for the Advancement of Peace at the Hebrew University in Jerusalem, I have this time to stress that the idea of this volume derives directly from my participation at the Vienna University-induced and convened Symposium on Commercialisation of Religion, held in September, 2023, at Nicosia University, organized by my esteemed colleagues Ednan Aslan and Areti Demosthenous and their legions of devoted aides. To them and to the many colleagues who animated the vivid discussions during that three-day conference, I owe my gratitude.

Raphael Israeli,
Hebrew University, Jerusalem,
Fall-Winter 2023

Introduction

What is the Significance of Commercialization?

Commerce, or trade, is by definition a bi- or multi-partite exchange of goods and other assets. Individuals, corporations and countries exchange goods, in buying and selling deals, in return for cash or other material assets. But when it comes to trading in ideas, or interests when conceding political or non-substantive assets like interest, reputation or prestige, accommodating statements or public support for one policy or another of other countries, we call that diplomacy or political exchange or foreign policy. Except when a country or organization, or entity, resolves to enhance its own prestige or reputation by releasing, launching or reinforcing a certain policy or belief, we call that propaganda (or use the euphemism "information" for that same purpose when it is intended internally). But all the same, when one of those tracks is embraced by any state or organization in the process lauding, degrading, demeaning or abusing a religious principle, we can view that as a "commercialization" of religion, i.e. the trade-off of something for religion in order to attain other, purposeful or incidental objectives. Take for example the October 7 at dawn rampage of the Hamas, a Palestinian affiliate of the Muslim Brothers which specializes in hunting and murdering Jews, similar to the Nazi hunters who collected Jews all over Europe and then herded them to their death camps in Europe. Just like the Nazis, they erected an entire ideological structure in the form of a *fatwa* (religious verdict[1]). That means that when a great and recognized cleric, like Khomeini's fatwa against Rushdi in 1989 declared his death it obtained on all Muslims; now Dr Mahmud al- Shajrawi, a Palestinian cleric in the Diaspora who termed as "splendid" the slaughter of 1,300 Jews, including entire Jewish families with their babies and their elderly, because their "blood was permitted", in Palestine and everywhere else, one day after the Hamas perpetrated on October 7, 2023, the horror of murdering them for the "sin" of being innocent Jewish civilians in peaceful villages east of Gaza, and led 230 of them, including babies and elderly as hostages to Gaza, thus lending legitimacy to their crimes, and posing a challenge to the Nazis as their most identical competitors.

Hence the necessity to expand the meaning of commercialization to include the exchange or trade off of anything that is not concrete and measurable while getting in return, either similarly vague assets or a material and substantive *quid pro quo*. Take the example of a Jewish boy who goes to a Catholic school and attends a class when the regional bishop shows up waving a $100 bill in his hand and urging the kids to give the right answer to his question and get the cash in reward. The question was: Who was the greatest man in history? But the Jewish boy alone gave the right answer: Jesus Christ. The wondering Bishop paid the cash but inquired why did the Jewish boy render this answer and did not mention instead Moses; but the boy responded coolly: Moses is Moses and business is business. In this comic situation, there was commercialization of religion: the Jewish boy made a business deal, in spite of his true beliefs, and the bishop gained in return a sense of dominance and superiority of his faith, at the same time giving an educational lesson to the school children of his diocese.

"Religiosity", meaning affectation of religion when the purpose

---

[1] O the next day, October 8, the fatwa was published in Channel TV al-Quds Today, of the Islamic Jihad in Gaza

is not commercialization of the true faith, because it only intends to affect religion to gain another objective. In some of its aspects commercialization then meets globalization since it aims, by definition, to spread its tentacles worldwide, with the aid of commercial means, like the pecuniarization of abstract and awe-inspiring religious beliefs into cash generating goods. We propose to explore here, for example, these two angles as they come to play by the Muslim-Brother inclined Hamas Movement, which came into the open during the First Palestinian *Intifadah* of 1987-90, and gained momentum in the wake of the Hamas *coup* in Gaza in 2007, which signaled its separation from and rivalry with the Palestinian Authority in the West Bank of Jordan. As its power crystallized and firmed up, Hamas, capitalizing on the fact that it spoke radical Islam, to which many Palestinians of the West Bank were committed, and being supported in that endeavor by other radical and revolutionary Muslims, notwithstanding their Shi'ite convictions (like Iran and Hizbullah in Lebanon), the Hamas leadership, both territorial in Gaza and global (based in Qatar and roving around the Arab and Islamic worlds), has openly challenged the PA administration and seeks to replace it. *Inter alia,* it has invoked the unifying symbol of Jerusalem, - *al Quds* and the first *Qiblah* in Islam, with its Pearl in the Crown- the Aqsa Mosque, the very location from which the Prophet of Islam had ascended to Heaven *(Mi'raj)* to meet with the former prophets and the angels) after he had effected his mysterious nightly journey (*Isra'*) from Mecca aboard his wondrous flying al-Burak. Jerusalem was made a tool by the Hamas to not merely rival the PA and the Fatah rule in the West Bank, but especially to indicate that unlike the "ineffective and submissive PA" and its aborted Oslo Process, the Hamas not only rejected any talks, negotiations or agreements with Israel, and vowed to battle against it "until victory", but it was also wielding a formidable missile and rocket-making capacity which imposed terror on the Zionists.

The strong Islamic Movement, which in Israel is headed by

Sheikh Ra'id Salah[2], an avowed branch, like the Hamas, of the Muslim Brotherhood, together with the Hamas activists in Gaza and East Jerusalem, not only supports and propagates the Hamas ideas in Israel and East Jerusalem, but acts energetically and also plays a dominant role in their commercialization within the Aqsa Compound and around it, thus playing the anti-Jewish sentiment in Islam and the anti-Israel and anti-Zionist instinct in Palestinian and Arab nationalism in order to mobilize them against the Jewish state. Sheikh Ra'id has been personally committed to this goal by his endeavor to drag the entire Muslim world into this scheme, raising money in Islamic countries such as Turkey, Indonesia and Malaysia which have no direct involvement in the Israeli-Arab dispute, while simultaneously arousing among Israeli Arabs the memories of their *Nakbah*, delegitimizing Israel's existence as in the Hamas discourse, attempting to revive the hundreds of lost Arab villages in Palestine in 1948, and manipulating the symbol of al-Aqsa by falsely "alerting the world of Islam of its impending undermining and destruction by the Israelis". Unless the Israelis are hopelessly impotent, the past half century of first the attempt to burn that monument in 1968 and then to undermine it to its ruin ever since, have so far ended in the full burgeoning of the mosque and the continuous growth of its masses of Muslim worshippers. Hamas and its supporters, inside Israel and Palestine as well as within the purview of the Islamic world, have been scheming by various avenues, some traditional and some recently in vogue, to diversify their ways of globalization, notably by making use of the group of the 57 Muslim Nations within the UN (almost a third of the total membership) and the Organization of Islamic Cooperation (OIC) to universalize and commercialize the many usages of Islam to attain their goals, resorting at various times, in various

---

[2] See R. Israeli. *The Templars of Islam: Ra'id Salah and the Islamic Radicalism and Political Violence*, Vallentine and Mitchell, 2008, London.

places and in various volumes to either finding solace in the glory of the unifying *Umma* and the Caliphate, or seeking consolation in borrowing from the new global trends of "wokeism" and "zombeism", to extract benefit from victimization. Naturally, widening as far as possible under the Muslim umbrella one's field of action, thus recruiting to the cause as large a proportion as possible of the worldwide Muslim population of over a billion and a half, to focus its attention on the Palestinian-Zionist, the Israeli- Arab and the Islamic-Jewish frictions and disputes, is certain to increase worldwide Islamic solidarity in this respect, as the May-June 2023 episode of the scuttling of Israel's participation in the FIFA *Mundialito* has demonstrated, caused by Muslim Indonesia's refusal to host Israel in the games, and the removal of the events to Argentina, where Israel made it to the half finals, much to Arab and Muslim frustration.

The Muslim Field of the Game in Globalism

Given that he goal of globalism is the elimination of national states and cultures and the transformation of Western states into a single neutral territory with unlimited financial, material and intellectual resources, then the human being in such system is doomed to turn into a cultureless, ignorant and thoughtless consumer whose mind is filled with all sorts of fantasies and uprooted concepts, that do not relate to any core of principles, ideas, convictions or traditions, nor are they anchored in any system of thoughts or beliefs. Human society (or societies) will then be guided not by reason, law, principles, morality or religion, but solely by their spontaneous desires and emotions, and in fact might turn into pets, with their fate depending entirely on the desires and whims of their owners, not much different from the robots that the Artificial Intelligence, and the zombies that the Z movies have been suggesting (threatening) to saturate our streets with. The universal Islamic faith and community (*Ummah*) does not recognize the division of the Believers into nation-states, and is consistently backed and nourished by practically all radical movements of Muslims who all aspire to the revival of the defunct Caliphate, to govern the entire Ummah, under one Caliph, as under the glorious Muslim empires of the Umayyads, the Abbasids, the Seljuks, the Samanids, the Timurids, the Ottomans and the Mughals, which would ultimately rule the entire world, only concurs with this aspect of globalization, but the agreement ends there, while all other points of contingency are vastly diverse, as the recent rise and dissolution of ISIS in Raq'a, northern Syria, in 2014-6, under the hostile impact of Western powers, has illustrated. Radical Muslim movements, locked between their universal ambition for a Caliphate on the one hand, so as to unify the Ummah, and for world empire on the other, with a view of fulfilling the quest of Islamizing the entire universe, have evolved on all continents, including in the lands of the Western Infidels, into centrist- essentialist blocs which occupy the front lines in all of the geographical, demographic and religious respects, for they are treated as the radical, aggressive, preponderant, Jihadi or "Islamist" trend in their lands of asylum; though also, for world Islam, as the peripheral blocs where all those aspects are viewed and experienced marginally, and therefore are regarded as the moderate, marginal, "Westernized", pragmatic and sociable Islam. But the real distinction between them is not essential or doctrinal, for both are nourished by the same sources: the Five Arkan (Shahada, Prayer, Fast, Alms and Pilgrimage) and the Five Usul a-Din: (Qur'an, Sunna, Qyas, Ijma', 'Urf), but only on the degree of their zealotry, the extent of their commitment and depth of practice, like the differences which distinguish between cadres of a political party, who are obligated around the clock, full-time, to fulfill the requirements of their faction with the utmost devotion, as their main preoccupation, and the rank-and -file, who vote for the same party and devote their thoughts to it on the eve of the elections, but other than that their daily thoughts go to their business, family or other civic obligations. And yet, they all consider themselves, and are viewed by others, as devotees of the same, Labor, Democratic or Republican Party. How the vast and varied landscape of Islam, with its over 1,5 billion population, spread over 57 Muslim-majority countries spanning the continents of Asia and Africa, and maintaining a minority presence in practically all countries in the world, manages to align itself on the side of the center or the periphery, the radical or the pragmatic, the militant or the quietist, that is what we are venturing to decipher, and detach its various codes of functioning in various parts of the world, under different regimes, conditions and circumstances. In each instance, we shall try to identify the mode of operation, which at times is impacted by general world trends, such as globalism and wokeism, or is subjected to the whims of a particular ruler, as to cave in to his demands for either sustaining radical Islam (like Qatar's Prince or ISIS's Caliph), or for combating it (like Egypt's President). For example, the trend towards wokeism among Black Americans is borrowed by various Muslim groups worldwide, like the Arabs in Israel, to claim that their victimhood justifies all means, including terrorism, to redress the wrong done to them while as the victims they are ipso facto exonerated from any blame; and radical Muslim Jihadis like the Boko Haram in West Africa and the Taliban in Afghanistan who argue that globalism renders the Islamic Jihad a universally justified global measure of retaliation against evil and injustice meted out to them either by their own domestic Islamic rulers or by the Infidels ruling them in their own lands during colonization, and their new refuge of immigration in the Western world.

The wide array of Muslim populations in the world, which nourishes, inter alia, the consistent growth of radical groupings and movements on every continent, mostly under the denomination of the Muslim Brothers or in affiliation with it, extends throughout the vast spaces of Asia and Africa, but also increasingly, among Muslim migrant populations since the middle of the 20th Century, first as guest workers to fill in the large human power deficiencies occasioned by W W II, and then as refugees, either real escapees from political or criminal persecution, or work seekers, or simple adventurers, or ideological Jihadists in search of expanding Islam, or criminal fugitives from their own regimes, or finally in search of improving their lot in the Western standard of living. In Israel, the situation is different inasmuch as a minority of its Muslim Arabs remained as natives of the land of Palestine when the state was founded in 1948, amidst war and displacement, where they have continually constituted ca 20% of the population, growing in numbers from 130,000 in 1948 to 10-12 fold that figure (ca 1,5 million) in 2022. But their impact, threat, friction, discontent and challenge to the Jewish majority and Zionist establishment are no different from those of other Muslim minorities in the world, except that in the Jewish state, they loom larger due to their high rate of 20%; to their militancy emanating from the direct conflict of their Palestinian people with their Israeli state, and especially emanating from their sentiment that they cannot relinquish their ambition to retrieve their lost majority by repatriating their refugees and revert to rule the land which they regard as theirs, or at the very least to be taken in as equal partners on its sovereignty in a bi-national state. Moreover, they believe that those aspirations are not only natural and historically anchored in the fact they had constituted the majority in Palestine before Israel was born, but that the Jewish state itself constitutes a tiny minority of 8 million Jews in the midst of over the 350 million Arabs (mostly Muslims) distributed in some 22 Arab countries in the Middle East and North Africa (MENA), and backed by 1,5 billion Muslims, in 57 Muslim nations, in the surrounding countries of Asia and Africa. They are at fault, however, like most of the rest of the world (many unaware Israelis included) in considering Judaism solely as a religion, often paralleling it with Islam and Christianity, which leads to their contention that Jews are not a nation and therefore they do not deserve a state (as claimed in article 20 of the PLO National Charter). They elect to disregard the fact that Israel was created by world Jewry, not Judaism, the parallel of other ethnic appellations (like French, Arab, Palestinian etc.). In this regard, they do not differ from the Druze or Assyrian minorities in the Middle East, which combine their ethnicity with their religion as one, and do not inter-marry with others in order to prevent assimilation. In our contemporary world, where the great powers are arrayed against one another: Americans against Russians and Chinese, while the latter are allied with Shi'ite Muslims (Iran); radical Muslims, both Sunnite and Shi'ite, are arraying their forces, under the cover of the unrelenting worldwide Islamic globalism, to launch a decisive war against Israel and Jewry, while the West is busy with the Ukraine; and Western ideas of liberalism and democracy are being eroded under the submerging waves of Islamic triumphalism, strange bed-fellows are wedded together and create a huge confusion in international affairs. For the purpose of reviving the universal Islamic Caliphate, as represented by the Muslim Brothers and their radical affiliates, radical Muslims, including the Hamas Movement which divides the Palestinian people, tries precisely to subsume under its roof in the future the Islamized Jewish state and the scattered Jewish minorities into their Muslim-ruled countries, but also to gnaw at the West's culture, hegemony and political existence until its *submission* (as Houellebecq 's novel suggests) . That is the reason why, unlike the PLO which officially rules the Palestinians in the West Bank of Jordan under the Palestinian Authority (PA), the Hamas leadership which has taken over the Gaza Strip since 2007, not only refuses to recognize Oslo, negotiate with Israel and deal with it, but clearly aspires to seize the entire and total leadership of the Palestinians, arguing, not without justification that they represent the majority of their people, as the elections of 2006, the last so far, had clearly demonstrated.

There are many other major sources, uses and means of commercialization in Islam, in addition to those directly emanating from the Pillars of Islam or associated with them, while at the same time facilitating the rapid expansion of Islam by trade and more rapid than before the rate of conversion to Islam of trade partners have been: dhimmitude that is enjoined in the Qur'an for subjugating the Scriptuaries (the *Ahl al-Kitab,* essentially Christians and Jews) under the rule of Islam; and the institution of the *Waqf* (holy Endowment), both of which had been important actors for activating the flow of money and goods in Islamdom, and expanding commerce and globalization in Islamic lands as a tool of extending the scope of the *Ummah* from territoriality, *da'wa* and governability into the economic domain.

a. **Dhimmitude,** (the term was coined in European languages by Bat Ye'or, in her numerous works on Christian and Jewish communities under Islam)[3] denominates the vast minorities of Christians and Jews who were subjugated to Islamic rule as the conquering Islamic armies were advancing during the process of conquest of Islam both in the first centuries of the Islamic expansion in the Middle East, North Africa, Central Asia, the Indian Subcontinent and the Iberian Peninsula (7th to 15th Centuries), and in the second wave of this expansion in the Balkans, Black Africa and Malay Asia(13th- 19th Centuries). While the occupied Christians, mainly in the Middle East and Anatolia, were to a great extent Islamized, exterminated or forced to move to other existing Christian countries, the smaller Jewish exiles, who had nowhere else to go, had been compelled to endure the *Shari'a*-imposed status of *dhimma* ("protection") which tagged them as "humiliated" and inherently prone to misery, as were the few Christians who remained under

---

[3] Notably, *The Dhimmi,* Fairleigh Dickinson University Press, Madison, 1985, translated into several languages

Islamic occupation to this day. Their inferior status which was symbolized and perennialized by the mandatory payment of the poll tax (*jizyah*) and by the exaction of many restrictions on their living, their cult, their dress, professions, and occupations, often leading them to perform the most impure works in society like tannery, burial of the death and the like, which did not immunize them nonetheless from periodic pogroms and acts of persecution, oppression and pogroms. This state of affairs, while customarily confining Jews (and Christians) under Islam to permanent misery and danger, held some promise nonetheless for some individuals whose individual talent and knowhow, supported by the common Muslim reluctance and contempt to practice matters of usury, to gain distinction in commerce, local and international, in diplomacy due to their mastery of some European languages and even in the high reaches of government in spite of their official reputation as "untrustworthy", cunning and prone to conspiracy and treason. Nonetheless, their contribution to commerce, the development of the Islamic economy and as go-betweens Islamdom and the Christian world was quite reputed in Istanbul (the Capital of the Ottoman Empire), In Monastir (in the Balkans)and in Fes and Marrakesh (the alternate capitals of the North African dynasties).

b. **Waqf**- emanating from *waqafa* (to stop, pause or block) is a Muslim concept, based on the popular response to the Abbasid Dynasty (750-1258) when it used to expropriate private property for the benefit of the public treasury, and many found refuge in the waqf (holy endowment) to block that measure and safeguard their property within their families or dedicate it to some charitable purpose[4]. There are several types of endowments, but all are governed by the Ministry of Awqaf due to the religious nature of this procedure and under the adjudication of religious law (shari'a) and religious courts. Due to the modern tax law that was adopted in most Muslim countries, the vast waqf sector was in fact depriving the authorities from a large portion of their income, therefore significant reforms were adopted to restrain the dent the waqf made on the public treasury. The main point for our purpose is the large part of this religious financial device in escaping the tax system of the country, thereby contributing to obscure deals and black market which necessarily impact the overall economic situation of the country.

According to Israeli blogger for the *Times of Israel*, Alexander Maistrovoy [5], who felt Israel was experiencing such a process amidst its struggle to reform its legal system to avoid the trappings of globalism, any human being in such system is doomed to turn into an infantile, ignorant and thoughtless consumer whose mind is filled with all sorts of ridiculous fantasies, such as "reptilian people," "zombie apocalypse," New Age beliefs" and "flat earth", wrote:

> …Under the pretext of "global warming" or "climate change," the economies of the leading states, their energy resources and modern agriculture are being destroyed. Under the pretext of "multiculturalism, equal rights for minorities and the rescue of refugees," ethnic substitution of entire nations is taking place. Under the pretext

---

[4] See Bruce Lawrence, "Waqf". In Keith Crim, *Abingdon Dictionary of Living Religions,* Nashville, 1981, p.802.

[5] Alexander Maistrovoy, "Revolution of Tanks'? Having Lost in Israel, Globalists Face a Dangerous Precedent: With the Stakes so High, will the Globalists turn to Violent Extremes?, *Times of Israel, Blogs, February 13, 2023.*

of "fighting racism, imperialism and white supremacy," globalists carry out a total destruction of the national history of Western states with their unique philosophies and cultures, as well as their brilliant scientific achievements, literature and architecture. Under the pretext of "equality of sexual rights of minorities," psychophysical anomalies are presented as the highest value, and the institution of the family and human psychology are being destroyed. Art becomes a disgusting caricature of itself. Monotheistic religions are being replaced by ridiculous pagan cults, and occult and esoteric practices. Young minds are subjected to sophisticated brainwashing that even the Soviet system did not know of. Finally, under the pretext of protecting democracy, cultural totalitarianism is established, in which "dissenters" are pushed to the periphery of public and political life, and declared racists, fascists or mentally ill people. The "fourth beast, dreadful and terrible, and strong exceedingly" of prophet Daniel, as if resurrected from the dark depths, has come into the world. All sorts of manipulations are used to take over the world, including an alliance between the "progressives" with their destructive agenda and "Islamists", primarily the Muslim Brotherhood and their sponsors: Turkey and Qatar. There is a ruthless persecution of those who are trying to save their peoples from cultural destruction: first of all, Hungary and Poland, perhaps the last strongholds of Western civilization in the Old World. However, the main tool of the globalists is now the judicial system, which was perceived by the fathers of democracy, from Alexis de Tocqueville, Jeremy Bentham and John Stuart Mill to Thomas Jefferson and Benjamin Franklin, as the main pillar of democracy. The judicial institutions of Western countries have turned into supranational structures, often not controlled by anyone, a kind of closed elite "priesthood." Those who try to get in the way of globalism immediately become the object of legal persecution, supported by the media, academia and the highest officials. Trump in America, Netanyahu in Israel, Silvio Berlusconi and Matteo Salvini in Italy, Marine Le Pen in France, Alternative for Germany, Sebastian Kurz in Austria, Andrej Babiš in the Czech Republic — these are the most striking victims of the modern auto-da-fé. The accusations range from fraud, as in the cases of Trump, Netanyahu and Babiš, to "illegally keeping migrants on board a ship," as in the case of Matteo Salvini, and alleged sympathies for Nazis and fascists, as in the case of Giorgia Meloni and Netanyahu. In some cases, politicians get vindicated, as happened to Marine Le Pen. Even so, she surprisingly softened her position on migrants. In some cases, as happened to Kurz, they are forced to leave politics completely. Israel is a unique case where the most popular statesman, against whom four cases were initiated at once, managed to return to power thanks to the support of the society. Moreover, he gave carte blanche to his Minister of Justice to implement a judicial reform, that is to deprive the judicial caste of the exclusive status and unlimited powers. In doing so, he jeopardized all the privileges enjoyed by the judicial elite.

And he concludes that:

If the new government wins the battle in Israel, the "bad example" could be contagious. Globalists see this as a dangerous precedent. Globalists cannot allow any legitimate government of any country to disarm their "sacred establishment," to take away their main instrument of power from them. This is a war of life and death, and this is what we are seeing today: mass hysteria, calls for defiance and rebellion, intimidation with threats of collapse of democracy, civil war and destruction of the state, political liquidation of key right-wing politicians, as in the case of Aryeh Deri [the unseated powerful Minister of the Interior from the National Religious Party]...[6]. What has been a universal goal for the globalists to attain their stateless world, is for Muslim radicals a mere means to eliminate the solid structure of Western states, including Israel, in order to fill that void and enforce their Caliphal world system. But they both converge on the immediate common target of precipitating the intermediate anarchy that is essential for each to attain its ultimate goal. It is a little like the messianic concept in all three monotheistic religions: the Jewish Messiah from Davidic descent; A second return of Jesus Christ; and the return of the Hidden Imam. All are expected at any time, and the more they seem amiss on their promise to return in order to rescue humanity, the more imminent that miraculous feat is awaited. But unlike those messianic expectations which may remain in suspense *sine diem*, both globalists and radical Muslims seem poised to act, as they already do, to precipitate each its process of world redemption.

By its close to suicidal activity, consisting of literally suicidal attacks against Israel, and launching massive rocket attacks from Gaza against Israel, the Hamas, knowing that the Jewish state's reaction would be so devastating that it would have to beg for a cease fire to rescue itself from total ruin, it at the same time props up its association with other

---

[6] Ibid.

Iranian "progressists" and Sunnite Muslims like Turks and Qataris, to advance the cause of Russia and China in their quest to overwhelm Western, notably American, hegemony in the Middle East and the Pacific. For that purpose, they strive first at taking over the West Bank from the dwindling Palestinian Authority which the US has taken under its protective wings, and capitalizing on their popularity as the intrepid fighters against Israel, at inheriting the administrative power over all Palestinians West of the Jordan River from the aging Abu Mazen (Mahmud Abbas). For that, not only do they permanently incite all activist Palestinians to create unrest against Israel so as to keep it on its toes harassed, on permanent self-defense, apologetic and blamed by world opinion for its "racist aggression" against Palestinians in "occupied" Palestinian territories, in contravention of international law; but they also focus on Jerusalem and the Aqsa mosque, spreading fake calumnies against Israel's alleged "schemes" to undermine it and replace it by the Jewish Temple that had been ruined by the Romans in AD 70, and on which site had the invading and conquering Muslims in the 7th Century knowingly constructed their mosque, claiming that it "descended" all ready from Heaven. Focusing on Jerusalem and al-Aqsa mosque not only attracts the attention of the entire Muslim world but also "reminds" the Christian believers worldwide that the Jewish state is intent on destroying their holy places, of which Islam pretends to be the best protector. Ensuring Christianity as their allies, no one can then rescue the Jews from perdition once again.

All creeds which are characterized as "Institutional religions" according to C. K. Yang's typology[7], and possess a founder (real or imaginary), worshippers, a doctrinal text, prayer locations and other places of worship, and an elaborate and complex ritual, have by necessity developed over the years commercial networks, either institutionalized or via private enterprise, all benefiting from their

---

[7] C.K. Yang, *Religion in Chinese Society*, University of California, Berkeley, 1967.

universality, and more so from their omnipresent and claimed omniscient activity, and their masses of followers, al destined to hold the Believers under their grip and extract from them endless sums of cash and goods which fuel the commerce markets, local and international. This phenomenon is known in the Monotheistic faiths as the sumptuous and costly rituals in the Christian Church, especially the Eastern Orthodox; the Islamic elaborate ceremonies, festivals and frequent (often daily, and repeatedly so) implementation of religious obligations; and the Jewish worldwide prominence of fabulous synagogues and the eye-poking international trade in Judaica. Popular religions, like Hinduism, Buddhism, and some pagan native rituals, have also their exhibitive aspect of commercialization.

Viewed in this light (or obscurity for some), one can observe in Islamic daily life in East Jerusalem, and in the rest of Islamic villages and towns in the West Bank and Israel Proper, especially in holidays and other festive occasions, an endless cycle of not only anti—Israeli protests, demonstrations, processions, Palestinian banner waving, posters and videos, and hear speeches, sermons and incitement in local mosques, public places and events like Ramadan, the Land Day and religious and political assemblies which gather to mark the Israeli occupation of Islamic territories and holy places or the claimed Israeli threats to harm them. Usually these assemblies are accompanied by fairs where food and other amenities are displayed, selling religious memorabilia and propaganda materials and raising the Islamic morale by the very assembly of many other Muslims to reinforce the impression of the cumulative might of the Muslim Ummah and to instill the certainty that no enemy power can overwhelm it or tame it or force it into docility or submission. Suffice it to roam around Jerusalem, Nazareth or Nablus and Jenin market places in such occasions, to realize how commercialization, which by nature attracts more participants than worshippers among the common people, plays such a great role in Islam. Similarly, the continued, and by now routine purchase of *Islamica* (Qur'an books, prayer carpets, the erection of exquisite new and more sophisticated mosque structures in artistic architecture, which are evident in the entire Islamic environment within and around Israel, all singing the past glory of Islam and celebrating its coming revival. Perhaps to top it all, the commerce of arms, both internally by rebels and gangs and Islamic movements like the Hamas, and internationally where most resources of most poor Muslim countries are dedicated to armaments rather than to fight poverty, illness, misery and illiteracy, is evidence of the priority lent to armed struggle for the glory of Islam and its instrumentalization of radicalism and the power of arms in enhancing commercialization in the Islamic Middle East.

CHAPTER ONE

The Basics of Commercialization in Islam

It is easy to account for the commercial links that can and are associated to various aspects of Islamic rituals, exactly as they are in all live religions which cannot operate in the real world without an economic base which often forces them to commercialize or worse- to trade off- some of their sacrosanct religious beliefs and principles in order to survive economically; or by choosing between various interests; or even worse- as they purposely breach the rules when they hope to escape punishment or when their lust for gain beats their religious fervor. Banning all those bad thoughts for now, let us look at the most innocent basics of commercialization of Islam, and any other religion for that matter, addressing those related to the Five Pillars (Arkan) of the Faith: Shahada, Salat, Sawn, Zakat and Hajj, as a corridor to enter into the thick of the matter.

a. In connection with the core of belief, the *Shahadah,* one can associate the enormous expenditure, by both Muslim states and wealthy Muslim individuals to finance the expenditure for the worldwide range of *da'wa* both within Muslim countries in order to expand Islamic education and reinforce weakly and hesitant Believers who may be lured by modernizing ideas of freedom of thought; and especially in the growing Muslim diasporas in Europe, where the temptation to assimilate into the dominant local cultures can become irresistible among the young and the inexperienced migrant workers who, overwhelmed by their imperative to adapt, may drift away from their religious duties. For that purpose, not only Muslims mosques and Islamic cultural centers which benefit from the Western freedom of worship to expand their omnipresence, but the independent Muslim education networks in the West, most prominent of them being the Turkish *Fethullah Gulen* in America and the various branches of the Muslim Brothers and other Muslim associations worldwide, have been lavishly financed by the very Islamic countries that often forbid Christian missionary activity in the midst.

b. In the area of the second *Rukn – the Salat* (Prayer)which was probably borrowed from the preceding Judaic and Christian ritual, with some adaptations, which also necessitated a house of prayer (the Mosque or *Masjid)* a large art-and- industry of architectural styles, of Islamic architectural ornamentation and building patterns has widely contributed to the globalization of construction economy. Auxiliary sub-industries were also invented, elaborated over the years, like the manufacturing of magnificent Qur'an books, with splendid illustrations and a large international market throughout the Islamic world, especially prior to the advent of the printing industry which expanded this form of art from rare works for the wealthy and the powerful to a worldwide distribution as a basic necessity in every Muslim house. So it went with the prayer carpet industry which branched off from the art of rug making and weaving in Iran, Central Asia and some nomadic tribes in other areas of the Muslim world in Africa and Asia.

Maybe the most prolific religious tenet in terms of commercialization has been the fast (*sawm)* of the month of

Ramadan, due, paradoxically, to the fact that while that long, arduous and trying ordeal was intended as a period of spiritual reckoning and monastic abstention, it in fact became in the popular lore and custom the era of gluttony and unrestricted consumption of food, which often enhances food purchases in Muslim market places many fold, even among needy families which would rather borrow funds to provide for the artificial prosperity which Ramadan occasions, to compensate, as it were, for the long hours of deprivation during the fast from sunrise to sunset, especially when the lunar calendar RAMADAN coincides with the torridly hot and horridly long and dry summer days. Since it is recommended that Believers who miss fasting days due to unexpected reasons or circumstances must fill in the lost days after the holidays, the phenomenon of material over-consumption can be observed in certain segments of Islamic society throughout the year, among those who travel intentionally on Ramadan in order to use it to their own benefit as one of the allowed causes for skipping fast.

c. The paying of Alms (*Zakat*), which had been introduced as a kind of tax on the ancient congregation (*Ummah*) of Muslims, to provide for the maintenance of the community and administration of Arabia, to substitute for the loss of tribal support if and when a tribesman joined Islam by abandoning the protection of his clan and nuclear famil . In modern times, as new systems of progressive tax collection have been adopted in most Muslim states, *Zakat* which cannot be nominally abrogated due to its holy status as a *Rukn,* has changed its definition and usage and turned into a charity used by the local Islamic Association in each village or town or city, to provide for social and religious needs of the place.

d. Internationally and commercially there is nothing that promotes travelling, purchase of memorabilia and tourism in Arabia, the cradle of Islam, as the *Hajj* (pilgrimage to Mecca), which is recommended annually as in old days when the congregation of Believers was confined to the Arabian Peninsula, but required only once in a lifetime, by reason of both the large distances to journey to get to the holy place of Islam and the limited resources at the disposal of most populace. Only in recent decades, thanks to the rapid and cheaper means of transport and the various aid programs by the wealthy Muslim countries to the needy, has the pilgrimage become somewhat more affordable to the masses.

At any rate, the highly honorable title of Hajj that the pilgrim is conferred on upon his return home, brings respect and reputation to the entire rural or regional Muslim community which had pooled its resources to finance the new Hajj's journey, is still viewed as worthwhile enough for the entire community to strive and sacrifice for. In the boiling cauldron of the Middle East, especially in the context of the Arab-Israeli dispute which never goes to rest in spite of the many concocted "peace deals", this pressure cooker seems permanently on the verge of exploding. On the Jewish Day of Atonement (Yom Kippur) of September, 2023, as the steep streets of Haifa, Israel, were desert, with all worshippers filling the synagogues to capacity, and a respectful awe filling the hearts and weighing heavily on the conscience and recollections of the veterans of the Kippur 1973 War, while children were playfully cycling up and down the empty streets; a band of undaunted Arab youth from neighboring Arab villages erupted mounting noisy motorcycles and scooters, with a great demonstration of contempt and defiance, just apparently to impress with their surprise and thunderous apparition, and prove to the dismayed Jewish majority that its rule and its holiest festivals are of no consequence for them. Incidents of defiance and religious eye-poking like this had happened in other mixed cities of Israel, where while the Jewish majority in usually respectful of Arab-Muslim holidays (like Ramadan) of the minority (and so are customarily the Arabs of Jewish holidays), from time to time an eruption of Arab violence, as had happened in Acre several years back on Yom Kippur, or during the events of May 2021, when Jewish citizens and institutions were attacked in an Arab orgy of murder and arson against their Jewish fellow dwellers and neighbors of mixed cities like Acre, Jaffa, Haifa, Ramlah and Lod. Events have peaked a fortnight later, when during the last Jewish holiday of the Tabernacles closing the season of Fall, 2023, a genuine pogrom against 21 Jewish villages around Gaza were raided by Palestinian Arab-Muslims of the inhuman Hamas creed, who massacred in one day close to 1,500 innocent Israelis, including women, children, the elderly and youth in the midst of a pop music party in the open. Over 230 of them were taken hostage to Gaza to be exchanged for the thousands of Palestinian terrorists who were convicted for murders they had committed in Israel. Thus, both parts of the Palestinian people: the Arabs of Israel and the Hamas of Gaza found themselves revolting against the Jewish majority ruler of the country, though acting within two vastly different levels of cruelty and savagery.

Chapter Two
Criminality and Commercialization

This is clear that knowing Jewish holidays and their sensitivities, especially the iconic Yom Kippur for prayer, atonement and fast, just like its Muslim parallel, the Ramadan, the Arab youth who perpetrated their offense understood exactly what they were doing, and had no other purpose than poke the Jews in the eyes realizing that except for scorn, friction and violence they stood to gain something from their Jewish State that they demonstratively despised, loathed and resented. For them, comprehending the importance of Kippur in Jewish consciousness was another good reason to hurt the Jews deeper, because to cause them to ache was, and usually is, much more gratifying to the Arab perpetrators than any resulting chastisement that might be deterring. For them, to show defiance of the ruling Jewish majority was a heroic act of bravado that made them oblivious of the punishment it might bring. In short this was a calculated act of commercialization of religion, inasmuch as Yom Kippur was so high in the minds of the perpetrators that they reasoned that the potential retribution might be equally elevated, and nonetheless they committed it. More importantly: One may wonder why this kind of Pogrom on the part of the Arab minority in Israel, seems to run counter to the customary course of events, when it is the majority who usually outrages and massacres minorities, not the other was around. It seems that only in the case of religious fervor, where commercialization takes place, i.e. a religious quid-pro-quo is in view, that a religious reasoning overrides the others. So acted the Muslim terrorists in Europe and the West in recent years, and so are acting Arabs/Muslims in Israel during these events. Similarly act the Uyghurs in China (a tiny minority of 12 million vs 1,5 billion), and the dastardly demonstration of savagery that the Hamas exhibited in its simultaneous surprise attack on 22 Israeli villages when their inhabitants were still in their beds on October 7, 2023 and massacred in the aggregate close to 3,000 of them.

In another context, it is known that the rate of Arab/Muslim crime against other Muslim/Arabs within Israel has reached exorbitant rates, with both sides charging the government of Israel of responsibility, while much of the blame is NOT connected to "regular" crime involving material gain that can be fought and eradicated, but in built in long family traditions and can only be defeated by long term education and enforcement, provided the majority of the Arab population collaborate with the government to struggle against this phenomenon. All the elements of alienation and dissidence (political, national, religious and cultural) which constitute a virtual see- through curtain between Arabs and Jews in Israel, permitting free peeking and infiltrating across in both directions, but remains nonetheless a divider, are further punctuated by a variety of cultural and religious hurdles which are so deeply rooted as to become immutable, and with rare exceptions are curable and reversible by persuasion, training, education or indoctrination. For those deeply ingrained qualities or characteristics or modes of behavior which can go so far as shooting at a rival who won democratically an election campaign, due to the resistance of Arab societies to deep penetration of what are the values of democracy, which not only are impermeable to the pressure to change, like an illness or otherwise deplorable deficiency, but stand up positively as desirable and favorable to the creed and belief system of their adherents, or are at the very least expressive of their inner selves, convictions and nature, and therefore not in need of change. One of the most conspicuous of those mostly soft crimes, which for the most part neither involves holding illegal weapons nor belonging to "organized crime gangs" whom apologetic Arabs in Israel usually blame for the crime rate in their midst, which they can impute to Israeli police's impotence and to the refusal of the Israeli government to budget the necessary funds to resolve the problem. They also customarily argue that when the Israeli authorities wish to resolve any criminal or security problem committed by or against Jews, they do it instantly. But they refuse to recollect all the cases where police failed, for example the months it took to find the culprits who attacked Christian churches, or the criminal Jewish terrorists who burned to death a Palestinian family in the West Bank, until the suspected Jewish youth were submitted to the same physical pressures meted out to the Arabs by the *Shabak* security agency. Most of those crimes concern cultural deeply-ingrained family-related crimes, which the Arabs regard as their customs and civilization, and therefore they either belittle them or disregard them as insignificant, and in any case resent the state laws that criminalize them, as do the Muslim immigrants in Europe today. More worrying, however, is when they act against the enforcement of these laws, as part of their resistance to the "conversion therapy",[8] though in this domain of social progress there is much more openness among the young generation, except for the radical Muslims who cannot contemplate any secular law that discards the Holy Shari'a or the centennial customs.

A. Polygamy

Most Arab families in Israel, as in the majority of Arab countries, conform to the modern state laws which forbid polygamy, save for

---

[8] R. Israeli, *The Vanity of Conversion Therapy:, The Delusion of Metastsizing Israeli Arabs,* Strategic Books, TX, 2022.

remote area when it is impossible to enforce those laws (or the practice of private harems of the rulers and the wealthy in some areas of the Middle East). However, in southern Israel, the Negev, where most of the Bedouins who live in the country live, the custom of bigamy and polygamy persists to an unknown scale, but is still estimated as still current beyond acceptable scopes. That is due to the sparsely dispersed Bedouin population of over one hundred and fifty thousand people, most of them concentrated in 7 townships which submit to urban planning and enjoy government services, but 40% of them are still illegally squatting in illegal settlements, devoid of modern services and seemingly also lacking law and order and the similitude of modern living and basic services. It is those remote and outlawed settlements, which keep growing due to the want of an agreed permanent solution, which probably shelter the plight of polygamy. In those places, there emerges a stratum of well to do aging Bedouin individuals who have few leisures or preoccupations in those vast deserts other than expanding their families and "acquiring" more wives, literally "purchase" young women from needy Palestinian refugee families, in the West Bank and Gaza, adding them to their private harems, taking full advantage of the precedent of the Prophet who allowed up to four wives simultaneously, provided he treated them equally (if that were possible).Several collateral issues arise from this Islamic Shari'a-permitted practice, which runs in contravention of Israeli and Western law and which is fought by the Israeli and European authorities but is considered by Arabs as "racist", "discrimination", "oppression" and "Islamophobia", though most of them respect the country's law in that regard. Bedouin wives, who are usually the older in the household from among the array of wives in the bigamist or polygamist Bedouin marriages, grow in a freer and modernized Israeli environment, more aware of the Israeli law, of their civil and human rights in Israel and of their enhanced position vis-a vis their husbands, and feel entitled to resist them and scuttle their fantasies of bringing home young brides;

1. In the expanded families, the newcomers, who become naturally the favorite spouses and dominate the household, come to unseat the older wives from their position, and this creates tensions and rifts which do not add to the family's health and sanity.

2. The newcomers, in contrast to the elder women who had gone into menopause, produce children who need care and who take precedence over their older predecessors, generating competition and friction, especially when the father leaves behind a substantial inheritance.

3. The plurality of children in the same household, which crowds the narrow space under the tent, often obliges the young growing adolescent women in the household to be married off and the boys to get out prematurely and look for their own livelihood. Some of them volunteer to serve in the security forces of Israel, others join criminal gangs which rampage the Negev and terrorize its inhabitants, often setting up road blocks and extracting "protection money" from frightened inhabitants, or break into private houses and steal or rob their contents.

4. The fertile young spouses often produce an uncontrollable number of children (in some cases 40 of them were counted in one household), which entitle the father to such high social security benefit income, that it becomes unnecessary for them to work for subsistence. All this is added to the concern of the Israeli authorities about upsetting the delicate demographic balance between Jews and Arabs in the Negev in particular, and all over Israel in general.

5. Evidently, the incoming Palestinian spouses are not all innocent brides who search for their new family well-being within Israel, for some security-conscious parties and authorities try to use them as willing or instrumental agents of subversion against Israel.

6. Finally, the Israeli government coalition formed since May 2021, which encompassed the *Ra'am* Islamic party, whose constituency's power base is among the Bedouins in the Negev, will be naturally handicapped in its attempt to remedy the situation, or at least reduce the pace of its deterioration

B. Family Honor

Much of the criminal activity that has plagued Arab sense of security, due to the recurrent, almost daily, acts of murder unfolding in their villages and mixed cities in Israel, involve what they falsely regard as the defense of "family honor", for these outrageously murderous attacks, especially against the women who are victimized due to the reigning belief that the honor of the family is symbolized and pre-served by the conduct of its women, only brings more shame and decadence to the entire Arab society which condones these acts. The motives which trigger similar horrors in Europe derive from the recurrent custom that a Muslim family of immigrants (typically from Pakistan or Bangladesh in English speaking Britain; North African in French speaking France or Benelux; Turkish in Germany), even deeply integrated in British, French or German society, lan-guage and culture, for the second or third generation, would long to marry off their adolescent daughter or son to a spouse from its country of origin. The reasons may hinge on a religious concern (usually Islam), in the face of its waning in the midst of the domi-nant European-Christian culture; or be ethnic-oriented, to preserve the continuity of the family within its original national heritage; or simply preserve the original cultural identity in the family line; or (most likely) following the cultural or family custom to marry off their progeny within the family, usually to cousins, or to close friends or associates who had promised their children in their childhood for marriage when they come of age so as to ensure the merger of businesses or keeping family wealth within the bounds of the joint family. The problem with this is that the young people not only no longer submit to their parents or elder's authority. But they often prefer to make their own choices and marry out of love and not for other family or expedient considerations, resulting in serious family rifts which may result in coerced marriages, or very often in the rebellion of young candidates for marriage against the imposed constraints and either defy, under the protection of the law of their host countries, their elders' desires, and run away from with their chosen lovers or simply refuse to conform to the established family and traditional rules . That may trigger, more often in the Arab and Islamic worlds than in Europe, and almost exclusively when the rebel is a woman, the syndrome of the family dishonor which necessitates redress, pushing one of the closest male relatives to erase the shame by eliminating the girl who had caused it. Other circumstances which also occasion murder, may involve the suspicion or just hearsay, that a woman, especially if already married, was seen flirting or just talking to another man, or consorting with him, or going out with him beyond the close supervision of her male relatives (usually father and brothers) who are shamed for failing to protect the family honor, and therefore they are the most urgently concerned with eliminating the source of the shaming outrage by killing the unfortunate victim, especially in cases when the "shameful scandal" has a visible outcome that cannot be hidden, like an unwanted pregnancy or when the illicit couple was caught together in intimate situations.

In Israel, many of the murders perpetrated against innocent Muslim women are attributable to decent common people, who are bound by their culture to perform their duty of defending their perceived honor, and not "criminal gangs", as the Arabs like to claim in order to prove that there is nothing cultural in their criminality, and therefore they believe that they are exempt of prosecution.

C. *Lex Talionis*

When this sort of murderous criminality occurs between Arab

families and clans, either due to economic interests, socio-political jealousies of plain criminal clashes, what is mostly feared among the various contenders is the pace and widening scope of this kind of crimes which bring shame on the families of the murderers because they trigger the endless chain of killings and retaliations *ad infinitum*, branching out to more and more distant and more and more innocent and totally unrelated relatives and associates who just happened to be there, or accidentally witnessing some of those criminal events. And due to their inability (or unwillingness) to break the circle of violence, for the last of a string of unrequited acts of murder which is thought to bring shame on the family, that open rift can last for months on end, unless a *sulha* (a ceremonial ending to the conflict by paying indemnities as negotiated and agreed upon by the intermediaries). But in the meantime, many victims have found their death. The late President Sadat of Egypt, himself a peasant from Mit Abu Kum, a village in the Nile Delta, recounted that in his village a rift could endure for centuries between families, involving violence and loss of life, about an unusable patch of rocky land just for the sake of protecting the reputation of the family when it was suspected as unable to defend its property.

All this amounts for a pious Muslims to believe, and often to state, that Shari'a law always overrides state law, and it often generates commercialization of religion which becomes a daily affair, which even when not practiced by common people who lead a decent life, is disregarded or covered up by family and neighbors, for to denounce a Muslim for his shari'a-sanctioned deed (for example, the murder of a female family members for the "dishonor" she committed) is in itself a sin. Thus every Muslim individual's inner torment, hesitating between denouncing the culprit or ignoring his own citizen's duty, becomes a sort of commercialization, weighing several contradictory reasonings before reaching decision to commit the murder or to denounce the murderer. The same has happened with Muslim terror against the mass murder in the Paris Bataclan

Theater in 2015, in the British Underground in 2005 or in the Israeli market place in any weekday when innocent people lose their lives because the holder of some other faith had decided to trade his belief for an act that may or may not be beneficial to him. It is only natural, that the culprit, who regards himself as a virtuous saint who responded to the call of his creed, should look elsewhere to find others to accuse, and for Arabs in Israel, Israeli policies or Police are unanimously accused of any of the crimes their criminals perpetrate. The feeling of guilt or at least of bad feeling would persist with normal humans once they performed their deed even if they assure the world that they performed their act of trading their religious duty for what they "did it in full conscience".

Consider this other revolting baseless accusation also involving a quid-pro-quo commercialization, via the manufacture of an abominable libel also done by Palestinian Muslims around Kippur, probably to spite Jews and to blacken their reputation to balance out the blame of mounting crime by Muslims against Muslims in Israel. It was made out with the "authority" of a former Arab MP in the Israeli Knesset, Walid Taha, who was happily cited by the Palestinian Authority and all other Muslims who waited for the occasion to accuse Jews of evil-doing, so as to demean and demonize them, compared to the noble conduct of the true Believers in Allah. The pretext was the rising number of killings in the Israeli Arab community. The newest libel was voiced by one of the regular columnists for the official PA daily, Bassem Barhoum, alleging that the killing of Israeli Arabs is carried out according to a plan devised by "Israeli forces" with the goal of creating fear and encouraging Israeli Arabs to "emigrate":

> It is clear that the Israeli forces, which stand behind this plan, rely on an atmosphere of strife, fear, and terror prevailing in order to make the Palestinian residents inside the Green Line (Palestinian term for Israel; see below)

think about emigrating and saving themselves and their families… The masked Israeli Arab killers are in fact "special Israeli forces from the [Israeli] army's undercover brigades," who are murdering innocent Arabs "in an intensifying systematic manner"… What we are witnessing today… is an act by a security establishment and dedicated intelligence forces that are managing the acts of crime in an intensifying systematic manner."[9]

This false condemnation, seen in its context, is connected, of course, to the concerted campaign of Hamas, backed by the Iranians, to raise the entire Muslim nation against the danger Israel is claimed to be posing to Al-Aqsa Mosque by undermining its foundations, in the process showing to all its inefficiency after its fifty years of such efforts, including the arson of the site in 1968, all in vain.[10] So, creating libelous charges in order to tarnish Israel's reputation is part of the unlimited struggle to trade lies, any lies, for any manufactured accusations their imagination can manufacture. On the way, Palestinian Arabs, especially the Hamas initiators of the libel, are inciting Israeli Arabs to take rebellious measures of civil disobedience in order to achieve destabilization and dismantling of Israeli rule in Israel/Palestine and replace it by Palestinian/Hamas rule. Thus, under the cover of seeking the "rescue of al-Aqsa", a great Islamic symbol being the third holiest place of Islam, the prescribed grand quid-pro-quo is the toppling of Israel altogether: a great religious achievement of trade-offs as envisaged by the PA official Daily, whose prospects are awesome enough to be heeded by Believers:

---

[9] Official PA daily *Al-Hayat Al-Jadida*, Sept. 5, 2023.

[10] In 1968, the attempt to burn the mosque was made by a lunatic Australian Christian tourist, but the Muslims accuse Israel, who on the contrary rescued the site; but since then, Israel is constantly blamed of digging down its foundations in order to topple it, but it stands as firm as ever.

When crime becomes a daily and organized act, this means that we stand before a fascist and apparent plan of ethnic cleansing . It is clear that the Israeli forces, which stand behind this plan, rely on an atmosphere of strife, fear, and terror prevailing in order to make the Palestinian residents inside the Green Line[11] think about emigrating and saving themselves and their families. This is tantamount to a great warning to those concerned and the decision makers. We are approaching the point of no return. Israel is now at the peak of its fascism, and it has a government whose entire task is to execute a comprehensive process of ethnic cleansing, a malicious process in which the victims appear like those slaughtering themselves with their own hands. Who said that these masked people who are spreading crime are not special Israeli forces from the [Israeli] army's undercover brigades?[12]

The same logic applies to any act of violence perpetrated against Israel and the Jews, for it is justified *eo ipso*, coming from Believers who can only do good, and directed against evil-doing Zionists who can do only evil. Trading good deeds of the Muslims, against the Zionist bad deeds, can only be qualified as virtuous. The Palestinian Hamas, in a horrendous demonstration of how capable they are to trade their libelous claims about the safety of al-Aqsa with the execution of the terrible surprise massacre and attack of 22 Israeli border settlements east of Gaza while their innocent residents were in their beds, resulting in the slaughter of close to 1,500 civilians, including babies and the elderly, and leading over 230 others to captivity in Gaza as hostages, with a view to demand the release of thousands of Palestinian terrorists who were tried and convicted for

---

[11] i.e. the Palestinian term for Israel; the Green Line is the ceasefire line between Israel and the neighboring Arab countries, 1949-1967.
[12] Official PA daily *Al-Hayat Al-Jadida*, Sept. 5, 2023.

murdering thousands of tried and convicted terrorists. In another case following a Palestinian terrorist's murder of 1 Israeli soldier and wounding of 6, and the knocking down of 3 Israeli civilians and a Palestinian teen in a car ramming attack, the Popular Front for the Liberation of Palestine (PFLP) called to "escalate the unlimited confrontation everywhere." The PFLP's goal: To make Israel "pay the price through the blood of its soldiers and settlers", all under the umbrella of incitement created by Hamas, to "defend al Aqsa" from those intending to undermine it:

> Our people is determined to escalate the unlimited confrontation against the occupation everywhere, to make it pay the price through the blood of its soldiers and settlers in light of its continued crimes against our people, and to thwart its delusions of stopping the wave of resistance.[13]

As is its policy, the PA presented the murderer in that account as an innocent "young civilian," who Israel "claimed" had carried out a car ramming attack:

> The [PA] Ministry of Health announced that civilian Daoud Abd Al-Razeq Dars [Fayez, i.e., the terrorist and murderer), 41, was shot by the occupation forces and died as a Martyr…The occupation forces shot young Dars claiming that he carried out a car ramming operation at the military 'Maccabim' Checkpoint located on the lands of Beit Sira, which led to the death of a soldier and the wounding of 5 others (sic., 6)[14]

---

[13] Ma'an, independent Palestinian news agency, Aug. 31, 2023.
[14] Official PA daily *Al-Hayat Al-Jadida*, Sept. 1, 2023.

Similarly, when Khaled Samer Al-Za'anin, a 14-year-old terrorist, was killed a few days earlier after he stabbed and wounded a 22-year-old Israeli on the Jerusalem light rail, the PA referred to him as "a young person who was shot and died as a Martyr. The designation of Shahid (martyr), though it has become customary whenever a Palestinian falls in an act of his terror, nevertheless stresses here his death for an Islamic cause. The PA also reported that eyewitnesses saw that Al-Za'anin was "executed". This means that his victims deserve their murder though no one ever accused them of a wrong doing, they were innocent people, while the terrorist who was "executed" clearly intended to kill innocent people. PA Chairman Abbas' spokesman Nabil [ironically meaning "nobleman"]AbuRudeina accused Israel of "murder in cold blood of [a] young Jerusalem resident," claiming Israel intentionally is trying "to bring about an explosion in the situation and drag it into the cycle of violence and escalation." [15] Adding to this, the PA Foreign Ministry turned the incident on its head, claiming that Khaled Samer Al-Za'anin was "executed" – and "barbarically attacked by settlers" while he was on the [light] rail and died as a Martyr while defending himself." The fact that the PA at times presents terrorists who try to murder Israelis as innocents, while at other times it brags about their "accomplishments" as "self-sacrificing fighters" and PA's soldiers, shows that trading with Islam, using the terminology of martyr and self-sacrificing Jihadi when convenient, is part of the "moderate" PA conduct, not only of the extremist Hamas discourse.

---

[15] Official PA daily *Al-Hayat Al-Jadida*, Sept. 1, 2023.

Chapter Three

Trading off Principle for Interest

Unfortunately, the recurrence of yielding a principle or an ideology, including a religious precept, for an immediate interest has been all too frequent to escape our scrutiny on all of the personal, governmental and the international levels. We have seen fanatic terrorists who endangered themselves to murder others "in the path of Allah", and we have witnessed that the immediate danger of perishing has deterred many individual terrorists from implementing their commitment to kill; we have noticed governments who pursued certain policies that contradicted their immediate interest, for the sake of some vague principle, as we have recorded others sacrificing long-held principles of legality, fairness, amiability and morality for the sake of some immediate gain considered crucial to their survival. In internal relations, especially in the Western Bloc during the Cold War, many were the "desertions" and betrayals between "allied" countries (remember the lethargy of the US when Saudi Arabia was attacked by Iran in the 2010s, while Russia rushed to rescue Syria militarily in the same period of time); by contrast the Eastern Bloc alliances and international treaties were much longer lasting and more likely to last, for it was more likely for the US to abandon an ally when convenient or necessary, than for the USSR to relinquish an ally. The former did it in the name of "freedom", especially in situations necessitating military involvement, the latter in the name of "loyalty under any circumstances" even when military complications loomed in the horizon. Are well known the contrasting cases of the US and Communist China in the 1970s and the 1980s, when Washington helped unseat democratically elected and avowed socialist President Allende of Chile and supported the fascist military dictator Pinochet whose rule lasted two decades; Popular Communist Beijing in those years backed the "fascist" military government of Pakistan in its confrontation with India, due to the mammoth menace of war between those colossal countries, and to the threat, and the real competition for Asian hearts between the two most populated nations of the world. Who does not remember the prostration of President Obama, the freedom and democracy preacher, before the Saudi King, the most absolute of monarchs, when he needed to secure petroleum supply to his country, in contrast with the determination of President (and his former vice President) Biden, when for years he refused to treat with Saudi Arabia, once the US had become independent in energy supply, when it become evident that the Crown Prince had a hand in the murder of the journalist Hashuggi. At the end, Biden also capitulated when his competition with Xi Jinping on Middle Eastern hegemony necessitated. The pertinent issue here is to demonstrate the religious Islamic vector as the trade off in any political demarche, local or international.

Actually, from its inception, the theme of Islam as the religion of Allah and its Prophet, evolved as a catch-all justification for anything that the new dynamic, expanding, ambitious, enthusiastic and effervescent new faith brought with it, from omnipotent Allah and His infallible Messenger who can generate no error, injustice or travesty, therefore anything related to them or citing them as having uttered or done, or not rejected when said or done in their presence or cognizance, sets a precedent and a standard for future doings by Muslims for all generations to come, the rules being set either by the Word of Allah in the Qur'an, or in the biography of the Prophet

(The *Sira*) and stories about his sayings and deeds(the Sunnah as described in the Hadith) as long as they are confirmed as solid (*Sahih*) by their chain of transmission, like those of Bukhari and Muslim. Therefore, suffice in every case to indicate the citation of the adequate reference in either source in order to make any subsequent saying or deed utterly justified and incontestable, including items that may sound horrific and uncivilized in Western eyes, but are indisputable in Muslim eyes, at least those claiming a fundamentalistic approach to the holy sources, i.e. a literary implementation of every word without accepting any mitigating commentary or interpretation which may be used in various times to justify any radical act or declaration. Examples abound: in Saudi Arabia and Iran, acts of execution or severing limbs or thieves, or of stoning defamed women for their "shaming of family honor", or for other relatively "minor" acts of heresy or apostasy from Islam that may sound as pertaining to freedom of thought in the West, but they are utterly and completely implemented in some Islamic countries like Pakistan and Afghanistan. Feminine "circumcision" which is universally loathed by most Muslim women, is still practiced in less fanatic nations like Egypt and Somalia, as well as the imposition of the veil and its varieties in most Muslim countries, and claimed, without solid foundation, by many practitioners to be required by Islam. But since in modern Islam some human-based considerations other than the Qur'an and the Sunna are accepted by state laws (Qanun as opposed to Shari'a), general and rooted customs like the veil and female circumcision, may be considered, not always justifiably, as universally accepted parts of the Shari'a.

The earth has been awash with a multitude of mutinous unrests, civil wars, domestic conflicts, internecine wars, interminable rebellions and international movements of itinerant fighters, which oblige one to wonder whether in civilizations other than Islam and the Mongols there has ever prevailed such a zeal for war as to make the outer boundaries and inner frontiers of Islamdom so bloody.

Moreover, not only were these numerous and multifarious wars fought simultaneously from one end of the Islamic world to the other, but they seem to be characterized by an uncompromising zeal and a unity of purpose that render them atrocious in their destructive violence, and horrendous in their consequences. It appears that all the notions of the sanctity of life and of the value of human rights, which were cultivated in the Western world in recent decades, following the devastation caused by the world- and colonial wars, have been pulverized by the reality of the Islamic and Islamic-motivated wars, where humanness, pity, compassion, decency and fairness have yielded to cruelty, murder, extravagance and one-upmanship in the conduct of war by mad clerical tyrants, of the kind of Osama Bin Laden, Abu Mus'ab Zarqawi, Hassan Nasrallah or Abu Bakr Baghdadi. Abu Marzouk, a leader of the Hamas, has deviated slightly from this norm of international Jihad when he affirmed his group's determination to confine its Jihad struggle to the boundaries of Palestine, namely only against Israel, instead of wasting its energies and resources on the international arena[16].The atrocious outrages that Hamas launched on 22 peaceful Israeli border settlements around Gaza on the early day of 7th October, 2023, where they caught innocent families in their beds and slathered more than 1,500 then led to exile in Gaza 230 as hostages, ought to remind civilized people of the menace constantly looming against any unfortunate people or country bordering on *dar-al-Islam*. In their fervor and zeal to kill and slaughter their ene-

---

[16] Hamas newspaper http://english.alresalah.ps/en/post.php?id=50

[1] March 2016. In fact Abu Marzook claimed that despite several Israeli operations against the Movement in different countries, the Movement remained adherent to its policy and retaliated with operations inside Palestine. He also stressed that Hamas does not interfere with internal Egyptian politics nor does it support or favor any Egyptian group, maintaining that it is the Movement's priority to guarantee the security of Egyptian borders with the Gaza Strip. "Palestinians are affected the most by any events in Sinai. Rafah crossing is Gaza's only connection to the outside world", he underlined.

mies, all the more so when they are Jewish, Hamas, like ISIS, Hizbullah and others, are prepared to forget about the injunctions of their own faith to avoid killing women and children, though it is not certain that being sold into slavery and forcibly converted to Islam, as Islamic jurists prescribe, can be accepted as any better fate than dying.

The historical record testifies that this apparent madness, which has increased in volume and frequency in recent decades, under the varying appellations of terrorism, rebellion, disturbance, upheaval, arrogance, conspiracy and outside aggression, all geared to make it appear so overwhelming and unnatural as to warrant outlandish measures against it, is nothing new in the history of Islam. What is new is that unlike in antiquity and medieval times, when might was right, and victory, conquest, expansion and domination sufficed to justify and consecrate the domination of occupied peoples and their oppression, nowadays the media war on airwaves and cyberspace has become part and parcel of war strategy, with a view of conquering the sympathy of world opinion and discrediting the reputation of the rival, at the same time that the battles on the warfront are being fought utilizing gunfire and spilling human blood. To wage conventional warfare, even in self-defense, using tanks, aircraft, bombs and explosives, has been discredited, while resisting and defying them with bare hands and sowing terror in the midst of the defenders, has been glorified and has gained the aura of prestige and fame of "resistance". Thus, the fervor to make Islam dominant worldwide has escalated among the radical Muslims to such a degree that they are prepared to absorb and sustain all the disrepute and loathing this brought toward Islam and Muslims, especially towards the horrendous mass murders in the West by avowed Muslim terrorists, as long as their main purpose to terrorize Infidels and make them lose their trust and pride in their Western cultures and to yield to the prevalence of the dominating religion of the future, that is Islam. In the wake of September 11 (2001), the Saudi Chief

Mufti, Sheikh Abd al-Aziz, who was aware of the damage caused to the reputation of Islam, showed readiness to trade some firmly held beliefs in return for loosening Western attacks on his faith, instead of defending the intrinsic merit of the religious value or the injunction of Allah and His Prophet, stated in an interview to the press what amounted to commercialization of Islam:

> Our monotheistic faith urges us to respect obligations and against their violation… The Prophet had said that those who kill allies will never enjoy the scent of Paradise…Ibn Hajr discussed the "allies" of Islam, who gain their status by paying *Jizyah*[17], or securing *hudnah*[18] or *aman*[19].It is incumbent upon Muslims to fear Allah, to think carefully and not to punish anyone for the faults of others, for our faith is built on justice[20]. One must think carefully because the consequences of such [terrorist] activity can hurt Islam and Muslims in this world and the hereafter… This kind of conduct is very harmful and tends to generate internecine wars, riots and destabilization of security. To conduct oneself in this fashion is

---

[17] This is the poll tax that dhimmis (Jews and Christians under Islam)were obliged to pay in return for their "protection" and as a sign of their humiliated status, hardly an ally in its straight sense. This trend of using Western neutral words in order to smooth the sense of Muslim terms, is part of the trade off of fervor against the prospect of improving the Muslim image in the eyes of the prevalent West, until a time when Islam will prevail, and such a need will be unnecessary.

[18] A temporary cease-fire or truce that was declared by the Muslim ruler when he could not overcome his enemies and was limited to 10 years, on the Prophet's precedent in Mecca, renewable *ad perpetuum,* until a time when Islam is strong enough to overwhelm its enemies. This is also a fair description of an "ally".

[19] This is a guarantee of protection accorded to non-Muslims under Islam.

[20] Once again, justice does not mean equity, fairness and equality before the law, but Islamic justice as explained in R. Israeli: *Justice, for whom?*, Lambert Academic Publishing, Germany, 2022 and Clinton Baily, "A Note on the Bedouin Image of *'adl* as Justice", *Muslim World,* Vol 66, No 2, 1966.

forbidden, due to the obligation to fulfill one's commitment, as stated above, due to the intimidation of Muslims it might provoke, and due to the scaring away of those who would otherwise seek [Muslim] protection....

Whoever possesses [*Shari'a*] scientific knowledge must explain the truth and open the eyes of people as to their duty to turn to their rulers and their *'ulama'* in times of internal strife…It is also incumbent upon scholars of the Holy Law to avoid rushing into discussing these serious matters which concern the entire Muslim Ummah and to leave them to those better qualified than themselves. The common people must avoid dealing with these affairs which are beyond their comprehension… We all know that the events in question [September 11, 2001] were ordained by Allah, and that Allah determines what is to happen with His immense wisdom, which may or may not be comprehensible to His servants. Allah may determine a good event that common people abhor or a bad one that people like… It is incumbent on all Muslims to spread the religion of Allah in the world but they must all know that Allah not only preserves His faith, but also ensures that it beat all others… We Muslims must preach for Allah and make sure that current events do not turn us from our mission.

These matters all back to rulers and doctors of the Holy Law because they understand the situation better than all others, master the written sources, know best how to attain our most vital interests and thwart the worst dangers. Hence the duty of all individuals to cluster around the *ulama* and their rulers. For when they say something and when they keep silent they know why they do so. We must beware not to listen to all voices we hear that wish only to kindle internal strife but carry with them no benefit[21].

Despite the reverend Sheikh's attempt to hide his approval of the act of terror, where most of the bombers of the American sites were Saudi, his manipulation of the smooth discourse taken from Western vocabulary, there is not one speck of humanity or sorrow for the thousands of American victims, nor a clear condemnation and damning of the perpetrators, only an acceptance of the event as act of Allah and a warning to the people of Saudi Arabia to abide by the established coalition between the King and the Wahhabi clerics who rule the country, because "they know best". This seemingly moderate cleric who apologized to his readership for being constrained in the interview, because he "knew when to keep silent".

When one resorts to open Wokeism where the one who believes in his victimhood, he also resorts to hell-raising terminology like "apartheid", "genocide", "neo-Colonialism", "racism", "Islamophobia" to force the accused Western world on its defensive toes and to justify itself or indulge in scenes of apology, which only make themselves look worse in the eyes of its accusers, who see in the apology of the attacked a "proof "of the Western sin and the rationalization to the accusations they launched toward it. Remote, naïve, sleepy and well-meaning Norway, which by hosting the Oslo Accords thought it was bringing peace and salvation to the world, and persists in allocating the Nobel Peace Prize annually, was jolted by the Cartoon Affair of 2005-6[22], not so much by the violence against some of its representatives and symbols in the Muslim world, but by what a notorious radical Muslim who had been generously sheltered by her for years, had the effrontery and ingratitude to say

---

[21] Tarad al-Amari, "Interview with Sheikh Abd al-Aziz about September 11", *al Watan*, Saudi Arabia,, 22 November, 2001, cited by MEMRI, Terror in America, No 44 (Hebrew).

[22] R. Israeli, *Retreating from the Mirage of Multi-Culturalism?*, Strategic Books, TX, 2018.

publicly to her media in that context. This chief of the *Ansar al-Islam* (Supporters of Islam) of Iraqi-Kurdish origin, Mullah Krekar, gave a press interview in the aftermath of the controversy over the derogatory cartoons of the Prophet Muhammad to the Internet edition of the Norwegian Daily *Dagbladet*[23]. In it, he expounded his views on the relations between Islam and the West. Krekar, whose real name was Najm a- Din Faraj Ahmad, came to Norway as a refugee in 1991, where he established his Islamic organization. While slated for deportation from Norway, he gave this interview to the press, which was representative of many others stated out loud throughout the European continent by other similar radical Muslim "refugees", or fugitives from the law of their countries of origin, or Muslim activists who regarded Islamic *da'wa*(mission, propaganda) as a sort of non-violent Jihad to propagate the faith while expanding Islam "peacefully" through subversion and demographic growth. In his words:

> On one side stands the Western way of thinking. This is a way of thinking that has taken its materialism, egotism and savagery from the ancient Greeks and Romans. This is a way of thinking that has altered true Christianity. An example of this is that Western Christianity [today] accepts men having sex with men. That was never accepted by Jesus. On the other side stands Islam, and the West has been attempting to take over and change Islam in the same way Christianity has been debased. There is only one civilization. But there are different ways to think about it, and our way of thinking of Islam stands in opposition to the Western way of thinking. Today, it is our way of thinking that comes in and shows itself stronger than theirs. Islam has a stable foundation:

---

[23] *Dagbladet,* 13 March, 2006.

one God, one Prophet, one Qur'an and one tradition. This generates hatred among [those with] the Western way of thinking, and leads the losing part to resort to violence. And that is the violence and war against Islam. Democracy is just an excuse- it is Islam that the West cannot stand… The same is with the hunt after Osama Bin Laden, it is just an excuse, it is Islam that the West cannot stand. The attack on Islam is like a hand. One finger is the war in Iraq and Afghanistan. Another finger is the incarceration of Muslims in Guantanamo. The third finger is the publication of the pictures of Prophet Muhammad. We must see things as they are, and those pictures [the Cartoon Affair] are only one part of the military fight that the West is conducting against Islam… By 2050, 30% of the European population will be Muslim…

We have no fear from the Western way of thinking, for it can never win. In Iraq, the two sides stand against each other. On the side of Islam stand men who love death and are willing to become martyrs for their beliefs. On the other side stand soldiers who fight for $1,000 per day. The number of dead American soldiers is proof of failure. The same is true in Afghanistan. From 2001 to 2004 there were five suicide attacks[24]. In 2005 there were 17. While the front line of the US and its allies is getting shorter, Islam is widening its front. The reports from Guantanamo show the same. They are trying to rip belief

---

[24] This author has coined a more adequate term for these fighters-terrorists: Islamikaze, a combination of Islam and the Japanese kamikaze of the Pacific War, where the pilots, like the Islamikaze, do not truly commit suicide out of a temporary loss of spirit or of taste for life, but on the contrary, are prepared to kill the enemy amidst the supreme act of sacrifice for the cause they believe in. See R. Israeli, *Islamikaze: Manifestations of Islamic Martyrology*, Frank Cass, London. 2003.

from the hearts of the Muslims, but it does not work. In Denmark they published cartoons [of the Prophet], but the result was only to encourage people to rally behind Islam. I and all Muslims are proof [of this]. They have not managed to change us. It is we who will change them. Look at the development of the population of Europe, where the number of Muslims increases like mosquitoes. Each woman in EU produces, on average, 1.4 children, while each Muslim woman in these same countries produces 3.5 children. By 2050, 30% of the European population will be Muslim.

Muslims who go to Afghanistan and Iraq to fight, that is an honor. It is an honor in itself if it violates the laws here in Europe. Those who say that Osama Bin Laden is a terrorist are themselves killing our women, children and civilians. This is what we see and know. We are not influenced by the US' words against Bin Laden since they are talking about somebody we know. We are fighting for the same goal, just under different circumstances.. The goal is Islamic rule over an Islamic state. Shi'ite Muslims have achieved this goal in Iran, and they are so strong that the West does not dare to attack them. This is the only way we can maintain a balance [of power] and achieve a lasting peace [under Islam]. Our Caliph is dead and we are orphans. Therefore we are fighting, like the Jews fought under David Ben Gurion, for our own state, a state ruled by a true Islamic ruler. Bin Laden is a good person to rule the Caliphate. Borders do not matter. Things are born and then they grow bigger. The essential thing is Islamic rule. That was why the West destroyed the Taliban rule in Afghanistan. They feared the Islamic state. The ruler does not have to be cleric, a good human being is enough and Osama Bin Laden and Ayman al-Zawahiri are among several good people. Weren't Jewish leaders also terrorists before they had their own state?

Muslims in the West and in Norway do not want to understand that this is not their country. The Muslim state will be their home, no matter where it will be located. Muslims in the West are like the Jews were. We are homeless and weak, and will remain so until we create our own country. Life here has no value for Muslims. Muslims can participate in elections and elect a Carl Hagen or Kristin Halvorsen, this in itself has no value for society. When we get our own country, like the Shi'ites created in Iran, we will have full political and economic control. We have no role to play in Europe at this point. Our position is to maintain our numerical strength. But now you are putting us in the role of the accused. It is you and the West who should be telling us what [the West] can do for us. The West should protect Islam, and not the other way around. I am protected by the law of this country, but this is not a law that protects Muslims specifically. Nor could it protect Muslims from the attack that these cartoons caused. It is not the West who is the victim in this case.[25]

This frank expression of Islamic thoughts and ambitions among radical Muslim activists, which were repeated in the ears of incredulous Europeans again and again, were echoed by no other than Turkish President Teyyip Erdogan during his official visit to Germany in 2011. His words urging Turkish immigrants in Germany, who form the bulk of the millions of Muslim *gastarbeiter* and "refugees", to preserve their particular identity (Turkish and Muslim), was seemingly similar to President De Gaulle's called upon the

---

[25] *Dagbladet*, 13 March 2006.

Quebec nationalists in July 1967 to preserve their liberty. But in the European context, Erdogan's call was much more scandalous and wide-ranging. Because while De Gaulle was referring to a single province in vast Canada which had only a local effect, Erdogan was addressing Muslims worldwide and a vast Muslim population of immigrants in Europe, some of whom entertained the dream of Islamizing all Europe, Erdogan in fact said in Dusseldorf to 10,000 Turkish immigrants during his visit:

> You must integrate, but I am against assimilation … no one may ignore the rights of minorities… individuals should have the right to practice their own faith. Our children must learn German but they must learn Turkish first…I want you to learn German, that your children learn German – they should study, get degrees. I want you to become doctors, professors and politicians in Germany.[26]

Similar encouragements that one can hear among Muslim Diasporas, in Great Britain, Holland, France as well as in Israel and Norway and elsewhere have no other sense than being part of a long haul plan or at least intent not only to take roots wherever they are in order to penetrate into government and the lucrative and prestigious professions, but to take it up ultimately, by way of jealously preserving their separate identity and faith. This means that it is incumbent upon them to appear as integrating into their host societies but at no price to assimilate into them. This has brought Muslims to the mayoralty of London, Amsterdam and many lesser municipalities in France and Switzerland, as well as their growing numbers in the governments and/or Parliaments/Congresses and local municipalities of many Western countries. Some of them are

---

[26] *Reuters,* Helen Pidd *in Berlin, Mon 28 Feb 2011 10.39 GMT.*

truly assimilated and they have become fully French, German, British and what have you, but others, especially pious Muslim radicals among them who may envisage the Islamization of European and American populations, may come to regard the rising Muslim elites in those countries as one stage toward the realization of their dream. Of great help toward that destination is the relatively large numbers of Western converts into Islam, citing the number of 50,000 in the past decade in each of the large concentrations of Muslim immigration in the "three great": Germany, Britain and France. Admittedly, some countries in Europe, which have awakened from the mirage of multiculturalism, like Britain, France, Italy and Holland, have installed some restrictions on the influx of Muslims, legals and illegals. But Germany has hit back by official counter-statements at the explosive remarks of Turkey's prime minister, who told his compatriots that they should learn Turkish before German and resist assimilation into German society. Nonetheless, Chancellor Angela Merkel, who had caused controversy in the previous month of October (2010) when she said that multiculturalism in Germany had "utterly failed"[27], invited in one million Muslim refugees in 2015, many of them from the Syrian civil war, with some of them causing outrageous abuses in their new refuge; only then has the extra caution in sheltering unlimited numbers of work migrants and others who pose as "political refugees", has been heightened throughout Europe.

Unlike warring nation-states and expanding empires, which in the past had launched campaigns across their borders against their enemies, then retreated to their core territories and engaged in the consolidation and defense of their own domains, nowadays the Muslim Jihadi movements have grown global, a true "army without borders", which keeps moving from one waning battlefront to an emerging one, their mobility, flexibility and adaptability to chang-

---

[27] Ibid.

ing circumstances being their greatest asset. This does not emanate only from the widespread distribution of Islam throughout the world, spanning 57 Muslim states in Africa and Asia, and more or less sizeable Muslim minorities in the rest of the world, notably in western liberal democracies, which are less able than others to resist the Muslim onslaught; but also from the iron-clad conviction in Jihadi circles that the imported western notion of nation states has revolved, and it is now time to let the universal 1,5 billion strong *Umma* of Muslims manifest itself once again, and world dominion be undertaken by a universal Muslim Caliphate. These movements of itinerant Jihad fighters have so markedly departed from the accepted norms of warfare, and deviated so far away from the conventional custom of war between sovereign nation states, that they have gained the epithet of "international terrorists", even among other conservative Arab and Muslim states which had thus far refused to recognize them as terrorists, and had rather attributed "state terrorism" to the West and to Israel, assessing acts of terror not by their violent means but by the nobility and usefulness of their purpose. Indeed, the Gulf Arab States have recently designated Hizbullah as a terrorist organization[28], in the same way Assad of Syria has called his opposition that is waging war against him, as "terrorist groups". As the six-member Gulf Cooperation Council declared Lebanon's Hizbullah a "terrorist" organization, it has amplified pressure on that Iran-allied group that exerts influence in Lebanon, and plays a key role in the Syrian crisis, fighting in support of Assad's regime. The Gulf monarchies took the action against Hizbullah members because of "hostile actions of the militia who recruit the young Muslim people (of the Gulf and elsewhere) for terrorist acts," GCC Secretary General Abdullatif al-Zayani, said in a statement issued in Riyadh. This novel process, which is fueled by

---

[28] *Alsharq Al-Awsat* (English) 2 March, 2016.

the vast universal recruitment of Muslim volunteer youth, both within the Muslim states, and often against their established governments, and among the Muslim minorities elsewhere, often against the active opposition of their authorities, is the challenge that this volume is undertaking to sort out, mainly based on case studies like the early conquests of Islam, and modern time Afghanistan, Iraq, Syria, Bosnia, Somalia, Libya and elsewhere, where the phenomenon of the volunteering "armies without borders" has dramatically manifested itself.

Chapter Four

Commercialization of Dhimmitude in Islam

When one consults the historical and legal documents relating to the mistreatment of *dhimmi*s in general, the Jews in particular, and especially the cruel, sadistic and inhuman punishments meted out to the "transgressors" of the Holy law, in the perverted eyes of the *Shari'a*, it turns out that Arabs and Muslims are not out there today, as they claim, solely in order to redress the wrong that was allegedly done to them and to the Palestinians; but they are today, as they were before, under a pressing psychological need to persecute, oppress and humiliate the *dhimmis*, who were at their mercy in Islamdom, and today also to erase the humiliating anomaly in their eyes, which permitted those Jews, the submissive and humiliated *dhimmis* of yesteryear, to emerge as a sovereign nation, which is able to defy them and stand up against them, in spite of its being tiny and vastly outnumbered. The mistreatment of Jews under Islam, especially in North Africa and in Spain, has been firmly established, despite the claimed inter-regnum of the "Golden Age", whose imagined myth under the independent Western Umayyad Dynasty, has been shredded to pieces recently[29]. The same attitude toward Jews in different parts of the Middle East, either under the Mamluks of

---

[29] See Dario Fernandez-Morera, *The myth of the Andalusian Paradise,* ISIS Books, Wylmington, 2015.

Egypt, or the Persian kingdom further east, or later under the unifying Ottoman Empire, has been a matter of some controversy. But the animosity of the Hamas towards the more than a thousand Jewish inhabitants of 22 Israeli villages around Gaza, who were assaulted in their beds at dawn, arousing the disgust and incredulity in Western civilized countries albeit the celebrations of joy that were witnessed across many Muslim and Arab nations.

The difference between those various approaches lay mainly in the terminology that those two schools are ready to resort to, when describing the very same Islamic societies that they studied, and the "protected" people (Christians and Jews who endured many centuries of oppression under them, providing one of the most prolific avenues for commercializing with that human mass as they did with goods, and often worse. However, since Christians could go elsewhere into the Christian world, thus practically end Christian presence in North Africa until colonialization allowed it to be renewed. But the Jews who had nowhere else to go until modern Israel was established in 1948, had to endure for one millennium and a half a sorry existence as *dhimmis* until they could depart. Some scholars claim that anti-Semitism was particularly suited for European Judeophobia, therefore Muslims could never be accused of anti-Semitism; at any rate, dhimmitude encompassed both Jews and Christians. Even in the periods when Jews were persecuted and decimated by Muslims, those scholars further claim, it was out of mere circumstantial misgivings about the Jews, and not part of a systematic ambition to eliminate them. The other school claims that, on the contrary, the notion of anti-Semitism was specifically coined for hatred of the Jews everywhere, and when one examines the history of Islam since the days of Muhammad and to our days, one cannot escape the perennial theme of the visceral anti-Jewish contempt, hatred and dismissal, which could only be dubbed as anti-Semitism. Today's mind-boggling fanatic hatred of the Jews, and the open vow of their annihilation (which was often implemented when feasible to them, as illustrated in the pogroms against Jewish neighborhoods, the last of which was perpetrated on 7th October 2023, when Hamas terrorists murdered at dawn more than 1,500 Israelis in the villages around Gaza), emanate not mainly from Christendom any longer, but from Islamdom (Iran, Turkey, the Palestinians, Hamas, al-Qa'ida, Hizbullah, ISIS and a few others[30]).

Be it as it may, the humiliating effect of the degrading and revolting *dhimmi* status of the Jews (and Christians) under Islam, has been universally recognized as having generated such a deep hatred and hostility towards the Jewish (and Christian) minorities throughout Islamdom, that anti-Semitism and hatred of any other faiths was an inevitable outcome, whether that terminology is referred to or not. The anxiety, mistreatment and deep and constant fear suffered by the Jews, which went in par with Jewish existence under Islam, had always cried for reaction on the part of the oppressed. This reaction began defensively in place, within the lands of Islam, against all odds, but ended up in the total divorce of the Jews from that environment and its abandonment, when it had grown entirely unbearable. As long as the Jews were helpless to alter their situation, they had no choice but to submit to it; but when Israel was born in 1948, it brought redemption to those unfortunate Jews, who massively immigrated there, if they had not sought asylum elsewhere before. To understand this process, one has to account for the years of Islamic conquest, expansion, annihilation of the existing Jewish (and Christian) communities, occupation, forced conversion, and cruel subjugation of the non-Muslim communities, which survived under the Islamic yoke of conquest and then occupation. When old Jews were beaten and humiliated before the eyes of their grandchildren, when cataracts of rocks could

---

[30] See R. Israeli, *Hatred, Lies and Violence in the Islamic World,* Transaction, NJ, 2013.

always land on Jews from nowhere, when peaceful Sunday picnics could always be disrupted by beatings and other outrages, or when the Jewish Sabbath and holidays could always be inexplicably interrupted by some Muslim thug or incited mob, who thought they could launch a rampage against the Jews, without the authorities interfering, or often doing so in support of the attacking murderers, those were all daily and persistent parts of a constant malaise, which undermined Jewish existence under Islam.

The greatest contributors to the unearthing of the original documentation, which has revealed the stunning mistreatment of the People of Book (the Scriptuary Peoples, namely Christians and Jews) come from various backgrounds, hence the possibility they afford us to cross-verify their findings, which stand in stark contrast to the myths of tolerance and co-existence that have been promoted by generations of Muslim politicians, scholars and clerics, and an entire generation of politically correct scholars, politicians and journalists. These deniers of the historical reality, who usually had an axe to grind, have elected to smooth over the documented truth rather than reveal it in all its ugliness, cruelty and inhumanity, which could, Allah Forbid! raise the ire of Muslim propagandists. Following on the footsteps of the legendary Haim Hirschberg, the pioneer among the dissident scholars, who were determined to tell the truth, was Bat Ye'or who created a new field of study that she termed "dhimmitude", where she elaborated in harrowing detail, in a series of books, based on hitherto unpublished original documentation, on the torments of the Christians (and Jews) in Islamic lands. The general picture, however, was even much bigger and much more painful than what the persecuted Jews themselves suspected in their particular locations. For example, it was especially debilitating to discover the grim reports about the decimation of one third of the Jewish people in the Nazi crematoria during W W II, to which the Palestinian Arab and Muslim pro-Nazi *Mufti* of Jerusalem, Amin al-Husseini, made a huge contribution that stains his, Palestinian, Arab and Muslim reputation forever, in the eyes of decent people across the world. No wonder, then, that when the alternative avenue of survival loomed to the Jews after 1948, in finding refuge in an independent Jewish state, most Jews of Islam unhesitatingly rose in one sweeping messianic wave, and moved there. They were simply tired, frightened, and disgusted from centuries of oppression and humiliation, which explains their massive and rapid exodus from the land they had inhabited longer than the Arab/ Muslim invaders, who subjugated them and rendered their existence into strangers in their country and their lives unbearable. The Jews of Islam, who were enslaved, despised, persecuted and marginalized for centuries, initiated their own saga of exodus from Islamdom, which was little reported and is little known[31].

The irony is that after the Jews had been settled in Morocco, for example since the beginning of the Christian era, before the Muslim conquerors came to occupy and oppress them, and they then returned to their ancient home in the Land of Israel one millennium later, they are now accused again of "occupying" Arab and Muslim Palestine. Similarly, other Jews of Egypt, Babylonia, Persia, and North Africa, whose flourishing settlements preceded those of the Arabs and the advent of Islam, were also compelled to leave their ancient patrimony and move to Israel, from which Arabs and Muslims now wish to evict them. The Arab/Muslim trauma that haunts today the existence of Jews in Israel/Palestine, is thus double- edged: Jews in Israel are accused by the Arabs of having displaced the Palestinians and replaced them, hence the urgent need to remove them from the land; and at the same time, by moving out from lands of Islam and seeking shelter in Israel, they have in fact committed the sin of nullifying the *dhimma* status which had governed them for more than a millennium, but renascent Israel has helped them to shake off. That Mus-

---

[31] See Raphael Israeli, *Pisces out of Morocco: the Saga of the Clandestine Jewish Emigration,* Strategic Books, TX, 2016.

lims should seek revenge for the loss of overlordship on "their" Jews in their lands, on the Israeli front which they now face in Palestine, only seemed natural to them, if disastrous all the same for themselves and for the Jews they are battling against.

The Fez (Morocco) Chronicles, for example, which were recorded for centuries by the rabbis and notables of the community, cannot be matched by any other primary source for the detail and accuracy of their reports. Had it not been for the horrors that were recorded day in and day out, and for the survival of the Jews who wrote them despite massive tortures, murders, and forced conversions, we would not have known today anything of that sorry history, which matches the much better known pogroms against the Jews in the Ukraine, Russia, the Baltics, or medieval western Europe. Moreover, those records would have been countered by avalanches of denials by Muslims, who have been accustomed to regard themselves highly, if inaccurately, and are loath to see their record stained in the eyes of the world. Just for comparison, already now, under the best conditions of memory conservation of the Holocaust, which is still fresh in decent people's minds, and whose survivors are still around to torment our conscience, Holocaust denial has sadly become universal throughout the Islamic world. These are shame cultures where politics precede decency, and where saving face takes precedence over honest and accurate accounting of facts and events of history. Muslim cultures, which had, for centuries, been preserving a self-image of "protecting the Jews" and "living in harmony" with them, and with protected minorities in general, cannot simply face with equanimity a documented scholarly deprecation and denial of their own writings, and of the positive legends they have been weaving for centuries around their treatment of the Jews, whom they had in fact always wished to either Islamize, or at the very least to preserve as *dhimmis* in accordance with *Shari'a* tenets. Several examples drawn from those chronicles could be cited and commented upon to give a hint of the taste of *dhimmi* treatment under Islam, but save for the documentation we shall see below, we leave that option to the interested reader to amplify his/her knowledge[32]. It is important to note, however, that persecution of the Jews dated from the early dynasties in Morocco, and this contradicts the claim of harmony and tranquility for the Jews, advanced by Muslims, (and some Jews, admittedly) today, and their false assertion that it was only Zionism which spoiled this idyllic state of affairs since the end of the 19th Century.

For example, in 1438 (quite a few years before the rise of Zionism), the Jews were expelled from the old city of Fez (*Fas al-Bali*), and they built their *mellah* (ghetto). From that time on, at every *inter-regnum* when the heir to power was struggling against other contenders to the throne, Jews were always the easy prey, with each party demanding extra taxes, ransoms and protection money from them, while committing massacres against them and intimidating them into conforming to the extortion imposed on them. In the years 1553-5, for example, the rulers levied money from the Jews to finance their domestic or internecine wars. When, in 1558, Muslim Turks invaded the *Maghrib*, they killed the incumbent ruler and massacred Jews, raped Jewish girls in the city of Sousse, took many Jewish prisoners back with them, if they remained alive, as slaves, and those were probably converted to Islam. Admittedly, horrors were done by Muslims against other Muslims too, killing them by the thousands and chopping their heads off beyond measure. But those were the accepted norms of action at the time against invaders from the outside, or rebels against the rule from within, and one can claim that there was no other way to repel the enemy or quell a rebellion. But Jews did not belong to either of these categories: They were native and preceded the Arab rulers in place, so they could not "invade " them, and they never rose violently against the

---

[32] See R. Israeli, *Back to Nowhere: Moroccan Jews in Dream and Reality,* Lampert Press, Germany, 2008.

ruling dynasty, in spite of the oppression which would have warranted such a rebellion. For one thing, they were too weak, unarmed and unhopeful of success. So, the cruel intimidation, oppression and outright elimination meted out to them, were not used by Muslims in defense from them, but, for some very specific ideological reasons deriving from their *dhimma* status. When, in 1562, the Chronicle reports, two Jews of Meknes, who quarreled with each other, had their arms amputated, that was well beyond any punishment which would have been meted out even to a Muslim thief, if at all, since there was no offense to the rule. That severe punishment was not even mandated by the king himself, despite its extraordinary severity; this goes to show that the deep enmity against the Jews seeped all the way down to the ranks. Under the conditions of those times, amputation meant almost certain death. Those two miserable Jews indeed agonized until their death. Ten years later, in 1572, disaster fell upon the Jews of Marrakesh, when the *Seder* night of Passover turned into a time of death.

In 1606, namely, once again, much prior to any talk about Zionism, the Chronicles of Fez tell us of eight hundred dwellers of the *mellah* who died of starvation after a vain search for food in the public garbage piles; so were they either condemned to starve within the ghetto, or to be massacred if they ventured out of it. In this situation, six hundred Jews had to convert to Islam to escape both starvation and murder. This meant that it was not a state of general starvation which reigned everywhere, but that hunger depended on faith. Namely if, as in the days of Torquemada in Catholic Inquisition Spain, a Jew wanted to live or just to eat, he had to convert, regardless of the Qur'anic verse so often cited to demonstrate "Muslim tolerance", and that Muslims are so fond of repeating, to the effect that "there is no compulsion in religion". Many Jews were led to slaughter, and sometimes their own children had to rescue them from those dilemmas by converting, while others committed suicide and died as martyrs. In 1610 the Jews of Fes were burdened by the ruler with a special tax of ten thousand ounces of silver, in payment for the ruler's "rescuing them from pillage by other Arabs", as if the other Arabs were not his subjects, or as if he did not owe any measure of protection to the Jews who paid their regular *jizya* poll-tax as part of their *dhimma* obligations. Moreover, since the Jews had no way to collect that enormous sum, within the one day which was allotted to them, the sum was doubled. So bad was the situation, and so insistent and cruel the oppressor, that the Jews had to cancel their *Yom Kippur* rituals in order to busy themselves with the collection of money, in order to satisfy the tyrant and save their lives. That atrocious measure did not sound much like the "harmonious and tolerant" mode of accommodating Jews, that Muslims often boast about. However, since that heartless oppressor was removed from power by his brother, the newcomer demanded the same amount, and the Jews were compelled again to violate their Tabernacles festival to busy themselves with the collection of the funds, which included the melting of the precious metals which decorated the synagogue, in order to fill the tax quota imposed on them from high .

Thus, many Jews were dispossessed of all their property (which was "traded off" to Muslims) and knew the intimidation of starvation. Traders among them, who were on their caravan's way, were also robbed and maltreated. As if man-induced calamities were not sufficient, an epidemic of plague killed another four hundred helpless Jews in Fes. On *Hanukka* of that year, merely a few months after the unfortunate *Yom Kippur* and the Tabernacles festivals were just experienced, another ten ounces of silver were levied on the Jews, who, in order to produce them, had to melt the gold and silver ornaments and embroidered covers of their Torah scrolls, an act of last resort and of ultimate despair. How pitiful and deeply aggravating it was to them, to see the Holy Book bare and naked, like the community itself, which stood on the verge of bankruptcy, that was added to the humiliation, shame and grief that all its members shared. All these extra exactions came in addition to the ten thousand ounces of silver of regular taxes, which were levied on the community annually, and to the wine tax which Jews had to pay in order to be permitted to produce it for their needs. During the festival of *Purim*, a few months later, while the Jews of Fes were busy trying to respond to another exaction of eight thousand ounces of silver, news from the city of Tedla came to cause further despondence and spoil their holiday, to the effect that Arabs had destroyed Jewish homes and burned fifty scrolls of the Torah, two thousand books of the Pentateuch, followed by three thousand more. Again on Pentecost, the Arabs, having learned by then that the holidays were the most vulnerable days on which to "squeeze" the Jews, struck again. The Arab governor of Fes demanded from the Head of the community another twenty five ounces of silver, and the Jews had no choice but to conform, if they wanted to extricate their president from certain imprisonment and death. Rabbi Saul Serero, the rabbi of the time, who also kept the records of his community, wrote with bitterness:" Had all the skies been parchment, all the lakes full of ink and all the forests pens, they would not have been sufficient to write all our troubles in full". This picturesque, if somewhat exaggerated description, which cried out from the depths of despair, was to repeat itself many times later in the Fes Chronicle.

At the same time, many synagogues were robbed and their treasures stolen. The members of the congregation had to stand watch round the clock near their houses of prayer, or pay protection money to thugs, to the point that they were so impoverished, that they could do nothing more, and decided to throw their lot in the hands of the Creator. This was done by prayer, fasting, and bringing their babies into the synagogues; it was hoped that the cries of the children would generate God's mercy. As a rule, the worst moments for Jews came during the transition from a ruling king to his children, who fought for power; any one of them who emerged victorious, could blame his Jewish subjects for not identifying with him from the outset, and exact from them taxes and ransoms as a chastisement. The Fes Chronicles are replete with the reports of the prayers for rain, which were heard from every synagogue of the *mellah* in the Fall, for fear that if rains were scarce, the Jews would be blamed, and made to pay the damages in consequence. In 1646, local troops were directly involved in the destruction of the Fes synagogues, in spite of all the bribes paid to the governor and his underlings to avert the disaster. The bribes sufficed only to rescue the Torah scrolls, but the houses of prayer were so utterly destroyed that they were found comparable, in the eyes of the local rabbis, to the destruction of the Temple (in AD 70 by the Romans). Therefore, lamentations were read and sung, as on the 9th day of the month of Ab, which commemorated the destruction of the Temple, the holiest place in the history of Judaism. On the next *Yom Kippur*, the two colleges (*Beit Midrash*) of Torah learning were also razed to the ground. These traumas and their likes are deeply incrusted in the hearts and minds of most Jews originating from Islamic countries, who constitute, together with their descendants, about half of modern Israel's population. Thus, in spite of the prevailing mood among some intellectuals in Israel today, including scholars in the fields of Islam and Jewish history, who preach leniency towards Muslims in general, and emphasize the mythical "golden age and harmonious existence of the Jews under Islam", those who had experienced that "coexistence" continue to be terrified by Islamic persecutors and hate mongers knocking at their gates to this day. That horror was amplified by the rampages Muslims cause when their Qur'an is desecrated and by the slaughter of Jews by Palestinians in October, 2023.

What was amazing, and may have attested to Jewish survivability and durability even under the most calamitous duress, was the expression "due to our sins", which usually accompanied the descriptions of those calamities, as if turning the guilt inwards would somewhat mitigate the disaster, once the blame was not directed to others but reflected on oneself. The Chronicle did not call for vengeance or retribution, for such were considered impractical and unfeasible against the powerful rulers and their incited and hate-seething crowds. In return for the houses of prayer which were destroyed, and the desecration of Jewish holidays by the Arab hosts, the oppressed Jews believed in full reliance on God who would "take our vengeance". Indeed, the praises of God for having preserved the Jewish communities from total annihilation, were the prevailing themes in that register of sad events. Accommodation with those horrible events, in recognition that they could be worse, was due not only to a fatalistic acceptance of one's lot for the misfortunes that occurred; there was also in them an element of hope and optimism that not everything was lost, and that renewal and consolation, redemption and better days, could be seen looming ahead beyond the murderous present. Indeed, in 1672, during the first prosperous years of the Alawite Dynasty which rules until our days, such words of comfort and faith in the future were recorded in the Chronicle; this was done under the relatively generous and benevolent kingship of Mulai Rashid and Mulai Isma'il, who alternated between their ancient capital of Fes and the newly established one in nearby Meknes. Jews were exuberant and attached great hopes to the future, teaching us that in the long series of massacres and forced conversions, robberies, and destruction, there were also occasional intervals when the Jews saw the light. Even faint stars looked bright to them against the backdrop of the very dark skies they had grown accustomed to contemplate.

Either way, it became evident once and again, that Jews depended for their very existence on their sycophancy towards absolute and corrupt rulers, who legislated, enforced their cruel laws and punished ruthlessly, all at once. Jews became unfailingly aware, every day anew, of their misery under this kind of oppressive rule, and of the hazards of sitting atop a bubbling volcano, which could burst at any time, without warning or transition. In the year 1680, for example, while everyone was asleep, the king decreed that all the inhabitants of the

Fes *mellah* had to be pulled out of their beds and sent to the surrounding fields, the very same fields which, on happier days, hosted their *mimouna* picnics which followed the *Pesach* festival. The reason was that a sword set with precious stones had been stolen from his palace. The horrified Jews, with their praying elderly, yelling infants and helpless sick, lay on the cold and barren earth, not understanding either of what they were guilty, or when that collective punishment would be abrogated. Only when the Jews were permitted to go back to their homes, and when they realized that nothing was stolen from their property in their absence, did they burst into celebration of the "miracle" which was done to them, for they were able to remain alive, while the torment, the terror and the menaces, heaped on them in the middle of the night, were considered "normal". Moreover, that inhuman ruling king, Mulai Isma'il, was considered "benevolent", and when one day, the news was released that he had just escaped from falling prey to lions during a hunting venture, they celebrated the happy occasion in great pomp and ceremony, abstained from work, decorated the streets of the *mellah* with silk materials, and donned their most festive outfits. On that day, they could even visit the royal palaces and enter the mosques with their shoes on, as they jubilantly reported in their records of 1699. But, in the same breath, they reported of Mulai Zaydan from the royal house in Tefilalt, who stormed the *mellah*, taking as booty anything he and his underlings found of worth, and imposed a fine of two hundred and fifty gold coins on that impoverished community. These were the two poles of Jewish existence, which implied that the more the helpless Jews submitted and bent their heads down, the more mistreated and humiliated they were bound to be at the hands of their rulers. Just for the "privilege" of remaining alive, they would hold themselves grateful to their oppressors for the "generosity" from which they had benefited. That was, in essence, the status of "*dhimma*" which we will have to clarify.

Our world is replete with misnomers, to an extent that old

notions have been confused with new ones, words lose their significance and expressions of political correctness have handily replaced factual accuracy. We use the same words to mean different things, to the point that we find it increasingly awkward to transmit certain messages, and we occasionally have to create new phrases and coin alternative words, in order to avoid misunderstandings. Cases in point have been the widespread usage of "Islamist" (to distinguish from Muslim), and "suicide bomber" where there is no suicide, not even the semblance of a suicide, to describe Muslim terrorists, or "Judeophobia" or "anti-Zionism", when one is embarrassed to be openly "anti-Semitic" as of old. For example, it is unconvincing that the Muslims are merely anti-Israel and anti-Zionist and not anti-Semitic, when Jews in the Diaspora are habitually attacked for no other reason whatsoever today, or were historically mistreated, beaten, massacred or forced to convert, until compelled to leave the lands of Islam, apart from the fact that they were Jews. Reverting to the right terminology, calling a spade a spade, is not only our duty to scholarship, which recognizes no biases, no self-serving ideologies, and no catering to political correctness, but also re-establishes straight lines of communication between authors and readers, and between scholars and their peers, and forces upon everyone in the field to play by the same rules. It is unthinkable, for example, that ideology-driven volunteers, who are ready to make the ultimate sacrifice for their convictions, should be denigrated as "suicide-bombers", however they may deserve denigration, or that anyone who lacks in courage to criticize any aspect of Islam, should hide behind the spurious excuse of merely bashing "Islamism", while "peaceful Islam" pure and simple remains untouchable and beyond reproach. One should also recognize that injecting massive doses of Islam into an already difficult dispute, has turned the description of the Arab -Israeli conflict (not the erroneously dubbed Palestinian-Israeli issue), and of the dark past of Jews in Islam, into an accusation of onslaught against Islam at large.

Listen to Bin Laden, to Iran's Ahmadinejad or to the horrors committed by the Almoravids and Almohads against the Jews of North Africa (10th to 13th Centuries, and we can connect between the fate of Jewry under medieval and early modern Islam, and the current conflict in the Middle East. Both were motivated by hatred and both created as their means lies, violence, libels and prejudice. Anyone reading the Hamas Charter or viewing the Hamas conduct on Israel's border with Gaza, cannot have missed this state of mind since many Palestinians have opted to elect this murderous organization to guide their destiny.

From the onset of Islam in the 7th Century AD, as the new religion was expanding rapidly through quick conquest of the entire Mediterranean basin, and beyond, where ancient and exhausted nations were disintegrating, Islam divided humanity into three categories, and the earth into two kinds of territory. At the center, of course, stood the Muslims, the humans closest to the ideal, due to their submission (*Islam*) to the will of Allah. The second category were the Scriptuaries (*ahl-al-Kitab*), namely people like Christians and Jews, who possessed a holy scripture, which was recognized by Islam until it was "distorted" and "forged" by its holders, and subsequently "amended and updated" by the revelations of Islam. As the years wore on, and as the conquests were expanded further afield, other people too, like the Hindus, were recognized as Scriptuaries. The outermost circle encompassed the pagans, who did not know one God. The lands where those various peoples dwelt, were differentiated as either the Islamic Dominion (*Dar al-Islam*), or *Pax Islamica*, that is the territory ruled by Islam, regardless of the composition of its population (for instance, the lands still populated by a majority of non-Muslims, like Andalusia, were still part of this category, as long as they were ruled by Islam); and the Dominion of War (*Dar al-Harb*), namely the land that was yet to fall under Islamic rule. Evidently, for practical reasons, these categories are not effectively operational these days, for otherwise the entire system of international relations, and international rules of conduct, would be chaotic, if every nation determined for itself its attitude towards others, as it pleased. But in pre-modern Islamic countries, including North Africa, there was no public opinion, and the rules of conduct were determined by *Shari'a* law, exactly the way some revolutionary Islamic movements are attempting to revive them today, or by the ruler. That law is theoretically immutable and not open to reform, pressure or whim of the ruler, even as some of those same rulers have occasionally deviated from those severe rules, depending upon whether they were personally more fanatic puritans, or more open-minded and benevolent beings. As a rule, under the Malekite puritanism of the Moroccan rulers, especially the *Murabitun* (Almoravids) and the *Muwahhidun* (Almohads) dynasties of the 10-13 Centuries, *shari'a* implementation was the strictest, and the suffering of the Scriptuaries reached its peak.

According to Islamic political theory, following the Jihad wars which generated the expansive conquests and the enlargement of *Dar al-Islam*, the Muslim ruler found himself managing the lives of three sorts of people: the Muslims, who occupied the masters' position, the submitted Scriptuaries, who were merely tolerated under certain conditions, and the pagans who were compelled either to Islamize, or to run away for their lives, until they would be subjugated in the next round of conquests, or be killed. According to this theory, which has been revived today in ISIS, or other territories managed by radical Muslim groups, only the first two categories could dwell in the Muslim Caliphate, while the pagans had to expeditiously determine their choices. They were converted to Islam in their majority, as were many Jews and Christians who could not accept their "tolerated" status. The pace of conquest was so dizzying, that the occupied pagan peoples had little time to ponder the new situation, and in general had to adapt to the new rulers. But the People of the Book, whose scriptures were recognized, had only to accept Islam's superiority by submitting to it, and were otherwise permitted to observe their religion under the status of dhimmitude, and to pay a special and demeaning poll tax (the *jizya*) in return for their "protection". On the face of it, Muslim societies in the Middle Ages were thus much more tolerant and open to Jews than was Christendom. This has created the myth of tolerance and of the "Golden Age"[33] of the Jews (and Christians) under Islam, as if they had enjoyed total freedom (that even the Muslims did not have), or total equality in the Muslim medieval world.

The status of *dhimma* (protection or dhimmitude) has gained considerable treatment in the Muslim judicial treatises of the Middle Ages. To be a *dhimmi,* not only signified the inferior class of the tolerated peoples, in contrast with the privileged Muslim subjects of the Caliphate, but meant also a lesser judicial stature (e.g. the evidence provided by a *dhimmi* was worth half of the Muslim's, and the *dhimmi* was legally incapacitated to bear witness against a Muslim; an inferior economic and social position (certain dirty jobs and occupations were reserved to the *dhimmi*s); a submissive political rank (Jews and Christians had no political rights and could not be trusted to serve in the government or the military); and a cultural handicap (Jews were always suspected of plotting schemes or mirroring Satan). When Muslim children were disciplined by their parents for their misconduct, the "threat" that the Jews would be brought upon them, was often used. That was understandable, because the Qur'an instilled the idea that they were "the descendants of monkeys and pigs", and discouraged any amicable relations with them or with Christians. Many of the limitations imposed on Jews (and Christians) were crystallized in what came to be known as the 'Umar regulations, which expressed the ambivalent attitude of Muslims to the Scriptuaries: On the one hand they were supposed to be tolerated and protected, due to their holy scriptures and

---

[33] This myth has been completely debunked in the recent study of Fernandez-Morera, Dario, The Myth of the Andalusian Paradise: Muslims, Christians and Jews under Islamic Rule in Medieval Spain, ISIS Books, Wilmington, 2016.

to their payment of the humiliating *jizyah*; but on the other hand, they were to be humiliated and tormented, due to their "forgery of the Word of Allah", unless they complied and converted to Islam, as most conquered peoples did. But one has to emphasize that those regulations were often violated, for the better or the worse. In Muslim Spain, where Jews attained temporary grandeur, served among the highest bureaucracy of the state, and distinguished themselves as professionals and intellectuals of the first degree, their stature was a huge improvement on their official status of *dhimmi*; but in Almohad north Africa and Mamluk Egypt, Jews knew worse periods of genocide of entire communities, massacres and extortions, forced conversions and a stifling oppression, even after they paid their poll tax and filled their obligations under the *dhimma*. During W WII, when It was Vichy France which ruled Morocco, the Muslims of Morocco thoughts that would be their "finest hour" when they could happily collaborate with the pro-Nazi government to implement racial laws and deport Jews, again taking advantage of the Islamic-Nazi cooperation, But both the America landing during the Torch operation and the parallel rescue operation of Helen Casez Ben-Attar scuttled that scheme[34].

There is no doubt that, compared to medieval Christianity, which did not tolerate any non-Catholics in its midst, and activated its infamous Inquisition to enforce conversions to Christianity, or to eliminate or expel Cathars, Jews, and other dissidents in the West, and committed horrible pogroms and expulsions against Jews in Western and Eastern Europe, the Muslim world was much more open and tolerant. It absorbed Jewish refugees expelled from Christendom, and generally did not persecute Scriptuaries in any systematic and constant way. This was possible, because while Christian society was uni-compartmental and supposedly homogeneous,

---

[34] Israeli, Raphael, *Helene Cazes Ben Attar: The Saga of how Moroccan Jewry Shelter Jewish Refugees from the Nazis,* Strategic Books TX, 2022.

allowing no diversity in its midst, the Islamic Caliphate was bi-compartmental which recognized, like under the Roman Empire, a place for others, though in a secondary or subordinate position, to be sure (like the slaves in Rome), but a protected and tolerated class (*dhimmis*) within Muslim society. Evidently, Jews of the time felt better protected under Islam than under Christianity. But to jump to a hasty and incorrect conclusion, that they "always lived in equality, harmony and peace", as Muslim propaganda would have us believe, is, unfortunately a gross hyperbole. The fact is, that the moment the Jews of Islam could leave their land, some sought shelter in the Western world, which had, in the meantime undergone emancipation, liberty and modernity, while Islamdom, as a whole, did not experience such developments; and some decided to migrate to the newly established state of Israel. It is true, that most Muslim countries, mainly under the impetus of the colonial powers, have formally canceled the *dhimma* in the 20th Century or slightly before, but the built-in hatred and contempt toward the Jews did not relent. The continuing Arab-Israeli dispute, and the revival of Islam and its norms in the 20th Century, have contributed immensely to the renewal of the traditional Islamic political thought concerning Jews, even though they have all practically left Islamic lands. All one has to do is to read the platforms of Hamas, al-Qa'ida or Hizbullah, to realize the full-fledged retrieval from almost oblivion, of the anti-Jewish ideology and vocabulary, and their euphemistic demand to "return the Jews (and Christians) to their former state (of *dhimmis*)". This has in fact been implemented in areas controlled by Hamas, ISIS and other radical Islamic movements.

The most insidious aspect of *dhimma*, however, beyond the humiliation and institutionalization of discrimination in the judicial, social, political, economic and cultural domains, has been the state of mind of fatalism and submission of the *dhimmis*, born out of centuries of inescapable persecution and oppression, on the one hand, and the mood of sycophancy and identification with the oppressor, which has turned this state of affairs into a "natural and immutable" situation, on the other. In other words, while it has been possible to extricate Jews from the *dhimma*, it is next to impossible to extricate the *dhimma* mentality out of some of the Jews who had suffered it. We have already described the mood of submission and sycophancy that had characterized Jewish conduct during the dark ages of their existence in the various *mellahs* (Jewish ghettos) of Morocco . For even after their exodus from that backward society, and their rootedness in the modern and advanced societies which absorbed them, where liberty and safety are guaranteed, there is among some of them a lingering habit of praising the Muslim rulers for their "benevolence" towards the Jews; it is as if the Jews owed their right to exist to those absolute and corrupt rulers, who held thousands of political prisoners in jail without trial. This typically Jewish parochial outlook, of judging rulers only based on their conduct towards Jews, and not on the basis of their universal and human rights records, is what distorts the thinking of those Jews today, who erect monuments in Israel to Moroccan kings, or praise Moroccan monarchs, and participate in their feasts and funerals, only because they were thought to be "pro-Jewish", or accepted bribes to let Jews leave their bondage there, or had otherwise collaborated with Israel. Furthermore, the *dhimmi* outlook has insidiously penetrated the domain of international relations, inasmuch as the political correctness cultivated by the media, academics and diplomats, has imposed rules of conduct which prohibit criticizing anything Islamic, including their repressive regimes, their backward societies, their corrupt leaderships, or their aggressive and discriminatory policies. We have been surrounded by a sub-culture of legends and lies, which holds Islam as "the religion of peace", in the face of the rampages of *Jihadi* Islam across the world, at the same time that it is the more militant trends of Islam which prevail today. The Rushdie syndrome, the hiding of European politicians in their own lands from the wrath of Muslim attackers, the kow-towing of European countries before the masses of Muslims, who threaten to submerge them and to change Europe to their tune, the violence used by Muslims across the world, the fear of western media and publishers to give vent to anything critical of Islam, and the wimpy supplications of the West for Iran to desist from its nuclear program, are all manifestations of this malaise. And if one dares to resist this *dhimmi* mode of behavior, one is dubbed "racist" or "Islamophobe".

The hypocrisy and sycophancy surrounding Jewish existence under those conditions, must be, in the final analysis, the main reason for their eagerness to relinquish all their past and heritage behind, and venture into a new life abroad. The same Jew, Habib Toledano, who reported, in the Fes Chronicle of the year of 1699, the celebration of the rescue of Mulai Isma'il from the claws of lions, also whimpered in 1701 about "the troubles we experienced under Mulai Isma'il, who exacted from Moroccan Jews one hundred silver pounds for the conduct of his wars". Of that, the Jews of Fes were to pay twenty two pounds, such an enormous sum that "our hearts melted, our knees trembled, our hands weakened, our eyes blurred, our bones broke… and the joy of *Pesach* turned into disaster. Many households did not read the *haggadah,* and those who did, intoned it like a lamentation". Following all those levies, pains, and whimpers, the Jewish community dispatched a delega-tion to the Court, with gifts to express gratitude, and to appease the ruler, who might be influenced to alleviate some of that burden. But it was all in vain, and they had to "cry and pay". To collect that money, the Jewish leadership imposed on the wealthy between six and ten thousand silver ounces each; the rabbis, who generally were penniless, had to pay "only" two thousand each. To get that sum, Jews again had to melt the silver decorations of the Torah scrolls, but felt that this act was so demeaning to the honor of the Torah, that they refrained from reading from those naked scrolls during the following feast of Pentecost. In the 1704 Chronicle, more reports of robbery, taxes and acts of cruelty against the Jews were reported. One Jew, who had hardly been married for a month, was abducted and burned alive. The local governor, who ordered the murder, also sent his underlings to exact a "ransom" for the dead Jew. Others of his underlings visited the *mellah* every day, to demand more taxes and gifts, or to collect cones of sugar, silk materials, food stuffs, and clothing, as if the Jewish pockets were bottomless; thus, anyone who had any authority or wielded any power, saw himself entitled to dip his hand and grab as much as he could. But when there was no other source from which to pay, delegations of Jewish notables went to the Court in Meknes to complain about this endless procession of exactions. The king ordered them flogged with lead-garnered whips, until two of them died, and the rest of them were ordered burned alive in the lime furnace. But he reconsidered and elected to hold them hostage until their community in Fes redeemed them with another twenty pounds of silver. Jews who could not pay were arrested, and they either died under torture, or announced their conversion to Islam in order to escape that hell. After all these horrors, the chronicler sang the praise of Mulai Isma'il at his death (1727), perhaps to signify that the other leaders were worse. He was specifically lauded for the security of trade in his times, due to his ruthless security forces, and for his "wisdom and intelligence". And on the circumstances of his death, it was mentioned that "due to our sins, he fell ill and died", as if the Jews' sins caused his death, or that they should regret the passing away of the despot. Maybe they sensed that the successors might turn out even worse.

Nothing could better illustrate the *dhimmi* state of mind than these dismaying reports. They were founded on the "miraculous" and the unpredictable in the permanently flimsy and threatened existence of the Jews, where the oppressed, who hardly maintained their breathing, were overly grateful to their persecutors and to God for their survival. They thanked the Lord that they were not compelled to convert from their faith, and that they could withstand the tortures, the hunger, the fears, and the threats, which accompanied their survival. They thought that things could always get worse. Sometimes they did indeed. In the *inter-regnum* year of 1790-1, for example, the Jews were compelled to leave the Fes *mellah* for twenty two months, and upon their return from their shelters in the mountains, or in other cities, or from hiding places in town, they began to build the ruins anew, to refurbish the walls which were breached, and to rebuild their private as well as their communal lives. After all this, the great luminary, Rabbi Yehuda Ben-Attar, sang the praise of the Lord for "all the miracles He performed for us, to our benefit. Let us sing in gratitude to the Lord, for we should not be ungrateful. We have seen with our own eyes and heard with our own ears, the miracles done to us, just like the exodus from Egypt". Shortly thereafter, in 1793, during the years immediately following the French Revolution, the rule again revolved, and new persecutions were imposed, on *Pesach* at first, in the town of Tetouan - whose Jews were robbed of all the provisions they had accumulated for the holiday, and many of them were killed, raped, burned and despoiled. These rampages spread to other cities and lasted until Pentecost, seven weeks later, when nothing was left to be despoiled, not even the honor of deflowered Jewish women, who tried to cover their nudity with extant pieces of burnt Torah scrolls. In the city of Oujda, the Jews who came out in festive Arab dress to welcome the new ruler, instead raised his wrath, because they were indistinguishable from the Arabs in the crowd, so he ordered the right ear of all Jews present, old and young, men and women, to be cut off, in order to tell who was who. Rabbi Shriki, a great scholar in Torah in that generation, to whom a high position had been promised by the king, if he converted to Islam, but he refused, was burnt alive, while the cruel ruler watched and sang. Other Jews were hanged alive by their feet at the entrance to the *mellah,* for all to see and be struck by terror. That king, Yazid Ibn Muhammed (1790-92), was known in Jewish sources as "arrogant and Jew-hater, like Haman from the Book of Esther, who delighted in chopping off the heads of Jews and hanging them at the city entrance. When his brother, Suleiman, took over the reign (1792-1822), the Jews regarded him as a "savior and redeemer".

And so, the lives of the Jews proceeded from one ruler to the next, one more or less greedy, cruel and evil, than his predecessor or his successor, to the point that periods of slightly less duress (there were no good periods) looked like a golden age. Namely, a king who did not indulge in massive massacres, or in frequently despoiling the Jews, was adulated as "benefactor" and "benevolent". The next century was not any better. In 1811, a large scale pogrom plagued the Jews of nearby Meknes, many synagogues were burned, with their books and scrolls inside, and so many houses were destroyed that families were compelled to spend the nights in the streets. The Jews were afraid to decry the ruin of their community, or to eulogize the dead in public, lest the authorities suspect that they identified with them. Despite the discretion of the mourning, reports were passed to the rulers, that Jews had built new synagogues, something strictly prohibited under the Umar Regulations. That prompted the authorities to destroy the new buildings, and impose fines for the violation of the rules. Only now, when one looks back at the past, but now better equipped with the learning, experience and an historical perspective, can one understand the significance of the deep sighs so often sounded by the resigned old generation of fathers and grandfathers, accompanied by the prayer: "May God pronounce our suffering plentiful!". When they repeated that prayer, their voices were shaky and painful, as if the entire weight of the universe rested on their shoulders. At the time, one could never fathom their individual and communal agony, which was imprinted, generation after generation, on their flesh, and not only on their recollection, in spite of the atmosphere of quiet, serenity and normalcy which they tried to weave around the younger generation they wished to raise and preserve. That saga of suffering, not only was recorded by the Jewish victims, but was also confirmed in the writings of their oppressors, who saw no wrong in their doings; for that was what the prevailing rule of the Muslim masters, was supposed to mete out to the inferior *dhimmis.*

That treatment of the *dhimmis* was enshrined not only in ancient Muslim judicial theory, but also in pre-modern practice. A 15th century Moroccan scholar, al-Maghili, described the day of payment of the poll-tax, which was levied on Jews individually and on their community collectively. On payment day, they [the *dhimmis]* shall be assembled in a public place like the *suq* (market place*).* They should be standing there waiting in the lowest and dirtiest place. The acting officials representing the law, shall be placed above them and shall adopt a threatening attitude, so that it seems to them, as well as to others, that our object is to degrade them by pretending to take their possessions. They will realize that we are doing them a favor (again) in accepting from them the *jizya,* and letting them thus go free. Then, they shall be dragged one by one (to the official responsible) for the exacting of payment. When paying, the *dhimmi* will receive a blow, and will be thrust aside, so that he will think that he has escaped the sword through this (insult). This is the way that the Friends of the Lord, of the first and last generations, will act towards their infidel enemies, for might belongs to Allah, to His Messenger, and to the Believers (Cited in Bat Ye'or[35]*).*

Four hundred years later, at the end of the 19th century, an Italian Jew, visiting Marrakesh, personally watched this similar scene at the gate of the *mellah:*

The Governor and the Judge planted their tents at the

---

[35] Bat Ye'or, *The Dhimmi: Jews and Christians Under Islam*, p.201.

entrance to the *mellah* and urged the Jews to proceed to the payment of the *jizyah* which they collected for the sultan… I was also summoned, and since I inquired whether strangers who enjoyed European patronage were also obliged to pay their part, I was told that others had already paid, therefore I agreed to conform too. After I paid the tax to the officials, I was beaten on my shoulder by the guards of the Judge [the act of payment, which is a religious duty, was overseen by the Judges, but law enforcement was assured by the Governor]. I addressed the two officials and told them that I was under the protection of the Italians. Thereupon, the Judge ordered the guards: "remove the kerchief from his head and beat him forcefully, and let him complain to whomever he wishes!" The guards obeyed, and beat me energetically. This kind of attitude to a protected European subject, only shows the local Arabs that they can mistreat Jews without any fear of punishment .[36]

Another European visitor to Morocco reported that *dhimmis* could not possess Qur'an books, or employ Muslim servants. In Marrakesh of 1880, an old Jewish couple employed a poor Arab woman as a house maid. When that was discovered, the old Jew, Jacob Dahan, was ordered beaten to death by the Governor, and his corpse to be dragged in the streets by soldiers. Only a high ransom paid by the Jews permitted his burial, but all his property was confiscated. Marriage or sexual relationships of Muslims with *dhimmis*, was also punished by execution, as was the fate of Jews who converted to Christianity and vice versa, the rationale being that if a *dhimmi* decided to relinquish his religion, his only alternative was Islam. In those days, Moroccan Jews were prohibited from leaving

---

[36] Ibid. p. 327.

the confines of the *mellah* wearing shoes, for among Muslims, their being barefooted made their humiliation obvious. Under the Almoravid Ali ben-Yussef (1106-42), the Jews were forbidden from coming to the capital Marrakesh and staying overnight, and if they disobeyed, they stood to lose their lives and properties. Jews could also be executed, if accused of insulting Islam or the Qur'an. Any Jew who raised his hand against a Muslim, even in the course of self-defense, had it cut off. Other horrific reports testified what the *dhimmis* were forced to do, in order to publicly demonstrate and perpetuate their state of misery and humiliation. For example, when in internecine wars of succession in Morocco, heads of rivals were cut off beyond measure, it was the Jews who were charged with emptying the skulls from whatever brains were in them, to allow the victors to hoist them on top of their long spears in their victorious parades. In other cases, where the victors wished to preserve the skulls of their enemies, they forced the Jews, intentionally on their Sabbath day, to salt the bleeding heads. One hypothesis places the salting as the origin of the word *mellah* in that forced occupation, given that *milh* is the Arabic for salt. Only due to the protests of western consuls to the sultan, did Muhammed IV consent, in the 19th century, to cancel this cruel practice. In the 20th century, the *dhimma* was abrogated by the French authorities, and many of its practices simply disappeared, much to the displeasure and bitterness of the Muslims, who did not forget that they had been in total control of their Jews, and could manipulate them to their whim. When Muslims were, in turn, under French occupation, against which they could do nothing, that was their opportunity to displace their frustration to the Jews and take revenge on them.

Abraham Almalih, the director of the *Alliance Israelite Universelle* Jewish Boy School in Fes, wrote to the HQ of his organization in Paris in 1911, on the eve of the French occupation:

I have the honor to acknowledge receipt of your letter,

which also included a message by Rabbi Vidal Serfati, requesting the intervention of the Moroccan Foreign Minister, who is now in Paris, to abrogate the current humiliating custom which forbids entrance of Jews to the territory of the Kingdom, unless they are barefooted. Unfortunately, the facts mentioned by the Rabbi are accurate, for the Jews are indeed compelled to remove their shoes before entering the borders of the Kingdom. Apart from the humiliation involved, it is unbearable that our coreligionists should have to wait barefooted at the entrance to the royal palace, which is damp and frozen in the winter, or brazenly hot in summer. Rabbi Vidal himself, who is in the habit of going to the Palace for the community's affairs, or to interfere on behalf of individuals, often returns sick after his prolonged waiting sessions at the gate. I believe that it would be difficult to get the sultan to consent for the Jews to come to the palace with their shoes on, because this would be a far-reaching concession that his pride would not allow him to make, especially that this stands in contradiction to the image Muslims have of themselves and of the Jews. (Cited in Andrew Bostom).[37]

Rabbi Vidal Serfati, whose name has been venerated among Moroccan Jewry, in fact did not say anything which was not known, except to confirm that the draconian sanctions of the *dhimma* were well in effect into the 20th century, and would not have been abrogated if not for the French occupation which imposed the change in an effort to civilize the territory it dominated in North Africa.

---

[37] Andrew Bostom, *The Legacy of Jihad*, Prometheus Books, Amherst, 2005, p. 31. For much more, on the humiliating conditions of Jews in North Africa, see Paul Fenton and David Littman, *Exile in the Maghreb: 10th to 20th Centuries*, Fairleigh Dickinson Univ Press, Madison, 2012.

The reporters in the Fes Chronicle had for generations recorded the exactions against the Jews, which had reached their peak under the Almohads (1130-1232), who brought destruction to North African Jewry (and Christianity too). They indeed slaughtered untold thousands, forced conversions, and imprisoned the recalcitrant survivors. The Jewish chroniclers, Abraham ibn Dawud, and the poet, Abraham ibn Ezra, depicted in harrowing detail the events under the supervisory authorities of the Almohads, who had forced Jews to either Islamize or to die as martyrs. Those who converted were kept under close supervision, lest they reneged and secretly abided by their faith. Their children were taken from them, and submitted to Muslim education, an exact antecedent to what was to happen three centuries later by the Spanish Inquisition. Maimonides himself was the most famous victim of that policy, when he fled Ahmohad's conquest of Cordova in 1148, found a temporary shelter in Fes, sometimes posing as a Muslim, until he found a permanent refuge in Cairo, under the Fatimid Dynasty, a more hospitable shelter for Jews of Islam. Jews were always proud of his heritage, for they had all heard of his greatness, but never asked why he fled, or had to hide, and to run away from one Muslim place to another. Only later did they understand that Moroccan Jews were themselves stateless, and in constant search for a permanent turf, which always eluded them, because Christian Europe was worse to them than was Islamdom; therefore, they could seek refuge only in other Muslim lands. Maimonides was unique in his learning of Hebrew and Arab culture, and was also a renowned doctor, so he could find a permanent shelter for himself, not as a persecuted Jewish refugee, but as a skilled and extremely learned and gifted individual, who easily spanned Arab and Jewish cultures, western and Islamic.

The great paradox is often cited in that the giant and unique Maimonides, who is often brought up as the paradigmatic example of the products of the Andalusian Golden Age of Islamo-Jewish coexistence, and of the cultural cross-fertilization between the two civilizations, had also himself become the archetype of its failure, and the most debunking manifestation of that utopian myth, which has been cultivated by many politically correct politicians and scholars, but, as a whole, as Fernandez- Morrero has convincingly demonstrated[38], had no leg to stand on. That Arabs and Muslims needed to cultivate this utopia for their self-image and propaganda needs, one can understand if not accept. But when Jews themselves fall into this trap, it is pitiful and self-defeating, and can only be explained as the paradigm of *dhimmi* behavior. Maimonides, who knew and understood the situation better than any contemporary, said that "the Ismai'lites (Muslims) have persecuted us and discriminated against us, and no other nation has humiliated and hated Jews more than them". The hellish and nightmarish Jewish existence under the Almohads, which remains incrusted in the memory of Moroccan Jewry, was not amended or made up for thereafter, and no effort was exerted by later dynasties to erase those atrocities completely. Quite the contrary, that dynasty lives among the most glorious in Moroccan history, on account of its expansionism and religiosity. Moreover, we have seen that even under the current Alawite Dynasty, which is supposed to be benevolent and generous, there were very dark days of massacres and cruelty towards its Jews. Namely, one does not have to take the Almohad period as an extraordinary aberration to an otherwise benevolent rule, but, on the contrary, as a yardstick to what would come after them. For, during all the periods when wars of succession raged, it was always the Jews who paid the price, while the brief periods of let-up were the exceptions rather than the rule in the long, sad, dangerous and ultimately destructive existential condition of Jews in North Africa. Solomon Cohen wrote about the heritage of that most inhuman of dynasties:

---

[38] Op. cit.

Abd al Mu'min, who inherited the founder Ibn Tumart, conquered Tlemcen in North Africa and killed all its inhabitants, including the Jews, except for those who converted to Islam. All north African cities, which came under Almohad rule, as well as all Spanish cities they occupied, were submitted to massacres and spoilage. In Fez alone, one hundred thousand people were killed, and another one hundred and twenty thousand in Marrakesh... The Jews of North Africa suffered greatly under their yoke, many of them perished, others converted their faith, and the rest did not dare to appear as Jews in public... This was also the fate of large swaths of territory which they conquered in Spain between Tortosa and Seville [39]

That entire register of horrendous events, under which generations of Jews (and Christians) suffered - sometimes more and sometimes less, according to the time, the place, and the whim and zeal of the ruler - was given legitimacy and consistency by the Muslim ideology, which sanctioned it. Officially, under the new modern Muslim regimes of nation-states, *dhimma* was abolished, especially under the pressure of colonial powers who imposed a more liberal order of things. But the notion of *dhimma* has never disappeared in practice, because the power of the *shari'a* law, which sanctioned the political theory of Islam, could never be overtaken by any western law. Much was said about the many mistreatments of Jews in Morocco after the coming of the French, meaning that centuries of Muslim hatred and contempt could not be erased by a few decades of western rule, especially since European colonial powers in Muslim countries were not themselves totally divorced from their own anti-Semitism of the European brand. Furthermore, the Muslim

---

[39] Bostom, p. 612.

revivalist movements in the contemporary world, have been clamoring for the renewal of the same imagery and terminology, as existed in classical Islam, meaning that the *dhimma* ought to again become part of the Muslim legal system. Indeed, sermons in mosques, even political speeches and fundamentalist writings, posters and leaflets, audio and video cassettes, demand this revival and make it a popular quest for some of the new Muslim states. What is difficult to comprehend is the conduct of many Jews, who, after regaining their sovereignty, are still under the grip of the *dhimma*. Some of them, who had never experienced this humiliating status themselves, have become enslaved by their naïve quest to gain recognition by Muslims, who fundamentally still despise them. Because, even though no more than very few Jews still dwell in the lands of Islam and feed Muslim hatred toward them, the fact that their kin have created a modern and successful state, which is the envy of Muslims, who cannot bear that their formerly submissive *dhimmis,* now occupy a place of honor among the nations, cannot be a source of satisfaction for Muslims to be proud of.[40]

The scenes of horror and fear which every Jew experienced since his or her childhood in Morocco, were not temporary and passing episodes, but a permanent feature in his or her psychological and behavioral make-up (as confirmed once again in the massacre of 1,500 Jews, entire families including babies and the elderly On October 7, 2023 in 22 Israeli villages east of Gaza at dawn, and others led to exile in Gaza as hostages). Jews in the Islamic exile were considered inferior ("the descendants of apes and swines") and,

---

[40] Two extraordinary and well-documented studies which were added recently to the vast treasure on the condition of the Jews under Islam, and have torn apart the myth of Muslims generosity and tolerance, must be added to the bibliography to get a more balanced picture on this state of affairs:

1.Dario Fernandez Ferrera, *The Myth of the Andalusian Paradise,* ISI. Wilmington, 2015*; and*

2.Paul Fenton and David Littman, *Exile in the Maghreb:Jews under Islam,* Fairleigh Dickinson University, Madison, 2016.

therefore, were condemned to eternal misery and subordination. But in Israel, their very claim to sovereignty contradicted the *Shari'a*, the most perfect of legal systems, originating from divine inspiration, when its validity proved questionable in the face of thriving Israel. The Muslims could have changed their minds, when they realized that liberated Jews can be successful and even challenge them in open societies; however, they elected to ignore those marks of success, and to continue to look down upon them, for otherwise, how could they feel superior to them? Hence the massive return of Muslims to the fundaments of their glorious past, for only there can they revive their pride in their culture and their dominance of the *dhimmis*. The Jews' decision to leave Morocco was, thus, a disengagement from a situation they could not bear, but which they could not alter either. They were yearning to live in a new world, where they would no longer need to cater to Muslims and act sycophantically to please them, in order to ensure their continued existence. But Jews could not imagine that the status of *dhimma* would pursue them to their old-new country. In effect, Muslims in conflict with Israel still consider Jews as rebels, who did not accept their due place of submission under Islam, and thus they transformed their anti-Jewish hatred into anti-Zionism and anti-Israelism, which amount to the same. For them, Zionism and Israel mean that the rebellious *dhimmis* have invaded a Muslim territory, in a quest to make it their base to battle Islam. Hence their yearning to return the Jews to the condition of "eternal misery" allocated to them by the eternal and immutable Qur'an, and that proposition is not negotiable. Islam does not recognize Jews as a people, therefore Jews do not deserve a state, and their movement of national liberation – Zionism, is discarded as "racism", Allah knows why. The end result is that the vicious circle of persecuting the Jews as *dhimmis,* first in the lands of Islam and then as rebels who need to be subjugated anew, has been closed in modern Israel. For now, for every attempt to humiliate Jews, they can, in turn, cause more pain and more humiliation to whomsoever attempts to harm them. For modern Jews, better to be accused of humiliating others than be the victims of humiliation themselves, though it would have been better if one could avert humiliation to either side.

As Muslims see it, the world is replete with hatred towards them, as evidenced today by the widespread claims of Islamophobia; and plots are constantly woven against them, hence their backwardness. They are the innocent victims who are never at fault, while all their woes and deficiencies are others' faults. Therefore, whenever Muslim honor, or that of their Prophet, seems to be hurt, like in the cartoon affair of 2006, or the *Charlie Hebdo* event of 2015, their vengeance is called for which justifies killing, rampaging and destroying the perpetrators. Believers of any faith, who are firm in their convictions, do not force them on others, nor are afraid to compete in the public square with different faiths. And when reality does not conform to their belief about the predominance of Islam, Muslims resort to violence to redress the situation. In other words, they do not live by the firmness and spiritual strength of their religion, but by watching what the others say about it to denigrate it, and they burst in violence when anyone wishes to contradict it. In Judaism there is a Talmudic saying that "if one wishes to elevate oneself, one ought to erect a mound for oneself, not dig a ditch for others". In Islam the focus has been centered on digging as many large and deep trenches to bury the enemy, rather than raise itself to their level. Thus, the main attention in the Islamic world has been, not how to elevate themselves in imitation of the strong, the advanced and the progressive, as the courageous Saudi thinkers and liberal Muslim writers have recently admitted, but how to bring them down, as Bin Laden and his ilk thought, in order to eliminate the humiliation of seeming inferior, compared to the success of others. Violence seems to have been elected in modern days to achieve that goal, as ISIS, Hamas, Hizbullah, Boko Haram and other radical Muslims, have demonstrated; and oppression, humiliation, despoiling and utter disparaging and dehumanization of Jews (and Christians) in Islamdom, during the past millennium, was the chosen way to debase the non-Muslims and show who rules the world.

Not much more has to be said to show how intimately locked into commercialization was the practice of dhimma, both literally and by expansion of the term: apart from the pogroms which could break out at any moment against the Jewish mellah, which usually involved destitution and robbery, by the local ruler and his lawless followers against the Jews and their properties, there were also the occasional periods of inter-regnum, when competing heirs to the throne all extorted from the Jews special levies of money and gold to finance their war of succession, numerous were the special levies of special taxes to provides for the needs of the rulers. Not counting the myriad ways of extorting money, which meant direct commercialization, where very little or nothing was given in return for that extorted money, many forced conversions to Islam were imposed, though there were other times when the authorities elected not to encourage conversion, for their lust to levy the "protection money" (Jizyah) often overrode the desire of a fanatic ruler (especially under the Almohads and Almoravids to rule over a purely Muslim citizenry, for the latter were exonerated from the poll tax, so the less payers the smaller the state income. But the most horrific of all these exaction was to either enforce upon Jews the choice between conversion and death (and they often chose the latter), and the almost equal act of humiliation that was described in the Qur'an, which for ever immortalized the miserable, impoverished and hopeless status of the Jew, though the dress restrictions, the ban for Jews to take up weapons even when necessary to their dangerous trading travels. No wonder that when they could in the 1960s to leave they did for the most part, and those who could do it[41] did clandestinely one or two decades earlier.

---

[41] Like this author who left Morocco in 1950.

Chapter Five

The Commercialization of Jihad

Islam, being established since its inception amidst the inter-tribal violence in the Arabian Peninsula, not only continued to grow and thrive amidst violence, the worst of it being the "War of Heresy" (Ridda War/s 632-4) but even came to construct an entire theme of "fighting in the Path of Allah", and rewarding with blissful rest in Paradise in eternity at the foot of the throne of Allah those who fell in that fight. Naturally, foreign critical minds would suspect that the Prophet needed his followers to fight for him to enable him to expand his faith, but for the believers he just did what Allah ordered him to do to toughen his fighters in order to prepare them for battle and to advance their readiness to go fearlessly forward to war, knowing that a reward of eternal bliss awaits them in the hereafter. Moreover, they understood that while this futile world is only a "corridor" to the eternal bliss in Paradise while the real existence materializes there, any Muslim fighting for anywhere would be deterred by war. Consequently, incentives to go to war were elaborated by the Prophet and included in the Qur'an as the world of Allah so as to sound more credible. These are precisely the themes promoted today to encourage and cultivate among the *Islamikaze*[42].

Fledgling Islam had sprung out of the Arabian Peninsula, follow-

---

ing the death of its Prophet in AD 632, and the conquering Muslim Arabs, who had been versed in the language and practice of tribal wars, and wandering between pasturage domains, never settling permanently in any particular land. Except for the scarce urban populations in the sparse commercial cities in the Arabian Peninsula, where it came into contact with alien cultures, it was an insular Arab pre-Islamic culture until it conquered new territories by force, and was driven into the imperative of developing new political concepts and a new vocabulary for dealing with the new permanently settled political, social and military realities. A new *genre* of political and military literature, known as the *Futuh al-Buldan* (the Conquest of Lands) evolved, which filled the existing *lacunae* in the Arabian concept of the world and its linguistic expressions. *Fat'h* (pl. *futuh*, literally "opening") henceforth designated the territories newly "opened", i.e. conquered and subjected, by expanding Islam, meaning that the opened land was not only destined to become and remain Muslim for all generations to come, but by the very fact that it was acquired by and for Islam, it became a *waqf* land, i.e. a holy endowment which will obtain at all times and in all the Islamized places until "the Day of Resurrection". The eternal quality of *fat'h* territory obviates the need to discuss its status every time anew, under changing political and military circumstances, for example: though the domination of the Muslim lands of Andalusia, Kashmir and Palestine has veered to non-Muslims, those territories will remain for ever of Muslim ownership, pending their retrieval from their present infidel "occupiers". The Hamas movement, for example, which today vies for the "rescue of the Palestinian *waqf* land from the hands of its Jewish "occupiers", has inscribed its commitment to this cause in its proclaimed platform of 1988. It says expressly:

> The Islamic Resistance Movement (HAMAS) believes
> that the land of Palestine has been an Islamic *Waqf*

throughout the generations and until the Day of Resurrection.; no one can renounce it or part of it, or abandon it or part of it. No Arab country, or the aggregate of all Arab countries, and no Arab King or President, nor all of them in the aggregate, nor has that right any organization, or the aggregate of all organizations, be they Palestinian or Arab, because Palestine is an Islamic *Waqf*, for all generations until the Day of Resurrection. Who can presume to speak for all Muslim generations to the Day of Resurrection? This is the status of the land in Islamic *Shari'a*, and it is similar to all lands conquered by Islam by force, and made thereby *waqf* lands upon their conquest, for all generations of Muslims until the Day of Resurrection.[43]

This is not only a declarative sanctification of the conquest by force for the sake of Islam, but also a defiance of all the powers that be in the world, for all times to come, signifying that the Muslim order, once established, stands immutable, eternal and unchallengeable, come what may. The immediate repercussion of this is that the holy war, namely *Jihad*, stands as the only remedy before the Muslims in defense of their divine heritage, and as the holy obligation of every individual Muslim to join fighting for. The Hamas Charter, like the ideologies followed by adepts of al-Qa'ida, ISIS, the Taliban, Boko Haram and other radical Muslim groups, explains both the rationale and the historical evolution of this tenet. Indeed, in the surprise attack of the Hamas from Gaza at dawn on Saturday 7th of October, 2023, they slaughtered in their beds over one thousand innocent Israelis, including babies and the elderly and led with

---

[43] Article 11 of the Platform of the Hamas. See R. Israeli, "The Charter of Allah,the Platform of the Islamic Resistance Movement", in R. Israeli, *Fundamentalist Islam and Israel*, University Press of America, Lanham 1993, pp. 123-170.

them to exile into Gaza another two hundred prisoners as hostages. That was nothing new compared to what they pledged in the their platform which elaborates:

> This [norm] has prevailed since the commanders of the Muslim armies completed the conquest of Syria and Iraq, and they asked the Caliph of Muslims, 'Umar ibn al-Khattab[44], for his view of the conquered land, i.e. whether it should be partitioned between the troops, or left in possession of its population, or otherwise. Following discussions and consultations between the Caliph of Islam, Umar ibn al-Khattab, and the Companions (*Sahabah*) of the Messenger of Allah, be peace and prayer upon him, they decided that the land should remain in the hands of its owners, to benefit from it and from its wealth, but the control[45] over the land and the land itself ought to be endowed as a *waqf* [in perpetuity] for all generations of Muslims, until the Day of Resurrection. The actual possession of the land by its owners is only one of *usufruct,* but the Muslim *waqf* will endure as long as heaven and earth last. Any measure in violation of this law of Islam, with regard to Palestine, is baseless and reflects on its perpetrators.
>
> "Lo, This is certain truth. Therefore, O Muhammad, praise the name of thy Lord, the Tremendous" (Sura 56 (the Event), verse 95).[46]

---

[44] The Second Caliph of Muslims (634-44), who ruled after the death of the Prophet. Under his stewardship Syria, Palestine and Iraq were subdued to Islamic rule.

[45] *Raqba* in the original, which could mean either control, supervision or guardianship, but also could read *raqaba,* meaning slaves working as serfs on the land.

[46] Article Eleven of the Charter. See ftn 3.

'Umar, being the second of the Four Righteous Caliphs who suc-
ceeded the Prophet (the others being Abu Bakr, 'Uthman and Ali)
and are second only to Him, has been one of the most valued
among them, and therefore an eminent authority for referral, in
case of disagreement, regarding the validity of any Muslim tradition, especially in matters of military expansion, administrative
precedents and wise and pious rule in general. It is to the first
Caliph, Abu Bakr, that the leader of ISIS, Abu Bakr al-Baghdadi,
alludes, and it is to the second, 'Umar, that the late Mullah 'Umar,
the chief of the Taliban in southeast Asia, referred . The notion of
fat'h has become so awesome that some heroes of Islam, like the
Ottoman conqueror of Anatolia and eliminator of the Christian-
Byzantine Empire, Mehmet II, who turned glorious Constantinople
into Muslim Istanbul, is proudly dubbed as *al-Fatih*, the Conqueror. Yasser Arafat, the founder and head of the PLO, called the
major component of his organization: *Fat'h* (the Conquest), the
acronym for the Movement for the Liberation of Palestine, which
if left in that sequence in Arabic would have made *HATF*, meaning
"sudden death", something that is less than attractive for a movement of national liberation, therefore the order of letters was
reversed to make up the glorious *FAT'H*. In the time of the Prophet
there was no doubt that participating in fighting and distinguishing
oneself in battle not only pleased him, advanced his prospects of
victory and expansion and brought glory to Islam, but also included
a vast booty from the mythical and fabulous reaches of Byzantium
and then Persia, the first Empires that fought Islam and were at first
convinced they could control, contain and tame it. A poor Bedouin
in Arabia of those days must have been fascinated by those prospects in those days and his commitment to fight for Islam must
have been emulated by the many who became enthused by the
rapidly moving army of camels and fighters, among them celebrated
commanders who became Muslim war heroes for many generations
to come. Since then, Jihad had become the supreme "striving" that

Muslims are obliged to exert, and became the religiously sanctioned way to perform many tenets of the faith, among them the *fat'h (conquest to expand Islam)*. For many years after the initial victorious wars of expansion, the Muslim world has been apologetic about the aggressive aspects of Jihad, arguing that the original and true significance of Jihad was spiritual, namely the constant endeavor of Believers to improve themselves. But there is no doubt from the many references to Jihad in the Qur'an, and more so today in the Hamas Charter and in the discourse of al-Qa'ida, Hizbullah and ISIS, and particularly in their real practice, that they mean war, battlefronts, killing, death, maiming and blood letting which have left Western civilization flabbergasted. One could hardly conquer territory by kind words in the times of the Prophet and his successors, as one can hardly bring down the Twin Towers today, or behead Westerners in ISIS territory, or massacre entire populations in Syria, Iraq, Libya, Yemen and Afghanistan, or terrorize civilian populations in Paris, London or Jerusalem, by "spiritual endeavor" only. The perpetrators themselves, before they launch their outrageous orgies of killings, or when they are called to task after the act, arrogantly elect to parrot their commitment to bloody Jihad, and for the most part never express either sympathy for the victims nor any regret for their own murderous acts of violence. That is the main road pursued by moderate Muslims to make the Jihad digestible to Western civilization, trying to disclaim the widespread attribute of "Islamic terrorism" that has become of household usage in the West.

Jihad used to be the communal obligation of the Muslim *Umma*, meaning that whenever any part of the community, at the time of the Prophet and thereafter, or anyone of authority, caliphal or clerical, launched the holy war, all Muslim individuals felt exempted from that duty, for the whole community's performance relieved the scattered individuals. That was called *fard kifayah*, i.e. a *satisfactory fulfillment* of the Muslim communal obligation. But latter day

Muslim radical groups, beginning by the *Muwahhidun* movement in Arabia in the 19th Century, via the Muslim Brothers and through the other Muslim radicals that derive from them, like al-Qa'ida, Hamas, Jabhat al-Nusra, the Boko Haram and even ISIS, have reinterpreted the obligation of Jihad as an individual one, so as to override the established Muslim authorities, like government-appointed Imams and pro-western rulers, who are reluctant (let alone unable) to engage in perpetual warfare with their surroundings. This fanatic interpretation urges all believers to "pick up a bucket of water and rush to extinguish the fire enveloping Islam" themselves, instead of waiting for unreliable clerics and rulers to take the initiative. This reading of Jihad also determines that its obligatory nature is personal (*fard 'ayn*), deriving from other jihadists in Islamic history, who either followed the example of the Prophet, or of other illustrious Muslim fighters, by launching themselves fearlessly into the fray, thus bringing glory to Islam. Then there developed in various parts of the Muslim world, traditions of *ghazi*s (raiders), *murabit*s (border settlers) and *mujahid*s (Jihad fighters).This is the motif that Muslim war volunteers are moved by, and this is what causes the thousands of young jihadists from all over Islamdom and from across the Muslim minority populations in western countries, to defy their elders, the authorities of their countries and the dangers they encounter at every step of the way, and flock to the Islamic battlefronts.

Fat'h having become the laundered term for legal, "natural", conventional, divinely-inspired and civilized Islamic expansion and acquisition of territory by force of arms, and *Jihad* as the religious justification for doing so ever so violently, the rest of the "secular" terms for wars, conquests and expansion, which fit the uncivilized behavior of the Infidels, remain confined to *Ihtilal* and *Istitan* (conquest and settlement, respectively), both carrying the connotation of taking root, electing to dwell somewhere. The former is usually translated as "conquest", the other as "colonization", and the two are related, and are removed from the adventurism, danger, excitement and enthusiasm which accompany a military campaign of expansion, or of *fat'h* for the sake of Allah, or the participation in the fulfillment of the religious duty of Jihad. The latter (*Istitan*) has grown into an essentially negative endeavor, committed by non-Muslims, and connected with imperialism or illegal settlement in others' lands for material gains, involving the exploitation and oppression of others, except if done by Muslims to expand their conquests and dominion. Thus, the colonial acquisitions of the powers and Israel's nowaday's settlements in the West Bank of the Jordan river, are *mustawtanat* (colonies), or *a'mal istitaniyya* (colonial acts), while the Islamic conquest and settlement of North Africa, Central Asia and the Middle East are considered legitimate and Allah-ordained acts of *fat'h*. Even the current flooding of Europe by Muslim immigrants (euphemistically dubbed "refugees") is viewed by many Muslim circles as new, non-violent forms of Jihadi *fat'h*, since new Muslim communities are being established and rooted in Christendom, and new territory is being added to Islamdom by "peaceful means", without risks being taken and blood being spilled in the immediate future.

Interestingly enough, *ihtilal* has become the standard term for both conquest and occupation, although those two meanings are conceptually differentiated: conquest connotes the violent phase of the military takeover of the others' territory, as in *fat'h*, i.e. the process of "opening up" enemy territory, while occupation denotes the administrative phase of managing and maintaining the rule of the sovereign power over the occupied territory, including the process of settlement when there is one, until the newly acquired lands are annexed to the Caliphate that was ruled from one center, or divided up between various sultanates, which eventually attained independence. After Nazi Germany conquered Europe, its occupation forces managed it and maintained it, often with the willful collaboration of some locals ("Quislings"), who acted on behalf of the occupying power; but when the Allies counter-attacked and liberated the occupied lands, granting sovereignty back to its original holders, its "occupying forces" remained in defeated Germany (and in Austria for that matter), whose constitution was rewritten and the political system de-Nazified, while the new government was trained for pacific rule, until it was weaned from the Allied "guidance" and made conducive to "peace" with its former occupiers. The same pattern was followed after Japan was defeated in the Pacific War and made to conform to the "peace" dictated and enforced by General Mc Arthur and his team.

Having settled for one kind of warfare or another, the warring Believers had to make the world order accessible and understandable, with every land occupied, and every human in the community, well defined according to the standards of the *Shari'a*. Those standards did not talk of individuals but of communities, whose members shared the same creed. At the very apex of the human pyramid stood the Muslims, those who have surrendered (*aslama*) to the divine Will, because they are the closest human beings to perfection, which only the Believers can attain as members of the universal congregation of Muslims- the *Umma*. Next to them are the People of the Book (*Ahl al Kitab*, the Scriptuaries), those holders of holy texts, like Christians and Jews, who stood in an interim position between the True Faith —Islam- and the totally godless pagans or *mushrikin* (polytheists, those who share the oneness of Allah with other divinities). Being in this mid-way position between the belief in one God, on the one hand, and their possession of holy scriptures which they allegedly forged and distorted over the centuries, on the other, the Scriptuaries are not to be indiscriminately massacred like the polytheists, but must be protected by a *dhimma* (protection/toleration) pact which, on the one hand, guaranteed their lives and properties in the Islamic realm, but obliged them to pay the *Jizya* (a poll tax), as prescribed by the Qur'an. This was both a sign of their submission to the rule of Islam, and also of their acceptance of their inferior status. In other words, this seeming act of "tolerance" of the *dhimmis* by Islam, was not to be construed in the modern sense of accepting the others despite their ethnic, religious or gender differences, without value-judging them, but as tolerating the other in spite of his inherent inferiority. This meant that both the Muslims and their "protected" *dhimmi*s were cognizant and accepting of the humiliating status of the Scriptuary people as a permanent and perpetual state of affairs.

To be a *dhimmi* under Islam did not only entail the demeaning necessity of paying the *Jizyah*, in utterly humiliating ceremonies which survived until the 20th Century, but also an entire set of restrictions and limitations:juridical, political, social and economic, which made the ruling Islam ever more attractive to the other subordinate faiths, and indeed encouraged over the years more or less massive conversions into Islam, some times voluntarily but often under coercion. However, while the Christians in their lands that were occupied by Islam could always find shelter in the shrinking Christendom whenever life became untenable under Islam, Jews and other minorities who had no other place to go, had to submit to the grinding pressures of the ruling Islam and do the best they could to survive. In this situation, the Golden Age of the Jews under Islam in Spain in medieval times, has often been invoked, in order to advertise the legendary Muslim "tolerance" of others. But as it was definitively shown by Dario Fernandez[47], it was more a myth than a reality. The entire misconception of that episode has emanated from the ill-understood differential treatment of other creeds by Christianity and Islam in medieval times. Indeed, in Christendom the world was uniform and came under the undisputed aegis of the universal Catholic Church, and anyone who deviated from that norm, be he non-Christian or sectarian Christian, like the Cathars, the Orthodox and then the Protestants, or

---

[47] Dario Fernandez, *The Myth of the Andalusian Paradise,* ISI, Wilmington, 2016.

other dissident sects, was considered beyond the pale and persecuted accordingly. The medieval Jews of Europe were expelled, murdered, burned and subjected to the horrors of the Inquisition under those headings, and therefore their lot in medieval Europe was bad bitter and untenable. In any case, since Jizyah was an important avenue of income to the Muslim state, very often It paid for Islam to leave Christian and Jewish minorities in Infidelity rather than force them into Islam due to the Jizya they paid than to induce or even force their conversion which would exonerate them from the poll tax. Besides, the Muslims would have been deprived from the pleasure and pride of the entire ritual of payment of the tax, which was performed publicly and intended to humiliate the dhimmis for their low status that was dictated by the Qur'an.

Conversely, the world of Islam was compartmentalized into Muslims and "tolerated" Scriptuaries, i.e. the Jews and Christians who lived in its midst, who were recognized and accepted, though in a secondary and discriminated against status. Therefore, for the most part, as long as Jews and Christians submitted to Islamic rule and played according to their assigned inferior *dhimmi* status, their lives and properties were, at least in theory, guaranteed by the Muslim rulers. To be sure, reality was at times more favorable and at other times more cruel than described by Islamic theory, when generous or otherwise interested rulers entrusted to Scriptuaries high positions in government, although they were supposedly untrustworthy, but under mean and sadistic rulers they were crushed, oppressed and persecuted, although they paid their poll taxes and fulfilled their *dhimmi* obligations. But at least theoretically they were protected, and their existential condition always fared better than the non-Christian minorities in Christendom; hence the misconception of this differentiated treatment of minorities in the two worlds. In other words, a guaranteed second-rate existence under Islam was rightly considered as far safer than a permanently threatened existence in Christendom. But in the long term, the difference developed in that while in Europe modernity has brought liberties to all faiths and creeds (the bouts of anti-Semitism and the horrors of the Holocaust excepted), the world of Islam, until colonized by the West, would have persisted with its *dhimmi* limitations if it were not coerced to cancel them. Worse, resurgent Islam of recent decades has been keen to restore those ancient norms of mistreating non-Muslims, as we see evidently today in the persecution of Christian minorities all over the Muslim world, and in the execution of Yazidis and westerners in the Islamic State, together with the re-enforcement of the *jizya* for Christians in ISIS-held territory.

The lands taken over by expanding Islam were basically divided into two domains: the *Dar al-Islam* (the Abode of Islam, or the *Pax Islamica*) and the *Dar al-Harb* (the Abode of War). While for practical purposes, these categories have no longer been valid after the Islamic empire fell apart, and Islamdom fell prey to western colonial powers, Muslim radicals in our days revive them whenever they can, either in rebel enclaves that fell within their jurisdiction, or in their fiery writings which seek to restore the strict laws of the *Shari'a* when and where possible. Not that they are inventing new rules, but they are simply re-invigorating old norms of Islam which had been eroded by foreign coercion of by domestic practice, reluctant as it may have been. In old days, the swift processes of conquest were followed by the slower and often less violent tribulations of Arabization and Islamization, the former by the very fact that it was Arab tribes springing out of Arabia, which made up the backbone of the military command and of the top administration. This has naturally brought about the spread of Arabic as the official language, and the settlement of Arab migrants in the newly occupied areas, who ultimately caused the Arabization of the population, and the establishment of new Arab cities, like Kufa and Baghdad, Fez and Rabat, Cairo and Qairawan, and many others, even though it took many centuries to achieve. For example in Egypt, Iraq and North Africa, which had been dominated by native Copts, Kurds,

Berbers (or Kabyles in another appellation), respectively, it took notables of Arab descent, who often boasted recognizable or invented pedigree, centuries to create local ruling dynasties before they could dub their respective countries "Arab". Arabization was naturally reinforced and followed by Islamization, which took over when the local ethno-national identity was eroded and the Islamic religious element prevailed, which guaranteed the continuity of the links that bound the Islamic *Umma* together.

Islamisation and its benefits has been the much longer-run, the lasting and living expression of the ongoing jihad, either peaceful or aggressive, whose international destiny has permitted the birth, the progression and the longevity of the Jihad itinerants until our days. As noted by eminent Islamic scholar, Nehemia Levtzion[48], across the barriers of climate and culture in Asia and Africa, Islam won converts and was adopted by entire ethnic groups in such diverse regions as Morocco and Indonesia, India and West Africa, although Islam was so assimilated in so many local cultures that it is considered a native religion in each of them. The main issue is, however, that diversity did not interfere with the fundamental unity of Islam, and the local forms of Islam are viewed as part of the same universal faith. Although we are here concerned with Jihad as the main form of expanding Islam, we have to be cognizant of the fact that in various areas of the world, it was Sufi mystics and Muslim traders who acted as the major agents of Islamization in areas like Southeast Asia, which were too remote to be conquered by militant Jihad. Nonetheless, as we speak today about Jihad as the major fac-tor of expanding Islam, we also mean it as the major factor of main-taining and preserving Islam, when in conflict-ridden countries, like the Arab world or Central Asia, or the Muslim lands in Africa, Islam feels it is threatened by environing cultures, and it takes local

---

[48] Nehemia Levtzion, *Conversion to Islam,* Holmes and Meier, London, 1979., pp. 1-23.

measures in self-defense. Examples abound: Boko Haram in Nigeria and Jabhat al-Nusra in Syria, the Shabab in Somalia and the Taliban in Pakistan and Afghanistan, and the universal movements of al-Qa'ida and the Muslim Brothers who operate trans-nationally. All of them attract Jihadi itinerants from the entire Muslim world and beyond, including from the Western democratic countries where Muslim communities have settled over the past few decades.

The idea of the world Muslim community as one *Umma* has no doubt constituted the solid base of Jihad volunteers, who internalized the recognition that fighting the Jihad war was an ethnicity- and culture-blind vocation, for the glory of Islam was universal, and the obligation to enhance it was incumbent upon all Muslims, no matter what nationality they hailed from or what country they dwelt in. For when one went to Jihad, one fought for Islam, not for any particular country, ethnic group or cultural background. For example, when Arabs sprang out of Arabia after the death of the Prophet (AD 632), and they conquered rapidly Egypt and the Fertile Crescent, they were segregated in garrison towns (the *amsar*) like Kufa, Fustat and Rabat (the latter specifically meaning that), which initially limited the contacts between the Muslim conquerors and their rulers, on the one hand, and the local populations on the other. And it was, according to Sha'ban[49], when those garrison towns became flourishing urban agglomerations, that the local populace from the surrounding countryside began to migrate and settle there as artisans and traders, and in any other needed menial jobs that those flourishing cities could offer. In the process, the native population, which had been originally separated from the *amsar* (sing. *misr*), became its own foremost agent of acculturation, i.e. Arabization in language and culture, and Islamisation in religion, once they converted into Islam. In other words, the Jihad

---

[49] M. Sha'ban, *Islamic History (600-75)*, Cambridge, 1971, cited in M. Sha'ban, "Conversion to Early Islam", in N. Levtzion, op. cit., pp. 24- 29.

fighters who came from Arabia to conquer territory and subjugate its population, may have unwittingly found that they were also the propagators of the faith, thus fulfilling incidentally the cause of Jihad in the Path of Allah. The only caveat is that when they settled down permanently, they were no longer Jihad itinerants and became "colonizers" who settled down for the long haul, while annexing their newfound land to Islamdom.[50]

In a somewhat different process, the Arab armies who conquered Egypt and North Africa and settled there, augmented their numbers by recruiting native levies who Islamized and swelled the ranks of the armies, ultimately merging into them. In Anatolia, however, the process of Islamisation was more violent and lasted many centuries, before a state framework was formed to lend permanence to the new reality, and the process of the nomadic itinerant Jihad came to an end. When the Ottomans ventured into the Balkans, however, they were already presiding over an organized state army, which launched the Jihad and conquered and settled the acquired lands, leaving behind ultimately, after half a millennium of Muslim rule, pockets of resilient Islam In Bosnia, Kosovo, Albania and the Sanjak. It was not until the Bosnia War (1992-95) that itinerant Jihadis from the Arab world, Iran and Chechnya were at hand again to assist the Muslim side of the war against the Serbs, and then retreat back to their countries of origin, or to the next battlegrounds in Iraq, Afghanistan, Syria, Libya and Yemen. The process of Arabization and Islamization having usually ended in local assimilation and the creation of new identities under Islam, the phenomenon of Jihad itinerants was necessarily a transitory one, even when it took centuries to exhaust itself. So when we transit into the modern era, we find that most Muslims across the world have already long ago taken roots in different countries and cultures, so when they venture in the name of Islam to fight for their coreligionists elsewhere,

---

[50] Levtzion, pp. 7-8.

they jump into the fray as nationals of other countries, and then usually move back to their countries of origin, unless they are pressed by the circumstances to follow up their venture into opening up other Jihadi war theaters.

In Iran, as asserted by Richard Bulliet[51], the early Islamization of the defeated Imperial cavalry and of the members of the landed aristocracy, who would rather convert to Islam following their defeat by the invading Arab Muslims, than undergo the humiliation of paying the *jizya*, contributed to the ultimate Islamization of most of Iran, and the settling down and assimilation of the Arab Jihadis, who were dispatched there to defeat the Sassanids, thus terminating after several centuries the role of the outside Jihad itinerants, and replacing them by the Iranian Imperial army. Nowadays, ironically, it is Islamic Iran which dispatches her Revolutionary Guards as itinerant Jihadis to Syria, Lebanon and Yemen, to lead the battle for the supremacy of Shi'ism in the Muslim world. In general, the victory of the Arab Jihad warriors during the initial expansion of Islam vindicated in their eyes their sense of superiority and pride in their language (the tongue of the Qur'an), and in their ethnic descent; conversely, the defeated and conquered cultures were probably subjected to the reverse feeling which interpreted their defeat as a sign of inherent weakness and inferiority. Hence the voluntary mass conversion to Islam among the conquered nations, and the facilitation of the assimilation of the Arab Jihadi fighters in their midst, under the winning banner of Islam. Therefore, the transitory nature of the itinerant Jihadi became natural, as the reputation of the Arab –Muslims became preponderant, resulting in the local populations' eagerness to hasten to merge with them on the one hand, and on the other hand enticing the fighters to settle down and become part and parcel of the local culture, once the rapid episode of conquest

---

[51] Richard Bulliet, "Naw Bahar and the Survival of Iranian Buddhism", in *Iran, 14 (1976)*, . Cited by Levtzion, p. 9.

was completed and the slow process of acculturation began. As Levtzion put it:" Success was Islam's best advertisement"[52], confirming that there was always success and glory to gain from participation in Jihad. In China, for example, Islam and Confucianism generated a confrontation between two very self-confident cultures that had a long history of swallowing others rather than being swallowed up[53] by them; therefore, after some initial gains there, the spread of Islam was contained as a minority heterodoxy.

But the pace of conversion to Islam within other cultures in general, was conditioned by the preponderance of the institutional and spiritual conditions of the previous religions, before their encounter with Islam, and by whether conversion followed Islamic military conquest, which enhanced the prestige of the victorious religion, and was done under the shock of their own humiliating defeat; or was slowly and gently seeping into the existing system without causing traumas. Levtzion claims that when the preexisting religions had been interlocked with the defeated imperial system in place, such as the Zoroastrian faith in connection with the Persian Sassanids, they suffered dramatically from the violence and humiliation of Muslim conquest, thus the collapse of the Sassanian Dynasty (226-651) inevitably triggered the destruction of the Zoroastrian hierarchy. Similarly, the Muslim conquest of Anatolia and the collapse of the Byzantines caused the Greek Orthodox Church, which provided the ideological underpinnings of the Empire, a devastating blow[54]. When analyzing the religious system in China, C.K. Yang[55] used the same concept to differentiate between "institutional religions" which had their own holy texts, clergy, places of

---

[52] Levtzion, p. 12.

[53] R. Israeli, "Islamization and Sinicization in Chinese Islam", in Levztion (ed) op cit, pp. 159-176.

[54] Levtzion, p. 12.

[55] C.K. Yang, *Religion in Chinese Society: A Study of the Contemporary Social Functions of Religion and some of their Historical Factors*, UC Press, Berkeley, 1967.

prayer and followers (like the monotheistic religions elsewhere, as well as Buddhism), and therefore their independent survival did not depend on the fate of the political system; and "diffused religions" like Confucianism, whose very existence was intertwined with the daily lives and customs of the folk, or with the imperial state rituals, symbols and mythology, like the ancestor worship in popular religion. Therefore, they had no independent existence outside the imperial system, and the collapse of the latter necessitated the erasure of the former. Levtzion, who used that parallel concept, would have probably dubbed Zoroastrianism and Greek Orthodoxy as "diffused religions", due to their diffusion into their respective imperial systems. But while in the case of Zoroastrianism, together with Confucianism, this would have been justified by their eventual marginalization, except as obsolete philosophical theories; at least in the case of Greek Orthodoxy, judging by its survivability despite the destruction of Byzantium and the decades of its oppression under the Communist system in Russia, and now under Erdogan's Turkey, it is much closer to the definition of "institutional religion", just like the Catholic Church, Islam and Judaism, hence the inadequacy of lumping together the Persian and Anatolian cases when responding to the Muslim assault.

Following A. Nock, Levtzion brings up a novel category of "adhesion" as an alternative to conversion[56], when instead of the individual rite of passage performed by every born non-Muslim to join the congregation of the *Umma*, a group, tribe or society chooses collective adhesion to the faith, as it had been done at the time of the Prophet, when entire tribes were considered as Muslim once their Chiefs swore allegiance (*bay'a*) to the Prophet. In this case, not only was the process of Islamization long and slow, but being adopted willfully out of conviction or of other practical considerations, it did not necessitate a military jihad to enforce it.

---

[56] Levtzion, p. 21.

Hence, when adhesion was concerned, though it was not the only classical peaceful way of spreading Islam, it obviated the need for itinerant Jihadists in its service to enforce Islamization. The obvious conclusion from this state of affairs was that Jihadi volunteers, who roamed the globe in the service of Islam, operated only in war zones where a military force was needed to subjugate recalcitrant or reluctant converts into Islam, like during the *ridda* wars in Arabia (AD 632-634), or during he conquest of North Africa which was opposed by the Berbers and Kabyles. Conversely, in areas like Southeast Asia, for example, where Islam was spread by trade, it expanded gradually and grew organically over decades and centuries, but no Jihad itinerants were ever needed to fight there for the cause of Islam.

In the world of Islam today, from North Africa through the Middle East to Central Asia, where governability is problematic, central governments suffer devolution, and instability, chaos and uncertainty take the place of steady rulers, it is the *Mujahideen* coming from afar to reinforce local Jihadists, who are trying to fill the political vacuum. This happens precisely in areas which had been subjugated by military means to Islam, meaning that the abrupt imposition of Islam by force, which was never accompanied by the erection of an agreed upon social contract that could insure harmony between the ruler and ruled, has been at the root of the current instability and torment. For example, in Arabo-Islamic Spring of the 2010s, when the populace revolted against their tyrants, forcing them to depart, and trying to place in their stead Islamic movements, the rebels were trying to begin all over again a process of spiritual reconquest of the lands that had slipped out of their jurisdiction, when under the rule of their various monarchies or military juntas. Thus, once again, like in old days, jihadi itinerants are pouring in, from all parts of the Muslim world, to try to return the lost areas of Islamdom to the fold. This has happened in Bosnia, Afghanistan, Syria, Iraq, Libya, Yemen and east and west Africa.

There, either an authoritarian/tyrannical rule is required to keep all pieces of society in place, or total chaos takes over and reigns. Places where Jihad itinerants were not needed in the first place, like southeast Asia, where Islamization was slow and peaceful, and penetrating into the grassroots over centuries, there has been even a measure of democratization taking root (e. g. in Indonesia and Malaysia), and they remain today the more or less quieter and stable locations where no Jihad wars are being waged, and therefore no Muslim itinerants are called upon to interfere there.

In the process of conquest and Islamization, the itinerant jihadis from the outside, who took over the local rule, were so badly outnumbered by the overtaken (and often hostile) population, that they ensured the loyalty of groups who wished to aid them, due to their suffering under the yoke of the previous rulers, and to their regarding the Muslim occupiers as liberators. A case in point were the Jews of Spain who had lived oppressed under Christian rule, and when the Muslim conquest was advancing from Elvira to Cordova and other cities, the Jews acted as local garrisons for the new Muslim masters, thus allowing the Muslim troops to move on in their campaign of conquest[57]. It seems strange that the Jews who had been accused since early Islam of enmity to Muhammad, and earned from him the titles of "enemies of Allah" and "descendants of apes and pigs", should suddenly become the close allies of Muslims. The plausible explanation seems to have been not only that the Jews indeed saw in the Muslims a clear improvement over the previous oppressive Christian regime, but also that the acute manpower shortages of the advancing Muslim armies, which were made up at that point of the itinerant jihadists from North Africa, forced them to compromise with the reality and make the necessary pragmatic adaptations, even in contradiction to the basic convictions of

---

[57] See Norman Stillman, *The Jews of Arab Lands, Jewish Publication Society,* 1979, Philadelphia, p. 159.

medieval Muslims. That leniency towards the Jews has also probably contributed to the relatively high position of the Jews under Islam in what came to be known as "the Golden Age", since the Muslim occupiers never constituted more than one third of the population in that Christian-majority land. Therefore, they had to use any alliances they could wield, in order to counter the permanent threat that the Spanish *reconquista* campaigns, which were constantly hovering over their heads during the 8 centuries of their rule over their continuously shrinking Spanish domains, until they were finally expelled in 1492.

Jews and Christians in many conquered areas aided indeed the raiding Muslims against existing local rule, and that also facilitated the process of conquest, since instead of allocating troops to battle or guard against the local populations, the latter were right away offered the deal of paying the *jizya* and spare their lives and property, a deal that was beneficial to both parties. Again, this procedure saved military troops to the Muslims, and lent incentive to the occupied *dhimmis* to align themselves with the conquerors in return for safety for their lives and security to their properties, in addition to their right to maintain their faith as long as they remained Scriptuaries in conviction and submitted to the rules of *dhimma*. This has allowed the itinerant fighters for the Muslim cause to pursue their military campaigns, instead of settling down for the sake of maintaining their rule, and in the process sinking into the delights of civilian life and suffering the resulting erosion of their jihadi zeal. A classic example of such a pact of submission that was signed by the Syrian Christians, was addressed to 'Umar, the second Caliph of Islam, and became the prototype of similar pacts of submission which outlined the benefits and privileges of the subjugated *dhimmis*, versus their obligations, and the limitations they undertook, which later came to be known as the Pact of 'Umar. This was also the paradigm of commercialization, since the clear trade off of ideas for material benefits got its first religious foundation:

In the name of Allah, the Merciful, the Beneficent

This letter is addressed to Allah's servant, 'Umar, the Commander of the Faithful, by Christians dwelling in such and such city. When you advanced against us, we asked you for a guarantee of protection for our person, our offspring, our property and the people of our creed, and we have taken upon ourselves the following obligations toward you, to wit:

> We shall not build in our cities or in their vicinity any new monasteries, churches hermitages or monks' cells.
>
> We shall not restore, by night or by day, any of them that have fallen into ruin or monasteries which are located in the Muslims' quarters.
>
> We shall keep our gates wide open for passersby and travelers. We shall provide three days' food and lodging to any Muslims who pass our way.
>
> We shall not shelter any spy in our churches or in our homes, nor shall we hide him from the Muslims.
>
> We shall not teach our children the Qur'an.
>
> We shall not hold public religious ceremonies. We shall not seek to proselytize anyone. We shall not prevent any of our kin from embracing Islam if they so desire.
>
> We shall show deference to the Muslims and shall rise from our seats when they wish to sit down.
>
> We shall not attempt to resemble the Muslims in any way with regard to their dress, as, for example, in their *qalansawa* (canonical cap), the turban, sandals, or parting the hair (in the Arab fashion). We shall not speak as they do, nor shall

we adopt their Arabic by names.

We shall not ride on saddles.

We shall not wear swords or bear weapons of any kind, or ever carry them with us.

We shall not engrave our signets in Arabic.

We shall not sell wines.

We shall clip the forelocks of our head.

We shall always adorn ourselves in our traditional fashion. We shall bind the belt (*zummar*) around our waists.

We shall not display our crosses or our books anywhere in the Muslims' thoroughfares or in their marketplaces. We shall only beat our clappers in our churches very quietly. We shall not raise our voices when reciting the service in our churches, nor when in the presence of Muslims. Neither shall we raise our voices in our funeral processions.

We shall not display lights in any of the Muslim thoroughfares on in their marketplaces.

We shall not come near them with our funeral processions.

We shall not take any of the slaves that had been allotted to Muslims.

We shall not build our houses higher than theirs.

(when I brought the letter to 'Umar, he added the clause: We shall not strike any Muslim).

We accept these conditions for ourselves and for the members or our creed, in return for which we are to be given a guarantee of security. Should we violate in any way these conditions, which we have accepted and for which we stand [to gain] security, then there shall be no covenant of protection

> (*dhimma*) for us, and we shall be liable to the
> penalties for rebelliousness and sedition.

Then 'Umar wrote: "sign what they have requested, but add two clauses that will also be binding upon them, namely they shall not buy anyone who has been taken prisoner by the Muslims, and that anyone who deliberately strikes a Muslim will forfeit the protection of this pact[58]". That same pattern had allowed for Jews (and Christians) to remain close allies of the Muslims in their conquests, as when Jews aided the Muslims in the conquest of Hebron, or when Jews and Christians elected to aid the Arabs in the conquest of Hums in Syria from the Byzantines.[59] 'Umar indeed rewarded the Jews by permitting to 70 Jewish households to return and resettle in Jerusalem, and ordered them to clean the Temple Mount under his personal supervision[60].

The main motivation for Jihadi itinerants to flock to the war fronts of Islam, was initially the rich booty that was obtained in the raids (*razzias*) against Byzantine outposts during the Prophet's lifetime, followed by the expansive Jihad campaigns launched after his death, and rationalized as an obligation of the Believers to fight in the Path of Allah, in order to spread Islam to the entire world. There too the booty continued to be cited by Arab sources as a major motivation for the itinerant Jihadis, though it was gradually diluted and becoming secondary to the dominant religious requirement of fighting for Allah and the expansion of Islam, since the *Mujahideen* knew and understood that more raids on the non-Believers produced not only a terrorized population that facilitated its being conquered, but also large scale flights of civilians, who feared the approaching raiders, leaving behind them possessions to

---

[58] Translated from al-Turtushi, Siraj al Muluk, (Cairo, 1872), pp 229-30. Cited by Stillman, op. cit. pp. 157-8.

[59] Stillman, pp. 152-3.

[60] Ibid., p. 154.

be preyed on. Modern Historian Dufourcq, citing his earlier Arab counterpart, al-Maqqari, wrote:

> It is not difficult to understand that such expeditions sowed terror. The historian al-Maqqari, who wrote in the 17th Century Tlemcen in Algeria, explained that the panic created by the Arab horsemen and sailors, at the time of the Arab expansion in the zones that saw those raids and landings, facilitated the later conquests, when that was decided on. "Allah", he says, "thus instilled fear among the infidels that they did not dare to go and fight the conquerors; they only approached them as suppliants, to beg for peace" [61].

Worse, prodded by the doctrine of Jihadi *blitzkrieg*, the continuous Muslim raids and migration into Christian territory in the Middle Ages, were instrumental in the disintegration of the Middle East, and then of the Iberian Peninsula and southern Europe. Ibn Hudhayl, a 14th century Muslim Granadan historian, wrote:

> It is permissible to set fire to the lands of the enemy, his stores of grain, his beasts of burden- when it is not possible to take possession of them -- as well as to cut down his trees, in a word to do everything that might ruin and discourage him, provided that the Imam deems these measures appropriate, suited to hastening the Islamization of that enemy or weakening him. Indeed, all this contributes to a military triumph over him or to forcing him to capitulate[62].This manner of enriching the fighters from the fruit of their conquests, which started as an

---

[61] Charles Dufourcq, *La Vie Quotidienne and l'Europe Medievale sous Domination Arabe,* Hachette, Paris 1978, p. 20. Cited by Bostom, p. 40.
[62] Cited by Bostom, p. 40.

innate stimulus and incentive to participate in raids and warfare, was later consecrated by no others than the first Righteous Caliphs, who were second only to the Prophet himself, when in the process of Islamic conquests they rationalized and lent a seal of legalization to the fabulous booty that was collected on the way. This is what 'Umar, the Second Caliph and one of the most venerated among them, replied to Muslim conquerors who demanded the sharing out of the lands of the Middle East:

"I thought that we had nothing more to conquer after the land of Persia, whose riches, land and people Allah has given us. I have divided the personal possessions among those who conquered them, after having subtracted a fifth, which under my supervision was used for the purpose for which it was intended. I thought it necessary to reserve the land and its inhabitants, and levy from the latter the *kharaj* (land tax) by virtue of their land, and the *jizyah* as a personal tax on every head, this tax constituting a booty in favor of the Muslims who have fought there, of their children and of their heirs. Do you think that these borders could remain without warriors to defend them? Do you think that these vast countries: Syria, Egypt and Mesopotamia do not have to be covered with troops who must be well-paid ?. Where can one obtain their pay if all the land is divided up, as well as its inhabitants...? His resolution to levy the *kharaj,* so that the revenue could be shared among the Muslims,

was beneficial to the entire *Umma*, for had it
not been reserved to pay the wages and food
of the warriors, the border provinces would
never have been populated, the troops would
have been deprived of the necessary means to
carry on the Jihad, and one would have been
afraid that the infidels would return to their
former possessions, since these would not have
been protected by soldiers and mercenaries".[63]

You then have all in one: justification for taking booty, incentive
to settle down on the front lines (*riba*t), rationalization for creating
a source of income to raise the conquest outlays, the encouragement
of the growing class of Jihad itinerants (supplemented, to be sure,
by mercenaries), the clear subordination and exploitation of the
conquered populations, and the firm favoritism accorded to the
Muslim master race. Fernandez-Morera, in his seminal study of the
Myth of the Andalusian Paradise, also recognizes that an entire
gamut of attractive incentives existed for the Jihad warrior to join
the ranks of the itinerant fighters: from dying as a martyr (*shahid*)
to enjoying the bounty of the spoils he took in combat. He wrote:

Doubtlessly, it was a strong incentive for a male warrior
fighting in the way of Allah, that he would take all the
property of those enemy fighters he had killed in combat, including his women, who would not be considered
free women and therefore could be taken as sexual slaves.
The willingness to die while killing the infidels, taught in
the religious texts on Jihad, gave Muslims a tactical
advantage over their enemies during the Islamic con-

---

[63] Cited in Bat Ye'or, *The Dhimmi*, Fairleigh Dickinson University Press, Madison, 1985, p. 185.

quests. This willingness to die is found, for example, in the words of the Islamic Caliphate's Arab commander, Khalid ibn al-Walid in 633, ordering the Persians to submit to Islam, or else: "Otherwise you are bound to meet people who love death as much as you love life"[64].

The first phase of Islamic rule founded on the itinerant Jihadi campaign of conquests, who had sprung out of Arabia, guided by the first Righteous Caliphs, was engineered in an ambience of expansion, quick victories, and the euphoria born out of the great enthusiasm engendered by the rapidly advancing Islamic venture. But as Islamic rule firmed up and settled down, and the tenets of the crystallizing *Shari'a* were formulated, the attitudes towards Jews and Christians were toughened. For, wherever Islamic government seemed assured and the need to ensure the Scriptuaries' loyalty and allegiance was no longer so acute and critical as previously in the early stage, the laws of dhimmitude became more and more demanding and humiliating. Muslim supremacy indeed often elected to dig a ditch of oppression and push there Jews and Christians, rather than to erect a mound to elevate itself over its ideological rivals. To be sure, in the times of 'Umar and thereafter, a dual attitude towards the Scriptuaries existed: on the one hand the constant repetition and reminder of the many Qur'anic suras debasing them, warning against them, humiliating them, and prescribing their misery, innate wretchedness and bitter fate[65]; but on the other hand, Caliphal proclamations of appointment of notable Jews and Christians to crucial functions, and later the nomination of Jews and Christian as officials in the Fatimid Dynasty, and the ascendance of Jews and Christians to high positions in Muslim adminis-

---

[64] Fernandez-Morera, *Dario, The Myth of the Andalusian Paradise,,* ISIS Books, Wilmington, 2016, p. 25. This phrase is often used in contemporary radical Islam, like among the Hamas, Hizbullah, ISIS and others.
[65] See e.g. 9:29, 5:51, 2: 256, 2:61, 4:44-6, 4:160-61, 9:30-31, 5:64, 5:82.

trations and governments as in the alleged Golden Age in Spain[66].

The reasons for this apparent hesitation and ambivalence towards Jews and Christians were many: when the Muslim rule became solidly established, with the Muslim majority of subjects assuring its domination in the heart of Islamic lands, the laws of 'Umar were more effectively activated, and the *dhimmis* more likely to be mal-treated, even when they duly paid their *jizya* tax in order to gain the protection pledged under those rules. But when the Muslim masters only constituted a minority, like in Spain, or in border areas until the process of Islamization made deep inroads into the ruled popu-lation, Muslim governments needed to maintain local alliances with the occupied peoples under Islamic rule, so that their status was protected even when they did not pay *jizya*. This may also have emanated from the reality when the conquering Muslims had as yet no experience on how to manage a huge empire at the outset of the conquest, and they were at the same time catapulted overnight to the position of rulers, therefore they had to rely on local elites and non-Muslim bureaucrats. All that while, the Muslim elites gained prominence and accumulated their experience in government, and the Muslim governor needed less and less the local elites' expertise. Naturally, as old non-Muslim elites in the occupied territories con-verted to Islam, that also diminished the need of the rulers to resort to non-Muslim bureaucrats. For fairness and balance one must also admit, that deviations from the *Shari'a* rules had occurred both ways: there were generous rulers, like under the Fatimids, who treated humanely, and even discriminated favorably Jews and Chris-tians in their administrations, while particularly fanatic and mean rulers, like some of the Mamluks in the Near East and the Muwah-hidun in North Africa, behaved cruelly toward their non-Muslim subjects even when they completed all their duties under the *dhimma* regulations.

---

[66] See e.g. Stillman, pp. 178-182, p. 201 etc.

In either case, the solidified status of the *dhimmi*s within the Islamic realm, like the relentless persecution of the pagans who remained in place in the process of conquest, unless they converted to Islam, were signs of stability and long haul durability of the Muslim rule, therefore no Jihadi itinerants were there to constitute part of the already completed process of *fat'h*, expansion and Islamization. Those who did volunteer to fight for Islam had moved on to the new frontiers of battle, in North Africa and Central Asia, where they were usually honored with the prestigious title of *Murabitun*, literally designating those who "camped" on the farthest Islamic boundaries and were the forefront of the continued fighting for the sake of Allah, and the pioneers entrusted with the holy task to widen the *Dar al-Islam* to the farthest limits. One of those "camping" frontier areas, just like the old *amsar* of the Middle East, was *al-Ribat* in the westernmost frontier of Islam on the Atlantic Ocean, which became Rabat, the capital of modern Morocco, just as Kufa and Fustat (Cairo) became thriving cities. When "camping" sites took in local population and became permanent cities, that meant that itinerant fighters for Islam had gone elsewhere to seek new frontiers, and that the non-Muslims who remained in the realm as Scriptuaries had moved into permanent *dhimmi* status, if they had not Islamized before.

In the course of time, ruling as masters over Jews and Christians, the two ideological adversaries of Islam which challenged its doctrine, was proof for Muslims of the validity of Jihad as the only way to practice monotheism, and therefore controlling those two sorts of infidels under the subordinate status of *dhimmis*, in a way reflected on the success of Jihad. In a way, Itinerant Jihadis fought in the Path of Allah in order to reduce the recalcitrant Jews and Christians into *dhimmis,* until such a time that they awakened to their miserable condition and saw the light of Islam. Therefore, the status of *dhimmi,* while being theoretically a transitory stage until its adherents Islamized, was in fact a permanent reminder, right in the heart of Islam, of the supreme nature of the Faith of Allah, and the justification for the pursuit of Jihad in order to prompt the non-Muslim Scriptuaries to join the itinerant *Mujahideen* once they had embraced Islam. Be it as it may, the humiliating effect of the *dhimmi* status of the Jews and Christians under Islam has been universally recognized as having generated such a deep contempt and hostility towards the Jewish and Christian minorities throughout Islamdom, that anti-Semitism and Christianophobia were an inevitable outcome, whether that terminology was used or not, to express and carry that meaning.

The anxiety and sense of subordination which went in par with Jewish and Christian existence under Islam, had always cried for reaction on the part of the oppressed, which began defensively in place, and ended up in total divorce from that environment which had grown entirely unbearable, while the then stateless Jews were helpless to alter. But one has to account for the years of Islamic conquest, expansion, annihilation of some existing Jewish (and Christian) communities, occupation, forced conversion, and the cruel subjugation of the non-Muslim communities which survived those torments for many centuries. As old Jews were beaten and humiliated before the eyes of their grand children, as cataracts of rocks could always land on Jews from nowhere, as peaceful weekend picnics could always be disrupted by beatings, or as the Jewish Sabbath and holidays could always be inexplicably interrupted by some Muslim thug or incited mob, those were all daily and persistent parts of a constant malaise which undermined Jewish and Christian existence under Islam. The general picture, however, which was much bigger and much more painful than the persecuted Jews and Christians themselves suspected in their particular locations. For example, more recently, debilitating to the ill-informed minds of Jews (and Christians) during W W II, were the grim reports about the decimation of one third of the Jewish people in the Nazi crematoria, to which the Arab and Muslim pro-Nazi *Mufti* of Jerusalem,

Amin al-Husseini, made a great contribution that stains his and Palestinian reputation forever, in the eyes of decent people across the world. No wonder, then, that when the alternative loomed of finding refuge in an independent Jewish state, most Jews of Islam unhesitatingly rose in one sweeping messianic wave, and moved there. They were simply tired, frightened, and disgusted from centuries of oppression and humiliation, and this explains their massive and rapid departure from the land they had inhabited longer than the Arab/ Muslim invaders, who had subjugated them and rendered their lives unbearable, after they had been made to believe that expanding Islam was their savior from the hands of their previous Christian oppressors.

The irony is that after the Jews had been settled in Morocco[67], for example, since the beginning of the Christian era, before the Muslim conquerors came to occupy and oppress them, when they returned to their home in the Land of Israel, they are now accused of "occupying" Arab and Muslim Palestine. Similarly, other Jews of Egypt, Babylonia, Persia, and North Africa, whose flourishing settlements preceded those of the occupying Arabs and the advent of Islam, were also compelled to leave their ancient heritage and move back to Israel, from which Arabs and Muslims now wish to evict them. The Arab/Muslim trauma that haunts today the existence of Jews in Israel/Palestine, is thus double- edged: Jews in Israel are accused by the Arabs of having displaced the Palestinians and replaced them, hence the urgent need to remove them from the land; and at the same time, by moving out from lands of Islam and seeking shelter in Israel, they in fact nullified the *dhimma* status which they had been assigned to fill for more than a millennium, but renascent Israel has helped them to shake off. That Muslims should seek revenge on the Jewish front now available to them in

---

[67] For the story of Moroccan Jews, see R.Israeli, *Pisces out of Morocco: the Saga of Clandestine Jewish Emigration,* Strategic Books, TX, 2016.

Israel/Palestine, only seemed natural to them, though equally disastrous, all the same, for the Jews and for Arabs . The renewed elan of radical Islam in our times, and the mobilization of Muslim Jihadi itinerants to return the Jews to their miserable status of yesteryear, while at the same time to blunt the nature of western "arrogance", indeed stand at the center of today's universal battle against worldwide terrorism, where Jihadi itinerants play a main role.

Chapter Six

The Quid-pro-Quo of International Politics

In general, Islamic societies, which have remained at the bottom of the international scale of human development surveys, owe that status in no small measure to their fixed ideology, having turned the Prophet and his life in distant Arabia a millennium and half ago into the ideal that cannot be improved upon, thus erecting obstacles on the way to modern and progressive state and society building. In consequence, the emerging alternatives to the crumbling tyrants of the Spring do not seem to hold much promise of extricating those societies from their accumulated multigenerational backwardness. This is only one aspect of the perennial contradiction between the principles of democracy and progress and the revival of political Islam, should free elections produce Islamic parties that would further dig in the past and strive to emulate it. Certainly, Islamic societies also include bourgeois sections that have lived in or visited other countries and have grown modern and Westernized enough to recoil from the prospect of seeing their countries thoroughly Islamized and thrown backward (e.g., Egypt, Turkey, Tunisia, and Iran). It is precisely in those countries that a mammoth struggle has been unleashed between these forces of change and the new Islamic forces that threaten takeover, over the back of the masses, via democratic means of participatory elections—which if successful can also be the last. The chieftain of the tribe was not alone in the leadership spot. At his side there was a poet (*sha'ir*), who acted as a kind of public relations man and spokesman for the tribe. His role was to preserve the oral records of his tribe, which essentially played and replayed its days of glory.

Paradoxically, the *jahiliya* (Era of Ignorance) collections of poetry, known as *Ayyam al-'Arab* (The Chronicles of the Arabs) have been recognized as one of the pinnacles of poetry and literary creation. For want of better, they have also become one of the important sources or the history of that period before the emergence of the Prophet. Again paradoxically, despite its sublime beauty and the richness of its expression, this literature was also stigmatized for smacking of the Jahili atmosphere and culture in which it evolved, when humanity was sunken in sin, loss, and disorientation until the messenger of Allah came to bring it salvation. In our context, critiques of contemporary Muslim societies, precisely some of those who kindled the Spring and led it, have accused their countries of having relinquished Muslim values to the point of reverting—Allah Forbid!—to a *jahiliyya*-like condition. Therefore, the remedy today, as of old, has been to readopt the thinking of the Prophet and to migrate, as he did from Mecca to Medina in AD 622, traveling spiritually if not physically to a purer Islamic society where the revival of Islam might become possible. This is the sense that Islamic Spring leaders wish to give to their popular movements, implying that like the Prophet, after they have revitalized the *Shari'a* state, the entire world would open up to a world Islamic revolution. Many of those Muslim fundamentalists had tried for years to precipitate this process through violence, but as they were crushed by their tyrannical rulers who were supported by the West, they metamorphosed into peace- and legitimacy-seeking parties, as during the Spring in some countries, and gained as a result the support of world public opinion. The poet was also the living oral archives of his tribe, for lack of written record. He stored in his mind his tribe's literature, stories, legends, and tales of heroism, in order to raise the morale of his kin, together with tales of other tribes' history that denigrated them as cowards who yielded to his own people's courage. He also was the author of the never-drying fountainhead of new epic tales and poems unfolding as the history of the tribe evolved, whether or not those events occurred or were inventions. In our days, Arab poetry readings still attract masses, and national poets enjoy a great reputation (Darwish and Ziyad, for example, were worshipped by Palestinian nationalists). And often the leaders of Islamic countries use poetry to mobilize the masses. Some of them, like Nasser and Sadat of Egypt, delivered speeches for hours in public squares, acting not only as the chieftains of their countries but also as poets of their tribes, who accuse their enemies of cowardice and heap praise on their own noble people and heroic armed forces.

Only in more recent times, due to the increasing requirements of security and the threat of terrorism, did tyrants retreat to their palaces (or tents in the case of Qaddafi) and content themselves with spreading their messages through the state media. The difference is that in old days the chieftains and poets grew organically out of the tribal milieu, due to their natural gifts, because in that situation it was nearly impossible for anyone to impose himself upon his kin. From many respects, this was a kind of meritocratic order, but instead of the public servants being tested and approved by the authorities (as in ancient China and modern England), the order evolved and was accepted by the elders' consensual silent agreement. Over time, however, as the Umayyads (AD 661–750) and the Abbasids (AD 750–1253) took over and imposed a dynastic order, Islam absorbed the idea of blood inheritance, which received a further boost from the emerging Shi'ites, who based their religion on the concept of the Twelve Imams. In dynastic succession beginning with Ali, these imams had imputed to themselves the sole right of inheritance of the rule of Islam. The idea of inheriting power rather than competing for it peacefully has taken such deep roots in Islam that even in republican regimes today, the tyrants who saw their masses rising against them during this Spring had destined their sons to inherit their rule after many years of autocratic power: Mubarak of Egypt, Saleh of Yemen, Qaddafi of Libya, Saddam of Iraq. Even in Syria, where the transition of power between Hafez Assad and his son was complete ten years prior to the Spring, it was that continuity that enraged the rebels, among their other grievances.

The chieftain of the tribe and its poet were bound to the concept of honor (*sharaf*). The violation of honor could not be ignored, for otherwise an undefended honor could appear as unworthy of defense and fatally harm the reputation of its owners. Honor was also related to the possession of assets and women, and a violation of either could trigger a chain of hostile acts between the contending parties, because leaving a violated honor unpunished would leave the matter hanging, yearning for a settlement, tied to compensation, or taking the life of a killer (lex talionis). This is quite different from the modern idea of retaliation for wrongdoing, or inflicting punishment for it, that derives from the Roman legal tradition. For in ancient Arabia, and in the Islamic world today, the very act of vengeance—for example in case of the violation of a woman's honor or of the killing of someone of another clan—is supposed, *eo ipso*, to calm down the boiling blood of the victim or of the owner of the defiled honor. (Honor killings among Muslim communities are well known not only in the Islamic world, but also in the West.) The idea of retaliation in the modern world, by contrast (e.g., bomb Berlin and Dresden as retaliation for London and Coventry, or Tokyo and Hiroshima as punishment for Nanjing and Manila), is to chastise for what is known as a war crime and to deter recurrence. This retaliation is not motivated primarily by a primal desire to take revenge, but by a calculated consideration to make the enemy pay such a high price for its deed that he is deterred from repeating it. On the personal level, or in cases of inter-family, inter-clan, or inter-tribal rifts, honor killings for a woman's immoral conduct can be accepted and understood in Islamic societies, and these killings occur all too often. But European societies and Israel, where large Muslim populations live, cannot take these murders indifferently, for they are bound in their Roman and Jewish traditions by their civil codes of law to punish any murder. However, when they punish murders as criminal acts of manslaughter, clashes unavoidably occur between the authorities and Muslim minorities, who, based on their own history and tradition, consider themselves entitled to follow their customs. These minorities consider the insistence of the law enforcement agencies on imposing the criminal code to be Islamophobia. The idea of justice (*'adala*) in Arab and Islamic societies is also derived from the ancient Bedouin culture of Arabia. Then, it meant the balance between the two sides of the saddlebag on the camel's back. Just as the camel—so essential for the survival of the Bedouin in the desert—should have its saddlebags balanced on its back lest it limp and be unable to stride through the sand, so no Arab can function in daily life if the wrong done to him in his eyes is not redressed. In such societies, justice has never had, and does not have today, objective yardsticks to gauge the damage caused by the enemy or the compensation required to achieve redress. It used, and still uses, only a subjective criterion for measure, and that is the self-satisfaction of the wronged party. Only if he feels that the proper compensation was paid, or a ritual of conciliation (*sulha*) is held, and his honor is upheld and not humiliated, would he agree to accept the redress. The result is the concept of a "just peace" that is largely unparalleled in other cultures, as if justice had absolute parameters, when in reality what is just for one can seem unjust to another. For example, today, Arabs and Muslims demand a just solution for the Palestinians, which means, in their terms, the elimination of Israel and its replacement by them. And since no country would agree to commit suicide, and a compromise on that cannot be achieved, no peace can be expected.

When President Sadat spoke at the Israeli Knesset in November 1977, he insisted on a "just peace," which should return "every grain of sand of Sinai" to Egyptian possession. It was not because sands are important in themselves, but because what he considered to be his should be returned without argument or bargaining, regardless of who started the war where that territory was lost, regardless of who lost the war, and regardless of who should make redress for the damages of the war. Indeed, Sadat would not even have come to Jerusalem had the return of the Sinai Peninsula not been pledged to him a priori. On another occasion, Sadat said that in the Egyptian countryside where he came from, clans used to fight for generations over a useless patch of rocky land, solely because without the justice of returning that land to its owner, peace could not return to the village. On the international level, any Arab leader Israel engages in early negotiations demands as a first step the return of the entire claimed land (for Syria the Golan, for the Palestinians the West Bank and Jerusalem), short of which no process can even begin.

Arabs often demand that justice should be done for their prisoners in Israel by releasing them, regardless of their criminal convictions. They also demand that any incarcerated Palestinian should be set free on Ramadan, because those are days of haram (forbidden warfare), regardless of the fact that they launched the October 1973 war on Ramadan, and not to speak of Temple Mount in Jerusalem (haram al-Sharif), where they allow no Jew to set his foot, because it is now an exclusively Islamic site, regardless of the place's history. That is justice in their eye. In other words, Muslims are the only ones to determine what is Muslim territory, including Temple Mount, regardless of archeological digs, history, and the claims of other religions. For only Muslim conquests (*futuh*) lend legitimacy to the status of a place, and any other takeover of the same territory by anyone else is ipso facto illegitimate and unjust. In ancient

Arabia there were market towns—like Mecca and Yathrib (turned Medina after the Prophet moved there in AD 622), where Muhammed established his rule; Khaybar, where a thriving Jewish community was deeply rooted well before the times of the Muhammed— that were managed by councils of elders (shura), in contrast with the wandering tribes that were ruled by their sheikhs. The Prophet's friends and closest companions (*sahaba*) also implemented such a shura around him, to dispense counsel and comfort, though his final say as the messenger of Allah was binding for all. When he was dying, and more so after his death, this council was the pool from which the first vicars (caliphs) were selected, and until the first ruling dynasties were established, it acted as the supreme authority in the fledgling Islamic state, under the leadership of the serving caliph. This patrimony is still so powerful that any contemporary Muslim state, movement, or organization nominates a shura to lead it as its supreme institution.

Hamas and the Muslim Brothers in Egypt and Jordan are led by such a council. Many of them regard this institution as the ultimate expression of democracy Muslim style, refusing to listen to Western preaching about the need for democracy, because they claim that the idea of collective leadership was invented in and by Islam. Saudi Arabia—which does not allow any sort of elections, not even rigged ones—preserves the institution of the shura (appointed by the king, not elected) as a high manifestation of democracy. Countries such as Egypt, which ran elections under their tyrant regime for many years (rigged at every turn, to be sure) also maintained an appointed shura as an upper house, to balance the authority of the parliament in case it was not rigged enough to surrender to the will of the ruler. And finally, when we look at the complicated tribal situation in the countries affected by the Spring, we can see that in certain places that old structure and those old norms are time resistant and repel the pressure for change in the modern world. In Iraq, where the Spring preceded by one decade its outbreak elsewhere, the Saddam

Hussein regime, ended by the American incursion, was replaced by a weaker and less cruel regime that no longer controls the tribes as did the departed tyrant, either through soothing statements or ruthless measures. Add to that the dismantlement of the Ba'ath's extremely coercive rule and of the army that had been the main arm of control of the Saddam regime, and questions have started to arise about the new democratic games that the Shi'ite revolution brought about by the Americans has been trying to enforce, and about the revival of tribalism under its aegis as never before. When Iraq was the Mosul and Basra Districts of the Ottoman Empire, the Shi'ites regarded the other minorities, like Kurds and Turkemans, who were also Muslims, as subjects of the sultan in Istanbul, while the Christian and Jewish minorities' status fell within the general Millet arrangements that applied to the entire extent of the Empire, which meant that the non-Muslim minorities were regarded as autonomous communities in managing their religious affairs. Now that an Islamic Empire is no more, and even the Ba'ath framework has collapsed, minorities were left hanging insecurely in the air, and in the general atmosphere of insecurity, no one can guarantee their future— especially in light (or rather, obscurity) of the massacres of Assyrians in northern Iraq, which the Shi'ite government is unwilling or unable to check. Only the Kurdish situation has improved in the post-Saddam era, since the Kurds have upgraded their autonomous status from the weak central government and have even ensured the presidency of the federal republic through their coalition with the ruling Shi'ites.

There is also a question about the longevity of the present system, which through elections has toppled the Sunnite minority rule and, for now, turned over the decisive power in the country from the bullet to the ballot. In Egypt, which was one of the first sites of the Spring revolution, it turned out very quickly that the Muslim movements of all brands took control of most events, while the military, who took over power in the intermediate period, were trying to rein them in and diminish their increasing demands: first to run to Parliament, then to take it over, then to run to the presidency, then to claim it and hold on to it. To Tahrir Square they rushed the venerated Sheikh Qaradawi, the most important and popular Muslim preacher in the Sunnite world, who did not hide his restorative message to revert to the ancient mold of Islam, thus widening the gap between the Muslim fundamentalists, who constitute the vast elected majority and represent the old conquerors and rulers of the country, and the ancient natives of the land, now the 10 percent minority of the Copts, who are scared stiff of the imposition of a Shari'a law in their land. The rift between the two is not strictly ethnic or tribal but religious, but since the two groups do not intermarry due to religious barriers, they have grown into two rivaling ethnic groups, with Copts fearing increasing harassment by the Muslim fanatics, as in the last years of the rule of Sadat (1970–81) when his image began to fade. In Syria and Lebanon, where communal and religious diversity was managed by the Millet arrangement under the Ottomans, the French Mandate that followed continued to distinguish among the various groups so as to facilitate *divide et impera*. For example, persecuted minorities like the Druze and the Alawites, who were no longer considered part of Islam, were encouraged to embrace military careers in the colonial army so as to be used to control the Sunnite majority. Those minorities, which usually had strongholds, like the Latakiya area on the Syrian coast or the Shuf Mountains in Lebanon, also ensured their survival through their appointment to key posts in the army.

After the independence of those countries following World War II, the appointed minority chiefs held onto their military positions in the national armies, and they often reached even the top leadership, like the Alawites of Syria, who were reluctant to renounce their positions during the Spring turmoil lest they be exterminated by a revengeful Sunnite majority rebelling against them. Their world of options does not include the Syrian national interest, but first of all Alawite sectarian interest, which they have been pursuing in the coalition of minorities with various Christian and Druze groups. The Alawites know that if they free the tiger which they are holding tightly, they would be immediately devoured by the enraged animal, hence their apparent readiness to fight to the finish. This is how the tribal tradition, which has been preserved in Syria due to its basic diversity, might enhance the reversion of the country to its tribal origin. In Libya and Yemen, as in Syria, a very prolonged and destructive civil war was necessary to bring down the tyrant. These countries provide the proof that in tribal societies there is a zero-sum game wherein when some group wins the upper hand, another loses. In Egypt and Tunisia, which are less marked by tribalism, the struggle was shorter and less fierce, because the stakes of survival of one party or another were not as high, and no matter what happened, the country remained one, under one regime or another. But in tribal situations, the elimination of tyranny can also produce the breakup of the political entity. Certainly, the advocates of stability would support the continuity of the nation-states as they were prior to the Spring, but it is not certain that can be achieved. It is a fact that Islamic troublemakers and stability breakers such as al-Qa'ida have infiltrated these tribal countries, seeking to gain something from their dismantlement—but not into the solid nation-states like Egypt, where the local strong armies can still maintain security and resist any foreign challenges. However, it is noteworthy that while Egypt proper can still deal with its security in spite of the Spring, the Sinai Peninsula, which is part of its sovereignty, has been relinquished to those forces of instability that seek confrontation with Israel. Indeed, numerous terrorist attacks have already been launched against Israel from there, and the gas pipeline from Egypt to Israel was blown up fifteen times in the space of one year, before it was finally disconnected in contravention of the long-term gas supply contract between the two countries.

The discovery in Israeli waters of vast offshore gas deposits has in the meantime turned the situation around. The Islamic instinct for restorative reforms every time a revolution looms harks back to the ancient Islamic heritage, with at its center its Prophet, who combined his prophecy with his actual rule of Medina, thus creating, by the grace of Allah, the perfect model of a ruler of the first organized Muslim community, by the most perfect of rulers, who received via the Qur'an the word of Allah, divine guidance to the ideal way of governance. During his early prophecy in Mecca, all the chapters of the Qur'an that were revealed to him were of an apocalyptic import, predicting that the end of the world was at hand, on the model of the great Jewish prophets, but the moment he migrated to Medina in AD 622 and began serving as the local ruler, the burden of government obliged him to tailor-make new revelations that more resembled the legislative character of Leviticus and Numbers. But once those revelations were sanctified by inclusion in the Qur'an, after the passing of Muhammad, they could no longer be changed or improved upon, especially after the Prophet himself had followed their guidelines. Since then, those prescriptions for good government have been engraved in stone as the ideal Islamic rule for all generations to come—ideal since the Prophet himself practiced them. For, unlike the prophets of Israel who were giant intellectuals, usually inimical to the royal rule and its greatest critiques, Muhammed was himself the ruler, some kind of philosopher-king, who understood the requirements of government and found solutions to them. Moreover, since he practiced that rule under divine inspiration and was himself infallible, his style of government could not have been afflicted by major errors or deviations that would require redress today. Quite the contrary, pretending to amend today what the most perfect of men did, would amount to insulting the wisdom and integrity of the messenger of Allah. No wonder, then, that the era of the Prophet has become the perfect model for emulation, both spiritually and politically. Granted, after him no one can claim the gift of prophecy since he was the Seal of Prophets; his tradition (*sunna)* became the ultimate model of emulation, and the greatest scare of all in Islam has been innovation (*bid'a*—doctrinal, not technical).

We change things in order to improve upon them, but if it is determined that the best occurred in the time of the Prophet, then what is the incentive to alter anything? The rationale is that the generations away from the Prophet keep deteriorating. In his time, the companions (*sahaba*) were second in perfection only to the Prophet himself, but their followers (*tabi'un*) and more so the followers' followers (tabi'u al-tabi'un), and so on ad infinitum, can only continually decrease in quality the farther they get from the Prophet's times. Therefore, people can no longer attain the hereafter thanks simply to their proximity to the Prophet, but due only to their own piety and good deeds. This is the basis for the doctrine that has been adopted by the two most puritanical schools of law (the Hanbalites and the Malikites), which reject the *bida'* and claim that after the worthy men who founded all four schools of law had passed away, the inspiration that moved them to legislate and innovate was terminated (namely the gates of ijtihad had been closed); therefore any innovation after them would be hazardous and against good counsel. Hence the precedents and verdicts of the past remain the exclusive reference for any judicial pronouncement, something that obviously precludes any free and open thinking, divine inspiration having been exhausted on earth. Paradoxically, then, the more the new generations become distanced from the Prophet and in need of new interpretations to meet the challenges and requirements of new modes of life, the more they are denied any such opportunities and have to rely on the irrelevant judgment of the ancients. A classical example is Egypt, which in the 1920s and '30s was more liberal, open, and democratic than today. Indeed, in these days of the Spring, as Islamic opinions and sentiments are reasserting themselves, the remnants of the liberal and democratic voices can hardly go on blocking the dam with their thumb to hold back the threat of the Islamic flood. To this trend there is one major exception, and that is Shi'ite Islam, where the ayatullahs, due to their ongoing link to the Hidden Imam, can still get divine inspiration. This is what enabled Khumeini to lend innovative interpretations to the rule of the mullahs, as part of his ijtihad endeavors (see following). Looking backward at the past and finding in it all sources of wisdom and references to action, all that good and devoted Muslims can strive for today, is to attempt to recreate, in as close a replica as humanly possible, the time of the Prophet, and this is exactly the meaning of the Salafi movements: pious Muslims who strive to emulate the ancestors (*aslaf*), from the generation of the Prophet onward. In Egypt, the Salafiya gained 30 percent of the votes to Parliament and came second only to the Brothers, who secured 45 percent of the electorate. These Muslim tendencies profoundly believe that the truth is embedded in the sayings and deeds of their predecessors, and that pretending to improve upon them is blasphemous—a baseless and vain thought. Hence the tremendous magnetic appeal of those movements throughout the Islamic world that do not advocate any new doctrine, but simply to revive the ancient, venerated, but neglected and forlorn precepts that made the glory of Islam in the past.

And unlike the legendary Muslim Brothers, who are equipped with long-term patience and invest in welfare to prepare a solid base for their future rule, the Salafi movements and their likes (the Algerian Armed Groups of the 1990s, the Egyptian Gama'at of the 1970s and 1980s, the Taliban, al-Qa'ida, and their ilk of the 1990s and 2000s) want everything and now, and are often violent in their demand for immediate application of their rule. The Brothers had in the past also embraced that road of impatience and violence in Egypt, Syria, and Jordan, but when they were crushed by the authorities and risked annihilation, they elected to lower their profile and pretend that they had been moderated, giving the false impression to uninitiated foreign observers that they had indeed changed their ways. But now that Muslim Brothers are gaining legitimacy as a consequence of the Spring, they will also gradually revive the venomous discourse of their founding fathers—Hassan al-Banna and Sayyid Qutb, who continue to be deeply venerated throughout the Muslim world—and in practice merge with the Salafis, there being no significant doctrinal and operational gap between them. No less detrimental for the obstruction of the future by the past, when considering the era of the Prophet the best of regimes and the most perfect of societies, has been the pessimistic state of mind this creates among Islamic peoples when they grow up to believe that the best existed and is gone and is irretrievable; therefore things can only get worse. This does not encourage effort for betterment, initiative, entrepreneurship, but a spirit of fatalism and doom that leaves the individual apathetic, lacking in incentive to move and change, and not attaching hopes to learning, science, and advancement. Even as the Spring proceeds, we watch the rebels against their tyrants not only cursing their oppressors and removing them from power but also doing that in the name of Allah, shouting war cries of Allah Akbar (Allah is the greatest) in response to bombardment and shelling by their rulers' artillery and jet fighters. That means that they leave the revolution in the hands of God, while they, who expose themselves on the fire line, are only tools in his hands. It is doubtful whether Lenin or Mao could have achieved their grand revolutions if they had counted on any god instead of taking matters in their own hands, risking their lives and the fate of their nations in the name of the alternative ideologies they pursued. The Islamic revolutionary passivity, as much as it sounds like a contradiction in terms, continues to lay at the base of the Islamic Spring today.

The pessimistic view that all has been decided from above also stands at the foundation of the annual UN reports on social and economic development, which have invariably cast the Muslim countries at the bottom of the world scale, in spite of the fact that these surveys are made by Arab and Muslim scholars who know and understand this hopeless situation—for otherwise the accusation would have smacked of Islamophobia on the part of scholars, who would be accused of ill intent. In these annual surveys, the same sad themes are recurrent; this built-in chronic backwardness is due to Islam and its ramifications— namely the status of women, the lack of human rights and freedom, and the Islamic form of government. The young people who have risen in rebellion in this Spring are aiming specifically at illiteracy, poverty, unemployment, and sickness, which only if eliminated could salvage the situation. Paradoxically, however, the desperate people who ignited the rebellion also support the success of the Islamic parties, whose regressive views and worship of the past have helped generate this accumulated national lagging behind, which it has become urgent to change.

Friedrich Nietzsche, who is supposed to have remarked that the worst enemy of truth is not a lie but a conviction[68], had meant to condemn religious belief, which is nearly impossible to argue against, much less to change, and this emanated from the transcendental focus of that belief in some supreme deity or another, out of reach to human argument or to any philosophical sophistry. Hence, the added power and immutability of prejudices, ideas, and emotions generated by religious sentiments, goes much beyond the conventional significance of woekism as "the behavior and attitudes of people who are sensitive to social and political injustice" . So, one can presume that the plight of the Blacks in America, where these trends and terminology were born, would be much more pronounced and brought to extremes among Black Muslims who embrace a religion itself in competition and conflict with the

---

[68] See in this context this author's *Perception, Conviction, Action,* Strategic Books, TX, 2023.

dominant Christian faith in America and perhaps less so in the midst of the Evangelical Blacks whose Christianity is shared with millions of White Americans, especially in the Biblical Belt of the southern states. For, while the conventional "woke" are only expressed through the social media between the various conflicting parts of society, all humans, arguing about social inequities, which are by nature arguable and given to mitigation and soft talk, the addition of religious controversy, which is by nature unbridgeable and absolute would necessarily exacerbate both the dissatisfaction of the victims and the response/reaction of their perceived "enemy". It was Dostoevski who noticed, a propos the revolutionary socialists of mid 19th Century France, that there was among them a peculiar category, admittedly in the minority, of "believing socialists" who were more dangerous than the atheistic ones[69].Aayan Hirshi Ali, the celebrated Muslim refugee from Somalia who self-exiled to Europe and made a meteoric political career in the Netherlands, and was later stripped from her Dutch citizenship, make some significant remarks about the encounter between the two cultures and detected what radical Muslims and Wokeism had in common"[70] .In the wake of verdicts of the Dutch court of law, following the murder of Director Van Gogh and the vindication of MP Geert Wilders in 2005, some Dutch ministers backed away from the integration policy and announced plans to cut funding for programs designed to help immigrants. Saying Dutch values must come first, Home Affairs Minister Piet Hein Donner told parliament that the government "will distance itself from the relativism contained in the model of a multicultural society." A June 19 (2005) poll found that three-quarters of the Dutch supported the cabinet's slashing of funds that went toward aiding immigrants. "In the 1990s, [just]

---

[69] Fyodor Dostoievski, *The Brothers Karamazov (*In French translation), Editions MInerve, Paris, Traduction Nouvelle, p. 83.

[70] Aayan Hirshi Ali, "What Islamists and Wokeists Have in Common, *The Wall Street Journal*, September 10, 2020.

saying 'a multicultural society should end' was ruled discriminatory," said Channa Samkalden, a lawyer at the firm Böhler Advocaten which specialized in free speech and freedom of religion. She was referring to the case of another anti-immigration politician, Hans Janmaat, who was prone to saying "full is full" and "our people first." Said Samkalden: "We've simply changed our minds on what's allowable." For Ronnie Eisenmann, head of the board of the Amsterdam Jewish Community, the latest twists in the Dutch culture wars reek of political strategy. "The fact that politicians say multiculturalism has failed doesn't mean you can ignore that a multicultural society exits," he says. "They're saying it because they want to cut funding." So, Muslim and Jewish organizations have come together to oppose a ban to ritual slaughter that parliament members approved, a ban that Wilders supported. But while Amsterdam's politicians may have been declaring the death of multiculturalism, the picture on the streets told a different story. At Sunday's Roots Festival in the Oosterpark — a musical celebration of all things cultural, stands selling Turkish kebabs co-existed happily with Dutch herring sellers and African artists. Key among the reversal of the liberal Dutch policies was the popularity of politicians Pim Fortuyn and Geert Wilders, who have attacked Holland's immigration and ethnic minorities policies, calling for a ban on immigration and an aggressive policy of assimilating minorities into Holland's libertine culture. The murder of Theo van Gogh at the hands of a Muslim radical after Pim Fortuyn's murder (2002) had solidified Dutch opinion against Holland's lenient criminal justice system, raising demands for the quick ratification of legislation analogous to the Patriot Act in America, for eighty percent of Dutch people thought that Holland was too tolerant of ethnic minorities. Theo van Gogh, the film maker, cultural commentator, and great grandnephew of artist Vincent van Gogh, was brutally murdered on an Amsterdam street. The assassin, Mohammad Bouyeri, was a Dutch Muslim of Moroccan ancestry. Van Gogh was riding his bicycle to work when Mohanmmad, dressed in a Iong *jellaba*, in itself an obvious politico-cultural message, hit him several times. Van Gogh begged for mercy, saying in Dutch, "Surely we can talk about this." Mohammad pulled out two butcher's knives. He slit van Gogh's throat from ear to ear with one knife and pinned a five-page letter to van Gogh's stomach with the other. The letter called for a holy war against the infidels. It was incensed about van Gogh and Hirsi Ali's released *Submission*, a film about the abuse of women in the name of Islam. Obviously inspired by it was *Soumission,* a novel by French writer Michel Houellebecq that was published on 7 January 2015, with German and Italian translations also published in the same month of January, indicating a Pan-European awakening since it instantly became a bestseller in France, Germany and Italy[71]. The film showed a Muslim woman dressed in a see-through burqa, telling her story of abuse within her marriage while verses from the Qur'an appeared on her naked body: "Men are maintainers of women because Allah has made them excel": and "'The good women are therefore obedient… Those on whose part you fear infidelity, admonish them, then refuse to share their beds and finally hit them[72] .Van Gogh and Hirsi Ali were critical of radical Islam, which ultimately caused the murder of the one and the exile of the second, because they observed that even as aliens in Europe, Muslims sought to impose their norms. Therefore, Van Gogh referred to Muslim radicals as "Nazis who wear kaftans and hide behind beards". Hirsi Ali had been brought up as a Muslim in Somalia, where she suffered female circumcision at the age of five. At the age of twenty, she fled to the Netherlands to escape from an arranged marriage. Penniless, and speaking no Dutch, Hirsi Ali worked as a janitor in a biscuit factory and as a translator before studying political science at Leiden University. In 2001, she wrote

---

[71] Michel Houellebecq, *Soumission,* January 2015 by Flammarion in Paris.
[72] Qur'an, Sura 4, Verse 34.

a report on 'honor killings' of Muslim women that also served as a severe indictment of Holland's thirty-year experiment with multiculturalism, describing it as a "'disastrous error" born of "misplaced guilt." Slamming Islam as a "'backward, 12th-century religion," a "'medieval, misogynist cult incapable of self-criticism and blind to modern science," Hirsi Ali revealed to the world that orthodox Muslim men routinely indulged in domestic violence against women, as well as incest and child abuse. To make matters worse, she argued that such behavior was covered up. If that was the sorry situation within Muslim immigrants into Europe, where the mitigating influence of the host cultures was expected to eliminate forced marriages and murderous crimes to uphold "family honor" and a number of other primitive habits, how much more grave was the situation in the native Muslim countries where the immigrants had fled from?

Hirshi Ali was also struck by the contrast between her native land and the country of refuge where she thought she was finding serenity and tranquility. For "the Netherlands was a country that worships consensus and peace, but here you have newcomers who are not integrated into the system." she said in 2004. "They exploit an open, liberal society to reach illiberal ends. Everyone knows the position of women in Islamic countries is horrendous, but the Dutch like to think it doesn't happen here. They don't want to believe that Muslim women in the Netherlands are beaten and locked up in their homes, or that girls are murdered for holding hands with a non-Muslim boy". The solution, Hirshi Ali argued, was for fundamentalist Islamic books to be banned, mullahs to be banished; and for Western societies to stop accommodating a culture that advocates the denigration of women.[73] But when the murder of van Gogh happened, which had been accompanied by the humiliating message left on his bleeding torso by the killer who

---

[73] John Henley, "Inside Story," *The Guardian*, November 4, 2004.

wore an Arab dress as if to challenge the European culture which sheltered him, while fear of accusing and blaming the culprits was dwarfed among the Dutch by the greater dread of being cast as "racists," the patient and liberal Dutch rose in outrage and set off a rash of attacks on Muslim schools and mosques. In retaliation, arsonists attempted to burn down churches in Rotterdam, Utrecht, and elsewhere. These attacks subverted the culture of tolerance in a country known for legalized hashish and prostitution, home to the Peace Palace, the International Court of Justice, and the International Criminal Court. Many Dutch were now concluding that their tradition of tolerance has suppressed an honest reckoning with the challenge of integrating radical Muslims into their society. Moreover, the Dutch public was distressed to learn that Bouyeri was a second-generation immigrant, born and raised in Holland, and educated in Holland's best schools. Bouyeri's transformation from a promising student to a jihadist followed an ominous pattern among young European Muslims, as it transpired in the British born Muslims who committed the Underground horrors in 2005. Bouyeri had been recruited into the Hofstad Group, a radical Islamic terror group composed mostly of Dutch citizens. The terror group was composed mainly of young men between the ages of 18 and 32. The name "Hofstad" was originally the codename of the Capital city of The Hague, where some of the suspected terrorists lived. The network was active throughout the 2000s.+- and parliament. Only thus, had Dutch and European awareness of a Muslim element, not content with being sheltered and integrated by liberal and tolerant Europe, had grown to the dimension of 10% of the total population (over one million alien-born, mostly from Morocco, among the over 10 million native Dutch. What was worse, rather than being docilely integrated into Dutch society, they were, in connection with other Muslim radical movements in Europe, envisaging and preparing to rise in rebellion and confront the existing order, thus meeting the general scheme of the Muslim

Brothers to Islamize the world. What made matters worse, as Robert Leiken wrote[74], "if jihad recruiters sometimes find sympathetic ears underground, among gangs or in jail, today they are more likely to score at university campuses and prep schools". In view of similar, and apparently all inter-connected, achievements all over the Western world where large Muslim minority immigrants have settled, it now appears that when they reach the demographic threshold, or come close to it, as in Holland, Belgium, France and Israel, the vague talks and dreams about Muslim dominion begin to crystallize into concrete schemes of rebellion, subversion, irredenta and Islamic takeover. Contrary to the expectations of politicians and sociologists, Europe is now a favored place for certain puritanical and radical movements within Islam, due the liberty it has. The dissonance between the fear, indeed a real panic in some European cities, from the rapid change in the landscape of their cities and their gradual takeover by a variety of languages, loud public conduct, the blunt disregard for rules and habits in the streets, and their concern for personal and public safety, and for the downgrading of the old cultural norms, and the compressed fear of expressing those concerns lest they be dubbed "racist" or "Islamophobe", leaves much of the native European population either paralyzed and complaining silently, or pushed to extreme right wing nationalist parties (watch the process in Italy, Germany, France and the Netherland) where they huddle for collective safety, retrieval of their old cultural norms, and the hope of national revival which alone can check the onslaught of the insidious Muslim takeover. In Europe, globalization takes the form of de-territorialized cultures and communities based on categories of race, religion, and lifestyle, to create supra-state organizations facilitated by the EU, NATO, multi-national cultural and economic groups, which also afford local communities of worshippers to expand their radius of activities and reach to other

---

[74] Robert Leiken, "Europe's Angry Muslims", *Foreign Affairs*, July/August 2005.

similar organizations of coreligionists, compatriots, professional colleagues and student associations. In the Netherlands, as in other European countries, Muslim enclaves are turned in on themselves, frustrated by poverty and inequality, inspired by the imagined community and ethno-familial culture represented by Islam. Under such conditions, imposed ghettoization is accepted, even desired by the seceding Muslim immigrants. Politicians in those countries, who act like fire fighters without long term concerns as long as they can extinguish blazes here and there in order to gain votes in the next elections, show little care for the long term effects the Muslim ghettoes will surely generate for their countries and societies, and do not invest much effort in the necessary long-haul planning to resolve their countries' basic problems. Therefore, they come to believe that the deep and long practical solutions for them must be devised for them in their present locations, but under conditions that would reduce daily friction and give them the feeling of liberty from oppression and some sense of pride and distinctiveness on the basis of equality, for one must differentiate in order to unite. Europeans were able to join in a union only after each of them accomplished its own independence and achieved its national goals, while preserving its separate territory, while the concept of 'thinking' is left to thoughtful scholars, publicists and journalists who worry about these dangers, even though politicians too take from time to time some demonstratively harsh measures against the Muslim threat in order to calm the moods of their home constituencies and to prove that they are "doing something". In April, 2014, for example, PM David Cameron of Britain, alerted to the subversive intents of the Muslims Brothers in his country, asked Britain's ambassador to Saudi Arabia to conduct an investigation into that organization, including allegations of its links to extremism and its impact on British national security.[75] But as if embarrassed by that revelation,

---

[75] Reuters, August 18, 2014.

the British government denied that a report had been produced by the commission of inquiry and delayed its publication "due to disagreements among ministers about its findings. It was other media, like the *Financial Times,* citing official sources, which said that the report had found that the Brotherhood should not be labelled a terrorist organization and had found little evidence its members were involved in terrorist activities. However, ministers who feared a backlash from their allies in the Middle East have stalled the publication of the report for several weeks. The main findings were completed by July (2014), as per the Prime Minister's request, and work was underway across government to consider the implications of these findings, a government spokeswoman said[76]. A spokeswoman for the Prime Minister said the government would make the findings public "in due course" but that it had never set out a timeframe for doing so. Probably the main reason for Cameron's reluctance was due to the Muslim Brotherhood, once Egypt's oldest, best organized and most successful political movement, had just seen hundreds of its members killed and thousands detained when then-army chief Abdel Fattah al-Sisi overthrew elected president and Brotherhood member Mohamed Mursi in 2013, following weeks of protest instigated by the Brotherhood that threatened chaos throughout Egypt. France, home to over 6 million Muslims, banned headscarves and other "conspicuous" religious symbols from schools and public institutions; Germany, has exacerbated the problem, on the contrary by allowing in one million refugees, mainly Muslim immigrants who sought asylum. In Belgium, some cities banned the veil in 2004, while Holland took the most radical measures reversing decades of liberal absorption of newcomers and embarked on a program to force 26,000 failed asylum seekers to return to their countries of origin within three years. In December,

---

[76] This author and his colleague, Zvi Mazel, were questioned on this matter by the inquiring British Ambassador to Saudi Arabia, at the British Embassy in Tel-Aviv during the Summer of 2014.

2005, its Parliament voted in favor of a Dutch language and culture test for immigrants seeking citizenship, and the Immigration Minister, Rita Verdoonk, was considering to ban burqas. In Switzerland a ban was imposed on minarets, an unfailing part of every mosque, due to the loud calls for Muslim prayers from their top, usually emitted by loud speakers which disturbed the sleep of the population at odd hours. At times, these bans and limitations were exacerbated by petty incidents which just exemplified for the European population the incompatibility of its open and liberal policy and customs with the conservative and puritanical reticence of the incoming Muslims, which occasionally caused startling reactions from the local native population which came to see itself discriminated against while the Muslim immigrants were favored. For example, when a Muslim student was turned down for a job in Rotterdam municipality, because he would not shake hands with women, he was allowed to seek from the Dutch "Equal Treatment Commission" a compensation of ca $10,000. British Home Secretary Reid talked tough at the Labor Party saying that he would not tolerate "No-go" neighborhoods in his country and that integration was essential for ethnic minorities, in view of the growing Muslim areas of London, Birmingham and other cities where the Muslim populations clustered around mosques to create ghettoes from which hostilities, crime and terrorism started to emerge that led to the July 2005, London Underground horrors.

The first *prima facie* conclusion one is tempted to draw from this rather grim picture is that multi-culturalism does not work, except for rare cases like Brazil where its special conditions made it seemingly possible so far. People are proud of their civilization they are on their turf, speaking their language, abiding by the customs of their dominant culture and religion, where no clashes recur with other elements in society which reject those norms. For decades, Europeans were accustomed to watch Muslims flocking to their countries (there was never a reverse stream from the West to

Muslim countries, and for good reason), either as foreign workers or as tourists, or visitors for study or business, but in all cases they were peaceful, quiet, respectful and grateful for the opportunity they were given to shop, visit, trade or learn in and from the host country. During their stay the visiting Muslims made valiant efforts to address their hosts in the local languages that they had bothered to learn. Only in the last few decades, the increasing Muslim communities in the West have accumulated enough membership and clout to gain self-confidence and assert their permanent stay as of right. That has raised their level of arrogance and the volume and range of demands from the Western governments. Muslim visitors, whatever their motivation, have become aware of that new mood. When they flock to Harrods or Max and Spencer in London, it is those firms, which are now partly owned by Muslims, which provide Arabic speaking salesmen to accommodate their customers. And many Muslim community leaders, while demanding more and more concessions to their culture and religion, and benefiting from the social security and services that their generous hosts afford them, have proclaimed their intention to change Europe to their tune, not to acculturate to its culture so as to become part of it. So has it been for Israeli Arabs.[77]

When two self-confident cultures, the host and the guest, are so different and one unwilling to give way to the other, collision becomes inevitable. And this is what has been happening in Israel and throughout the Western world with the Muslim minority, and to a certain extent with the Black community which remains salient and difficult to assimilate due to its color stigma. To circumvent that difficulty, champions of multi-culturalism, like Tony Blair in Britain, and American leaders on both sides of the political aisle, have advocated the co-existing and mixing of populations, creeds

---

[77] See R. Israeli, *Suicidal Democracy (2019)* ; *Expedient Identity (2020)*, both by Strategic Books, TX.

and cultures which would end up, they hoped, in a total, peaceful and happy merger of all into one nation, under God, indivisible. But as far as Muslim communities who have migrated to the West since mid 20th Century are concerned, it simply does not work. This is due to the widening gaps, not only In the socio-economic domain, but mainly by reason of the impossibility to merge one into the other, as it is impossible to mix water and oil, for the latter will always float to the surface while the former will sink to the bottom. And that is cause for perpetual conflict. At the end of World War II, President Harry Truman appointed Joseph Schechtman[78] as his representative to resolve the enormous refugee problem and displaced people during and as a result of the war where this clash of civilizations was endemic in many countries. After much thought based on experience in Europe, trial and error, consultations and talks with the various refugee populations, like the German minorities in the Soviet Union and Central Europe, the Greeks in Turkey and others, and examining the various options open to him, he came to the conclusion that the choice was between keeping the minorities in place, often against the will of the majorities, thus perpetuating the state of friction and conflict between the two indefinitely, what we would call today a pro multi culturalist approach; and the radical and permanent solution of population transfer, often against the will of the minority. The former, which would be dubbed humanitarian, because it wants refugees to remain settled where they are, undisturbed to the extent possible, their human rights and desires gaining priority over all other considerations, regardless of the long term consequences of continued misery, bloodshed and conflict; but the latter, which looks and sounds reprehensible to human rights champions, who elect the short range to make people accept their existing situation

---

[78] J. Schechtman, *Postwar Population Transfers in Europe 1945-1955,* Oxford, 1946

and avoid any change, but is viewed as the fundamental solution for the long run to end the tensions once and for all. Therefore electing that the German minorities be removed back to Germany, mainly from Russia and Czechoslovakia, as were Greeks who remained in Western Turkey following the rise of Ataturk' s new republic from the ashes of the Ottoman Empire, or the millions of Muslims and Hindus who were, willy nilly, removed all over the Indian sub continent when Pakistan separated from India upon attaining independence in 1947.

Nobody disputes the temporary misery of the suffering millions, nor was anyone obtuse to the terrible suffering of the displaced millions. However, after a generation or two, when the removed populations settled down, reconnected with their kin, language, religious base and culture, they could no longer imagine to have remained behind and subjected to the state of conflict their parents or ancestors had grown accustomed to. For the solution is permanent, people are no longer in a state of oppression, bitterness and unfulfilled expectations, and asking for rights and dreaming of a day of liberation from their oppressors, which became by the day more improbable and unfeasible. What displaced Greeks would elect today to return to hated Turkey's rule, or uprooted German to Russian, Czech or Polish rule ? More strikingly, what Israeli Jews today (save for a small minority) who had originated from one hundred different diasporas even before the state was born in 1948, would consent to revert to the antisemitism, persecution, humiliation and ultimately annihilation that they had suffered for almost two millennia under Christianity and Islam? Similarly, had the Palestinian refugees been permanently settled in their host countries over the past 75 years, none of them would have been still confined to a life of abject poverty in refugee camps, awaiting the implementation of the illusory, but constantly promoted, "Right of Return". Instead, many Arabs today would rather force on Israel the repatriation of those refugees and their descendants, who have grown 6 or 7 fold since 1948, not because they are converted to multi culturalism, which has remained a taboo in all Arab and Muslim countries where they constitute the majority, but as a way to set foot and expand demographically, as they proclaim and do in Europe today, in order to take over ultimately. However, even in the unlikely situation where massive population transfers are carried out, voluntarily or coercively, and both the dispatching and receiving countries agree to the deal, the likelihood that most settled and long established minorities would agree to move back to their mother countries (like the Hungarians in Rumania or in Serbia or the Turks in Germany, or the Indians in Britain, or the Blacks in America, remains very slim, to non existent. This has been the world historical experience, which has become a conventional fact of life. It remains to find the proper framework for each particular case towards its ultimate solution, if one is ready to ignore existing norms and think outside the box. Solutions can be found in secession, as the Czechs and Slovaks, or as the component members of former Yugoslavia have wisely found out, or federal and confederal forms of government, like the US and Canada, or cantonal arrangements like Switzerland, or other kinds of associations on cultural, linguistic, religious or ethnic grounds. The essential purpose of all these attempts is to eliminate multi culturalism where it does not work, and provide satisfactory relief for both the predominant majority culture and the various under-privileged and humiliated minority groups. The problem is notably with Muslim minorities in Western lands where're the hosts are not ready to deviate from the principle of equality before the law while many Muslims believe that every law, country and civilization must bend before the shari'a and accommodate them, failing which they are obliged to manipulate (or commercialize) their faith in order to adopt it to the demands of the host culture until the day when they succeed to attain their state goal to change the hosts to their tune rather than altering their own rules and beliefs.

Federal, confederal and cantonal solutions require a territory which the differentiated minority considers as its turf, and where its language, religion and mores can be practiced without inhibition or handicaps. In Canada, this is done in Quebec, where the French ethnicity, French language and Catholic religion are pursued, while the federal commitment is achieved by the dual language training that is customary in the public service and by the federal government that provides the state services and protection to all. Other Canadian minorities are supposedly willing to accept to integrate into the country 's political, social, linguistic and cultural values of the Anglophonic majority and will assimilate in time, except for some radical Muslims who have been raising their own demands as they do today in western Europe[79]. For the Muslims, who are spread all over that vast country, cannot claim, for now, any territory as their own, just like in Europe, therefore any demands they make or long term menace they pose, will come from Muslim individuals or groups and local congregations of Muslims, backed by their religious and community leaders, not focused on any particular territory. In the US the situation is complicated by the fact that in all 50 states of the union, there are Blacks who are promised equal rights under law, but whose concentrations in certain towns and slums in the large cities have aggravated the situation, rendered the pledge of one nation under God not only unrealizable, but also worsening due to the continued frictions, explosions of rage and manifestations of racism that have become part of American life. If only blacks could claim a territory of their own, maybe their status could be upgraded as they exercise their autonomous rules over their turf. But even if that could be achieved, remains the problem of Islam in America, which in many ways overlaps with the black issue, through the growing community of the black Muslim groups which are supported by the mushrooming Muslim organizations of

---

[79] R. Israeli, *Muslim Minorities in the Modern States,* Transaction, NJ, 2009.

North America. Therefore, as Black Americans certainly prefer to stay where they are today, after they had shed their centuries of slavery and added to them more than a century and a half of more discrimination and humiliation, and have become worthy natives of the land, they must find a territorial answer to their plight. For example, if two or three states of the US where a large Black population exists, could be declared as designated to become, by choice of those who so desire, Black states within the union within a given time frame, and that in the meantime other people can move freely in, if they wanted to be included, and out if they did not. In the course of years majority Black states will take shape voluntarily, with their own administration, police force, institutions, churches and what have you, and can no longer complain of humiliation and discrimination. Their representatives in the federal institutions will ensure their fair share in the US resources and protective stature.

As to other Muslims in America, except for the Blacks among them, most of them recent immigrants who can be faced with the same choices as the European Muslims, either they accept the European values and relegate their Muslim beliefs and emotions to their individual concern and resign to their minority status in Christian societies, or they go back to their countries of origin, if Muslim regimes and mores are preferable in their eyes to European, Canadian, American or Australian culture. After all, those countries were hospitable to them when they arrived as refugees, or just as immigrants, in order to improve their lots, for those destinations were their choice, no one had asked them to come. They might not like what they found, but then they should rather go back than try to impose their norms on the host countries. One cannot be so ungrateful for receiving such hospitality by demanding the change to one's tune the initial conditions one had chosen to come under, like demanding the erasure of the cross from the Scandinavian, Greek or Swiss flags, or impose on hard working people the screams of *Muazzins* in mosques during the early hours when they want to sleep and Muslims want to pray. It is understood that one feels easy with the familiar landscapes one grew in, with well known and desirable sounds, smells and sights, but one cannot expect one' s host society to ply to one' s mores and whims and ignore its own, under the threat of violence or accusations of Islamophobia or racism against anyone resisting those unreasonable demands.

Unlike the Muslims in Israel, who claim that they are the native population, which is fact originates from migrant Arabs, and used to constitute the majority that was invaded by Zionist Jews, and therefore they preserved their native rights and have no obligation to respect the laws of the invader, Muslim immigrants in Western countries, do not advance such a claim, and therefore they have to submit to the preponderant laws and mores or depart. Muslims in Israel are different in yet another aspect. Since they identify themselves as Arabs and Palestinians, not only Muslims, they find themselves aligning unconditionally with Israel's enemies, making their own situation untenable. For example, their representatives in the Israeli Parliament are all on record as favoring the Palestinian "Right of Return", which if implemented would render Israel in the long run another Arab and Muslim country. What country in the world would countenance the presence in its midst of a subversive population aiming at ending its existence?. Therefore, putting an end to the pervert idea of suicidal multi culturalism in the Jewish state, is imperative more, and more urgently, than in all other Western nations in view of the increasing Arab Muslim population there, the growing intransigence of the Islamic Movement which does not hide its annihilationist intention against the state in which it resides, and the continuing link between Israel's Muslims and other Muslims worldwide who announce openly their hostility to the Jewish state, like Iran, Syria, Lebanon and Turkey on occasion. In Israel therefore, where Muslims dwell in three large concentrations, namely the Western Galilee, the central Triangle and the Northern Negev, where their numbers may be a base for territorial claims for autonomy and then secession, there exist the fundamental conditions for *irridenta* on their part, and for their permanent aspiration to link up with their country s enemies, at its detriment. They claim openly that they are Palestinians in a state that has occupied them, so there is no reason for them to remain "forced Israelis", unlike their European counterparts who have sought their countries citizenship, though their intentions are not necessarily different. Their permanent solution is then irrevocably related to the fate of the Palestinian people. To wit, if and when the Palestinians find a national or federal arrangement within the Arab world, the Israeli Arabs must be included therein, and all those who would elect that course, should become Palestinian nationals, either while continuing to reside in Israel as aliens, or by moving into the Palestinian territory or by having their turf in Israel exchanged for another Arab territory where Israeli settlers dwell presently. Squeamish bleeding hearts, who are seemingly concerned will the problems of all peoples except their own, would then cry racism, Islamophobia, inhumanity and the like, but watching the West coming to terms with its problem of multi culturalism, which has so far caused crime, tensions, violence and terrorism, one would elect to hear the cries of abhorrence from those who oppose remedying the problem once and for all, than watch for themselves the continuation of bloodshed and terror if the present uncontrollable situation is permitted to escalate.

One of the major reasons for the eventual collapse of all empires, both in antiquity and in our days, was the ultimate impossibility of maintaining many countries, cultures and religions under the boot of one hegemonic power, what today is equivalent to multi culturalism, with one difference, namely in past Empires one culture predominated and ruled, be it Assyrian, Babylonian, Chinese, Greek or Roman, Ottoman or British, while the lesser cultures and ethnic groups submitted to the hegemon, usually constrained by the force of arms, and often tried to acculturate to the dominant culture by

Hellenizing, Sinicizing, Romanizing or Ottomanizing. But when the Empire grew weak and no longer able to impose its predominance, the various groups, ethnicities, and religions assumed their independence, or parts of them remained within the boundaries of the emerging independent national states as minorities, like Jews in ancient Rome, Ottoman Muslims in the Balkans, Greeks in Turkey or Indians in Britain or Arabs in Israel. That is also the lot of the Tibetans and Muslims in China, the Rohinga in Burma, the Chechnyans in the Russian Federation, or the Arabs of North Africa in France. Conversely, modern multi culturalism is not imperially imposed from above since there are no longer dominant empires, but is adopted as a joint voluntary arrangement between former empires and their formerly occupied populations, on the presumed basis of agreement and equality, without one striving to dominate the other. All this is operational except in the case of Muslims, where their Caliphal empires: Abbasid, Fatimid, Ottoman, Moghul, were all based on religion, which combined empire with faith, and strove constantly to convert all the conquered peoples into Islam, save for Christians and Jews who were relegated to the status of the second class *dhimmis* as long as they did not Islamize, and duly paid the humiliating poll-tax of the *Jizya*. That was the most efficient way to ensure the monolithic Islamic nature of the empire, at the detriment of the ethnic, linguistic and cultural traits of the occupied peoples which were permitted to thrive. Thus, Islamic empires were multi cultural in many ways, allowing a rich gamut of cultures, languages, ethnic groups to keep to their mores and modes of life as long as they submitted to Islam which united them, again except for the *dhimmis* who preserved their creeds, as long as they recognized the suzerainty of the ruling Islam, although they were constantly lured to Islamize by the attractions of integrating into the prestigious ruling system. Other non Muslims, like the Slavs of Eastern Europe and the Balkans, were subjected to the Ottoman *devshirme* system, under which children were taken from their parents, raised as Muslims and trained as future soldiers fully devoted to the Sultan, and they later constituted the core of the famous Janissaries, who often returned to their countries of origin as the government's functionaries and served as the long arm of the Sultan and an eminent means of Islamization of their kin. Thus were founded the Muslim populations in the Balkans, which today destabilize countries like Serbia, Macedonia and Montenegro, and ensure the independent Islamic presence in Europe in such countries as Bosnia, Albania and Kosovo. This was the way this tolerated ethnic multi culturalism led, paradoxically, to the ultimate Islamization which denies multi culturalism.

At the height of its rule, the Ottoman Dynasty had also yielded to another kind of multi culturalism that was imposed by the Capitulations system which in fact subtracted millions of its nationals from its jurisdiction when it relinquished them to the authority of the foreign consuls of the European powers who pretended to protect them on Ottoman soil. Thus, the *dhimmi* status lost much of its acuity, and some of the erstwhile persecuted minorities, or at least the most disfavored among them, found themselves almost immune to the Ottoman reach. *Prima facie*, that was a manifestation of the renowned Ottoman "tolerance", but in fact it was a clear demarcation between the mostly Muslim population that was loyal to the Sultan's rule and the potentially disloyal and subversive elements which were always suspected of collaborating with the foreign powers and undermining the Ottoman rule, unlike the *dhimmi* status which delineated the Christians and Jews as inferior, all right, but they were still included as a legitimate component within the Caliphate. Besides, Capitulations were imposed by the European powers under the pretext of protecting members of various religious denominations, Russia as the protectors of the Orthodox Church, France of the Catholics, etc. When the Young Turks government abolished the Capitulations at the outset of the W W I, many non Muslims, including Christian and Jewish immigrants and refugees who had settled in Ottoman territory, like Palestine, felt suddenly exposed to deportation, accusations and suspicions, or worse. Ultimately, although most of the Ottoman multi culturalism was based on an ethnic and linguistic diversity within a religious unity, which recognized Islam and Ottoman values as the dominant religion and culture of the Caliphate and the *dhimmis* as an acknowledged, though second class, part of the Empire, it broke up with the rise of nationalism in Europe, including the independence wars in the Balkans. Exactly as the great empire of Austro Hungary broke up and new national states rose, so did the diverse peoples and cultures of the Ottoman empire, including the Muslims among them, who realized that if in Turkey Turkish nationalism could emerge, then why not an Arab, Kurd, Caucasian or otherwise, although they were all Muslim, the common denominator that used to unite all of them as Ottoman subjects. The Arabs even refined further that idea by differentiating between ethnic nationalism, dubbed *qawmiya*, i.e. ethnic descent, real or imagined, and territorial nationalism, deriving from the European concept of the *patria*, a fatherland that they dubbed *wataniya*, *watan* being a concrete land turf. While the former is purely Arab, though multi confessional for there are also Christian, Alawite, Druze etc. Arabs, the latter is totally territorial, for there can be Jewish, Christian, Druze, Kurdish, Alawite, Syrians, Iraqis, Moroccan and what have you. All those countries are self declared Muslim, while their non/Muslim nationals are tolerated minority religions. That is how far as Muslim and Arab multi culturalism can go, and never would an Islamic or Arab majority country admit a civil and secular egalitarian state for all its ethnic or confessional groups, Islam being officially declared as the "state religion". That demand is only put to other countries where Muslim minorities dwell.

To sum it all, when everything is taken into account, we must make two major differentiations. On the one hand, between Western and religious Muslim handling of multi culturalism, and on the other between religious and multi culturalism in general. On the first account, while the West has genuinely and honestly tried to experiment with multiculturalism in order to accommodate the influx of Muslim immigrants into its territory, on a secular basis and on an assumption of equality, if the migrants should abide by its laws and the general framework of its culture, while keeping their religion to themselves as individuals in the private domain, in other words if the incoming Muslims should acculturate and become loyal and useful citizens in their countries of asylum, then all is well, and multiculturalism should prove a success. For the Muslim asylum seekers, however, once they reached a demographic critical mass in certain areas and their visibility in the streets of Europe became annoying to the native populations who no longer recognized the familiar landscape of their country, suspicions and alienation began to set in. When they understood that they could now influence the politics of their countries of shelter by their massive votes and demand the implementation of their own agenda by their hosts instead of themselves plying to the existing one, they thereby started to unhinge the assumptions on which their immigration was done and absorbed. For the hosts soon realized, that their guests were not only adamant to preserve their dress, their conduct, their language and their mores in the public square, but they also built more mosques and Islamic centers where they educated their youth for Islamic piety, which generated more radicalism, and for hatred of Western culture which soon paved the way to violence and terrorism, instead of inspiring it to loyalty and respect for the laws and rules of the countries that had taken them in. That rebellion by the guest population against the dominant host culture which had sheltered it, is tantamount to wokeism in contemporary parlance.

On the second count, it is for Muslims unbearable to live under non Islamic rule, and all Muslims are required to dwell only in countries of Islam where their pursuit of their religious obligations can go unhindered. This seems strange in view of the fact that many more Muslims flock to Western countries as immigrants or visitors, than Westerners in the reverse direction, and for good reason. Westerners know that in Islamic countries they would be held in contempt and mistreated, and subject to unrest, illness and poverty, while Muslims flee their native countries for the security, prosperity and freedom they can obtain in the West. But when the latter settle in the West they cannot countenance to be ruled indefinitely by Infidels, therefore they strive to change it by more Muslim immigration, by imposing elements of *Shari'a* laws or aspects thereof in their countries of shelter, and to maintain their own neighborhoods, Islamic centers, separate and woke-inspired educational systems and economic networks so as to erect Islamic enclaves that would one day be able to undermine and take over the host culture. Judging from what some of their radical leaders said openly, they have every intention for their Islam to triumph, and certainly to shun the "moderate" European Islam that some EU politicians and officials have been toying with. So, while Europeans were busy wasting their time to differentiate between "good" and "bad" Muslims, with the aim of earmarking the former for collaboration in the future, and casting he latter in the role or criminal outcasts. They forgot that the perpetrators of the London, Nice and Madrid horrors were often moderate good Muslims who grew up in well to do families, and committed their misdeeds not for gain, as do other criminals, but for no other remuneration, and amidst putting their lives of the line, than accomplishing a religious task that was instilled in them in their mosques, of terrorizing the West and triumphing over it. In other words, where there was a Muslim community, it will always be accompanied by the potential for misdeed in its midst of radicalized and committed minds against the hated West and the "Westoxicated" culture it has been spreading in the world. All this while they had not been asked to move to West that they shunned, but chose and begged to come in in order to undermine it.

To put it bluntly, the Western view of multi culturalism has been rejected lock stock and barrel by the Muslims, because for them it is not a matter of only ethnic, linguistic or cultural disagreement, but a serious issue of a yawning and unbridgeable ideological and religious gap that separates them from their host countries. Western pundits have to understand that their attempts at dialogue with Muslims in order to calm down their frustration and their complaints of Islamophobia and racism, will not help. For here we have two different systems of thought and two contradicting approaches to life and to religion, the difference between quantitative and qualitative norms and principles. When a regular conflict exists between two conventional rivals, it is usually about territories, assets, influence or prestige. These issues are either decided by war, or by negotiation around the table, where by a method of give and take the belligerent parties can come, or are compelled to come, to an agreement. But when the conflict is ideological, like the one between Capitalism and Communism, as still manifested today int he American- North Korean rift, which has been generalized between that rigid authoritarian regime and the open West, negotiation is impossible because it is inevitably driven into a deadlock, as the Trump-Kim vain encounters (2017-8) have proven.

All the more so between Islam and the West, because each plays under different rules of his game. For example if a Muslim actor believes that Allah has invested him with a certain duty or allotted to him a certain land in perpetuity, like Andalusia, Kashmir or Palestine, there is no chance in the world that he would have any reason to relinquish his obligation to retrieve what he believes is his. And even if he yields temporarily to overwhelming circumstances, he will try again until successful. This is a qualitative approach, in which there is no point to negotiate, because a Muslim cannot negotiate, let alone cede to the enemy, any land that he believes was allotted to him by divine will. For negotiations mean a readiness to compromise, and one cannot compromise over divine rulings. Then why waste time in negotiations?. If one reads the Charter of the Hamas or the platforms of other radical Muslim movements, one is struck immediately by the frankness, conviction and self assurance in which these articles of faith are worded. To the Western mind, which tends to reason logically in the best cases, such obdurate positions taken by radical Muslims, which often border on suicide, are seen in the Muslim world as manifestations of courage and obedience to Allah, which in the West are viewed as foolish activities of Muslim terrorists, such as those by Hamas, ISIS, al-Qa'ida or Taliban have been illustrating daily. And this has not prevented thousands of Muslim youth who have grown in the West to flock to the ranks of ISIS and the other terrorist organizations, though they volunteer to fight basically against their countries of abode to which they return, if they survive, to continue their struggle that undermines the West.

Therefore, Western countries as well as Israel have no other recourse than tightening the screws on the existing Muslim populations, and certainly preventing by all legal means a further increase of their Muslim population (except by national growth or religious conversions into Islam), if they wish to ensure the survival of their national culture, and in the case of Israel even its very physical survival. Muslims are betting on long haul demographic processes and on the open and democratic liberalism of their host countries in order to grow unhindered and deliver their *coup de grace* when the appropriate time comes. The menaced countries must respond in the short and medium ranges in order to exactly nip in the bud those threatening tendencies before they become impossible to reverse. It is evident that harsh and discriminating measures against part of the existing populations in liberal democratic countries will be seen, and rightly so, as undemocratic, anti-liberal, inhuman, racist and what have you, but when it is a matter of national survival, emergency measures are imperative. We are in officially an undeclared war, though radical Muslims have declared that war and are acting as a belligerent party in it. The US, for example, had interned its Japanese citizens during W W II even though they not pose, even remotely, any threat to US existence, and its Supreme Court had endorsed that step, arguing that the perception of danger, not the actual one which can be given to various interpretations, was sufficient to justify that emergency measure in view of the state of war. The dangers today to Europe and especially to Israel, are so imminent and so great, and certainly greater than those jeopardizing the US domestically in that war, that no squeamish attempts at pacifying and accommodating the Islamic world will be equal to the job. After all, with the application of these new harsh measures, which might be justly regarded as collective punishment, those Muslims will be still freer, safe and prosperous in the West than in their Muslim countries that they have fled. And if they genuinely resent those measures, they always have the option to return to the countries they came from. After all, don't we all submit to the collective punishment meted out to us when the acts of terror against us are indiscriminately directed at all innocent people just for being what they are, and not for any wrong doing that can be attributed to them. And aren't we all suffering from the search in our belongings just because Muslim terrorists are threatening to blow us up. Yes, when public security obliges, then collective punishments of this sort become inevitable. A variety of measures are necessary, part of which are immediately applicable, others are to be envisaged for the future:

- No more Muslims will be admitted from the outside into Western countries, except for extreme humanitarian cases, which themselves have to be carefully monitored. Enough Muslim refugees have infiltrated into Europe and Israel who have later turned to terrorism against the countries which rescued them for humanitarian reasons. And enough Arab terrorists who got Israeli medical and humanitarian aid, turned against it when they had the opportunity to do so.

- Citizenship to Muslims in the countries of shelter should not be allocated indiscriminately, but case by case, based on the services done to the host countries by the immigrants, on their fulfilling fundamental conditions like knowledge of the language, permanent employment, understanding of the local political and social system, an impeccable criminal record, a signed commitment to abide by the local law and to relinquish imported mores like forced marriages, polygamy and honor killing, and proven utility to the absorbing country. Those who falter in these tests have to be unceremoniously repatriated. If they run a risk of persecution in their country of origin, that is the concern and responsibility of their country of origin, not of the country of shelter.

- The Muslims who are permitted to stay, provided they fulfilled all their civilian duties to their adoptive state, should be closely monitored, especially in their educational and religious institutions which have become the hot houses of terrorism. Classes and sermons in mosques and hatred material are to be approved by local authorities before they are diffused. It is true that these are precisely the traits that differentiate between the authoritarian regimes which they have fled and the democratic countries of asylum, but in view of the fact that many Muslim immigrants wish to impose on their host countries their own laws and customs, they must also bear the consequences of the harsh measures of control customary in the countries of origin.

- To the extent possible, Muslims must be banned from concentrating in growing slums and special quarters, like the Arab villages in Israel or the *cites* around Paris, where hatred is fomented, plots against national security are concocted on the one hand, and on the other hand the concentrated masses of

Muslims in one place lend a sense of strength, safety, immunity and separateness to the ill intended actors.

- The separate systems of education for Muslims have to be ended, and they must be integrated into the national educational network. For it has been proved that educating Muslim children in a different language than the national one, and instilling into it a separate set of values and historical ethos, necessarily produce a different category of citizens not tuned to the needs of the nation or to the thinking of its citizenry.

- To the extent possible, areas where large concentrations of Muslims already dwell, new territorial concepts of optional cultural and linguistic autonomy have to be devised, maybe on a cantonal basis, so as to give vent to cultural differentiation for those who find it difficult to completely integrate on the one hand, but not to hurt national unity on the other. A minority number of Muslim cantons, among a majority of cantons of the predominant culture will ensure that whatever the demographic changes the majority rule in the country will be preserved for the long run.

The overall salient lesson from all this is cold, simple and straightforward. As long as there is a dominant culture that is embraced by the majority of the citizens of any country, homogeneity in politics, culture, language, mores and ethos can be assured, on the basis of commonality of values and a joint familiarity and mentality of the people, then the likelihood of an unwritten social contract which ties all residents together is high, and the stability, law and order and happy voluntary citizenship can be ensured, a constitution is agreed upon which regulates life, and an independent judiciary is in place to adjudicate cases of disagreement peacefully and authoritatively. And when new immigrants are added to the existing situation, they must be asked to comply with the existing order as a condition to joining it and becoming part of it. This is usually the situation in free liberal democracies, where this order of things had grown during centuries of evolution, and that is the secret of their tremendous attraction to migrants from the less fortunate parts of the world, including the Muslim, Arab, Third World and less developed worlds. Under those regimes, the rule is either maintained by the force of coercion, or is doomed to devolution, chaos, war, disagreement, dissent, subversion and unrest. Those are ideal grounds for division and clandestine wokeism, while it is paradoxically in free and liberal societies that wokeism was born and has thrived in the first place into the open public square. Under authoritarianism, there is no social contract that keeps those splintered societies together, and to the extent that there are constitutions, they are usually the stated blueprints of the dictator, which are erased once a new dictator takes over from the previous fallen one. Instead of restricting the ruler, the constitution is given to his whims and changing moods. The result of that situation is what we see today in the Islamic world, from Afghanistan to Somalia and from Morocco to Iraq. What Muslims create on their own turf in term of values and mores, they certainly import with them to the West when they migrate to it, therefore Muslim minorities are usually, with some exceptions, so immensely at variance with Western culture that taking them in as an experiment in multi culturalism, as Holland did, is a great risk of ending in failure. Experience has born that out. One of the great obstacles that militates against blocking the way to further Muslim encroachment on Western territory is the UN, which champions the cause of the immigrants and fake refugees, via its own refugee organizations and its constant pressure on Western countries to accommodate the growing flow of populations from the poor south to the rich north. The UN has even created its own special agencies, like the UNRWA specifically for the Palestinians, which instead of resolving this 70 year old sore issue, has perpetuated it by turning it into a permanent insoluble political problem when it transformed the concept of refugee, which by definition is a unigenerational status, while one searches for and finds a settlement somewhere, into a career that is inherited from generation to the next, so that the Palestinian refugees are now in their fourth generation and have grown from their original 700,000 to over 4 million today. Too many vested interests have grown within the UN to prolong the life of that vast organization, which provides many lucrative jobs and positions of power, thus refusing to disappear by achieving its initial purpose of a final settlement of the refugees. The UN will not change or reform by itself and it will continue to sustain its organizations, agencies and fake jobs and perform as a theater of the absurd, unless shaken up, broken up and remade. Syrians and Libyans, Iraqis and Iranians, will continue to head human rights and disarmament commissions, preach to the world their version of peace and democracy, pretend that they fight terrorism while they instigate it, and encourage their impoverished and destabilizing crowds to move to the West in order to ruin it from within. It is as if the mafia were put in charge of public order. What must be done if to revamp the world organization by the US unilaterally if necessary, or through the collaboration of America's democratic and close allies, like Britain, Canada, Australia, India, Japan and Germany, and also little Israel, as founders of the Union of Democratic States, if possible. In the new Union, which will inherit today's UN HQ in NY, every member country will weigh according to its real strength: demographic territorial and economic, and only liberal democracies can be admitted based on a list of tests, like what membership in the EU or NATO requires today .Among other changes will also be the regulations of population migrations, the return to the familiar national states, and the end of the automatic majority of small, corrupt, undemocratic, sycophant, and valueless countries, which today rule the UN, often under the guidance of the authoritarian world powers. The present UN and its agencies and organizations will move elsewhere and continue to play its skewed role, under the aegis of the world dictatorships and their finances. At the end it will become redundant and wither, as more and more countries strive to pass the requisite tests in order to join the growing reformed Union. It is worth the trial, and there is no one more fit to wreck the boat and lead this revolution than a non conformist American President.

CHAPTER SEVEN

The Organization of Islamic Cooperation (OIC)

It is difficult to Imagine an arena where Islam can produce a more fertile and pregnant with intrigues as the process of commercialization of religion that is churned out within the than the United Nations. The process of Islamization which has been in progress since the initial conquests of Islam in the 7th Century and down to the radicalization movements of the 21st Century has unmistakably been geared to globalize and universalize the Faith, in the belief that it has been ordained by Allah to encompass the entire human race to the exclusivity or all others. Thus, all the conquests, missionary efforts and gentle ways of expanding Islam via commerce have converged to the very impressive outcome of 57 Muslim countries and over 1,5 billion Believers, but also upon a large (an increasing) Muslim community of Muslim immigrants to the West, some legal and others "undocumented, who are incrementally joined by many thousand Europeans who are attracted by the success of expanding Islam and convert. It is not only the wealth of the petroleum producing countries, most of which are Muslim, which impresses and attracts the converts, but also tagging it as the faith of the future, compared with the sinking role of religion in Western societies, and in the face of the apparent loss of the will to struggle and to stand for values that they encounter in the West, compared to the unyielding resilience of Muslim aggression and militancy in various fronts simultaneously.

One of the most impressive fronts where the Islamic united force comes to bear is the United Nations where the group of Islamic states constitutes over a quarter of the total membership, a bloc of 57 countries which consult among themselves and exercise arm-twisting when necessary, through money and energy- dispensing politics, in addition to the number of votes they can recruit to support any cause or scuttle others not to their taste. Indeed, we often find resolutions that are adopted in the OAI periodically tabled in the agenda of the UN by the Islamic group which has learned to maneuver its diplomatic power to suit its purposes, notably against Israel, which is condemned repeatedly and perennially by the sheer weight of the Islamic bloc. The HQ of the OIC sits in Jedda, Saudi Arabia, and any idea or whim of any member of the Conference can be reflected without delay in the UN resolutions, which Israel and its allies are powerless to scuttle, while all the Secretary Generals ls of the world Organization, except for the second to serve, Dag Hammarskjold who was killed in a tragic accident on duty in the Congo in the 1960s, do little or nothing to mend world crises or to redress global travesties or disasters, for all they care is to be reelected for a second term that can be ensured only via catering to the powerful Islamic bloc. Hence also the odd dominance of the Islamic bloc in various key commissions of the UN such as disarmament, Human Rights and the like.

The travesty of justice within the UN, which is generated by the Islamic bloc which permanently pressurizes, via soothing, cajoling, arm-twisting or even threatening, the other nations to conform, signals to the Muslim world its power to turn any event their way; most Muslim commoners across the globe, when watching on the media conferences of the OIC or of the Islamic bloc in the UN, are enamored with the sight of the corporate power of Muslim Heads of states or foreign Ministers or Ambassadors, who by convening together and taking fateful decisions, which are later globally spread by well rehearsed propaganda machineries that disseminate rumors and manufactured lies as "breaking news", which get the support of some Western nations, are persuaded of Islam's world power and of the global projection of that powerful image that can only reinforce its aura and prestige as to make it the "faith of the future", regardless of the veracity of its themes, for what counts in the UN are the vote counts, not truth or lies. Iran is just an example, that even business-minded and "politically correct" and "policy pragmatic" US and Europe can comprehend. However, except for the Abrahamic Pact Islamic countries, which have sworn a new avenue of relations with Israel, in the rest of the Islamic world, even in countries like Egypt and Jordan who ostensibly signed peace with Israel, the undercurrent of hatred, antisemitism and hostility remains firm toward Jews, Zionism and Israel, because of the backbone of perceived injustice which makes up the building blocks of those sentiments. The Palestinians, who are the closest to Israel geographically and the most integrated in their society, know it inside out and realize the fallacy of many of their insults against it, still maintain the high degree of enmity that obtained in the last century, since the beginning of the Zionist settlement in Palestine and because of it. The rejection of Israel is not conditional or limited or transitory: it is total, immutable, irreversible and eternal, as reflected in the next two official samples of the PLO publications:

a. Under the title" "The PA honors fencers who refused to compete against Israelis", the Chairman of the Palestine Olympic Committee Jibril Rajoub, and the Chairman of the Palestinian Fencing Association Daoud Mitwali honored the Kuwaiti fencers who refused to compete against Israeli fencers, considering their refusal an "awe-inspiring and noble position" and "appreciated" by Rajoub, almost

30 years subsequent to the Oslo Accords, where mutual recognition was accorded and approved.[80]

b. Under the heading "The Palestinian rejection of Israel's right to exist", The Balfour Declaration of 1917, which recognized the Zionist project of establishing a "Jewish Home" in Palestine, once again expressed its rejection of Israel's rights to exist, condemning the declaration, accompanied with elaborate conspiracy theories. The common theme of all the statements, is the denial of the internationally and historically recognized connection of the Jewish people to the Land of Israel and the rejection of the legitimacy of the State of Israel, in any borders. Leading the barrage was the PA Ministry of Information which claimed that the declaration was "the crime of the era" which "exceeded the crimes of colonialism", and called on the Britain to "be ashamed of their sin". The [PA] Ministry of Information said that the black Balfour Promise in its 105th year is the crime of the era, … this unjust promise is a dangerous precedent in the history of international relations… that … exceeded the crimes of colonialism… [81]

This demand was echoed by the official organ of the PA, which wrote: "through Britain gave that which it did not have ownership over to one who has no right, we are still paying the price of this ominous declaration's consequences in political, material, humanitarian, geographical, and other terms, and Britain must correct its historical mistake and recognize the sovereign and contiguous State of Palestine whose capital is Jerusalem, and the [Palestinian] refugees' right of return."[82] The PA Presidential Guard posted a similar message on its Facebook page. Under these circumstances, it is

---

[80] Nan Jacques Zilberdik, PMW, Nov 9, 2022

[81] Maurice Hirsch, Adv., PMW, Nov 7, 2022

[82] Al-Hayat Al-Jadida, Nov. 1, 2022

obvious that especially Palestinians, and generally other Arabs and Westerners who have been compassionately following the plight of Palestinian refugees for decades, must have come to the conclusion that the Palestinians must have been dealt a great injustice, and that no step or demarche that Israel can do or had ever done in their regard, has been the farthest away possible from justice. Viewed in that light (or rather obscurity), as eternal victims, who can do no wrong, the Palestinians feel entitled to retaliate in any fashion they deem fit, including what we regard as terrorism, which is for them the only way for them to gain the world attention and to have their unjust plight remedied in a supreme act of justice. The fact that more harm can be done to others (who deserve it in their minds) in the process, is of no importance and no relevance, because nothing that could be afflicted on the unjust demon, could equal or obscure all the horrific acts of injustice he had committed.

Nothing illustrates this better than the Easter 1983 Poison Affair in the West Bank under Israeli rule, which encompassed in one both the physical and metaphorical aspects of poisoning, and which brought injustice, bias, prejudice and hatred to their highest peaks in the name of false justice and decency, for the poison that was spread intentionally and promoted psychologically and politically, emanated from a trumped up anti-Israeli accusation of maliciously poisoning Arabs by Israel, which was made up, cultivated, inflated and propagated around the world, before it fell flat and vanished like a punctured balloon. This is a story, not unlike the perennial blood libel[83] or the more recent *Protocols of the Elders of Zion,* which had won currency around the world, not due to their veracity or likelihood, or to the just and righteous lessons to draw from them, but only because certain milieus were either interested to spread them, or were themselves eager to believe them. This poisonous story (literally), though its shares with its antecedents the blurred

---

[83] See R. Israeli, *The Blood Libel and its Derivatives,* Transaction, NJ, 2012.

boundaries between reality and fantasy, has no heroes, only cowards. It is replete with bigotry, calumniation, double standards of morality, professional dishonesty, political sycophancy and sensationalized press reporting worthy of the yellowest of tabloid. Not only was justice trampled cynically upon world arenas, but even when the hoax was revealed and proved, very few of the world media and of the world institutions (UN, Red Cross, Arab and Muslim organizations) had the decency to apologize, to recognize the injustice they had meted out to an entire nation, and make believe that they had erred innocently and led astray by others. The story is not devoid of drama and intrigue. For although no preconceived plot was revealed which triggered it, events did evolve in as a *deus ex machina,* acquiring their own logic by themselves and leading to an inevitable end. The detailed narrative as recounted by this author[84], reveals a Kafkaesque situation where cause and effect are not connected, non-sequiturs pose as logical reasons, usually credible and decent professionals are amiss on their duties, and all threads are woven, as in a mysterious hand, into a powerful and irresistible *toile de fond* of misapprehension and deception. The breathtaking scenery creates a vivid reality that is so much overwhelming than the imagination laying at its source, that it looks and sounds plausible. Once again, reality being freed from the shackles of human imagination, turns more fantastic than reality itself.

On 21 March, 1983, the Israeli electronic media reported *ad nauseam* during the entire day to their stunned audiences a bizarre event which immediately obscured the other happenings of the time. The first dispatches[85] reported that at the girls' middle school

---

[84] R. Israeli, *Poison:Modern Manifestations of a Blood Libel,*Lexington, Lanham. 2002.

[85] The first reports were flashed repeatedly on Israeli TV, the Voice of Israel Radio, and the three major dailies: *Haaretz, Maʾariv and Yedioth Aharonot.* Specific references, commentaries and interviews will be mentioned below.

of the village of Arrabeh in the Jenin District in the northern West Bank under Israeli administration, a mass poisoning had occurred. It was said that briefly prior to the beginning of classes at 8:00 AM, a student aged 17, ran to the window for air and coughed, complaining of a sore throat and breathing difficulties.. Later on, she felt headache, drowsiness, and stomach pains. She was sent home, but within two ours six more students, all girls, complained of the same symptoms. Some among them claimed to have smelled a strong odor or eggs and/or fish. The rest of the students soon panicked, classes were disbanded to allow the girls to vent their pains and express their feelings, and the alarmed teachers clustered in the "infected" classroom, the very the source of "poisoning". At 10:00, the district health authorities arrived on the scene and tried to probe the source of the discomfort. A hypothesis about a gas poisoning floated in the air, but nothing was found to substantiate it was found. But in the meantime, 17 more girls was struck with the same symptoms, and some of them burst into tears, vomited, fainted and were transferred to the Jenin Hospital. The emergency services discharged them soon thereafter, having discovered no medical reason for that mass discomfort. Some among them were again seized by the discomfort, when they learned about the hospital's decision to release them. At 11:00. The school closed down, but more cases of "disease" were announced among the students in the following hours. That afternoon, Palestinian and Israeli doctors were on hand to inspect the classrooms, and it was reported that they had detected a nauseating odor. Some of them said that it was a sulfurized hydrogen smell, others thought the smells emanated from the school's toilets, still others opted for "ozone pollution". On Tuesday, 22 March Dr Ubeid, the Palestinian Director of Health Services in the West Bank, then still under Israel's Civil Administration, before the Palestinian Authority was established (1994), accompanied by an Israeli nurse, came to the school in question, and confirmed having sensed a sharp odor which irritated his nose and eyes. The press reported on that day 34 cases of blurred vision among the students, which implied that perhaps it was the result of tear gas, often used by Israeli forces to quell violent riots.. The next day, when Ubeid again inspected the school, this time with a team of specialized pollution fighters, there was no trace of any poison to be found. Nevertheless, the Palestinian doctor remarked that some of the hospitalized victims did show signs of clinical poisoning. On Friday, when no classes are usually held due to the Muslim Sabbath, a teacher who visited the school could still report a strange odor lingering in the space between the village and the neighboring Israeli military camp just east of it. On Sunday 27 Match, the Israeli Ministry of Health sent a mobile laboratory to the scene, but no odor could be detected any longer.

However, the symptoms of gas contamination were no longer confined to Arrabeh. On Saturday, 26 March, 56 girls at the Zahra middle School in Jenin, complained of a similar malaise and were admitted to the local hospital and to a private clinic in town. More students from the adjoining village also flocked to the district hospitals which became crowded beyond capacity, and soon had to refer their patients to other medical institutions throughout the West Bank. By the weeks end, some hundred patient remained hospitalized in the main city hospital where they inhaled oxygen, to overcome their respiratory difficulties. Most of the patients during that first week were young women (247 out of 367, namely 67%) but there were also cases of young men and some adults afflicted by the discomfort. At the beginning of April, 310 girls from Hebron, in the southern part of the West Bank were hospitalized with what came to be known as the "Jenin Syndrome". Some serious cases were referred to the better equipped Israeli hospitals, notably Rambam in Haifa. Upon admittance to the emergency ward, the patients were subjected to a regime of oxygen breathing, glucose infusions and tranquillizers. And usually, a short time later (hours or sometimes minutes), their condition improved. But in

Israel the issue had grown into an excruciating process of self-ques-
tioning,, at times even self-flagellating, and throughout the initial
states of the crisis much empathy was shown toward the innocent
young people who had fallen victim to that unknown and mysterious mass illness. The authoritative and respected Haaretz daily
wrote:

> More than 300 female students from five different
> schools have been poisoned on the premises of their
> schools. According to the military circles estimates [for
> the entire West Bank was under Israeli military govern-
> ment], poisonous substances had been spread on the
> window sills, or sprinkled on the curtains of the class-
> rooms. Laboratory tests by Ministry of Health officials,
> by chemical warfare specialist of the military, and by
> police experts, have not been completed yet, but there
> are indications that nerve gas was used in the affair[86].

The Israeli psyche was profoundly shaken by this sort of candid
and sympathetic writing, which was duplicated in all Israeli media
and immediately jumped upon by the international media, who
found an easily available "explanation" to that riddle. They were
quick to interpret the yellow substance on the window sills as "evidence" of the "poison", and none of them bothered to initiate an
analysis of it in order to find out. And when Israeli authorities did
and released the "sensational" finding that it was simple pollen which
dropped from pine trees in that Spring season, they all burst in
laughter, at the "ludicrous Israeli attempts to escape the world blame
for their crimes against the Palestinians". Paradoxically, it was the
Israeli public which raised questions about the ethics of war, about
the conduct of Israeli troops in occupied territory and hinted to even

---

[86] Front headline of Haaretz, 28 March, 1983.

darker questions that no one dared to ask, under the horrifying memories of the Nazi death camps of W W II, merely three decades earlier, which a large chunk of the Israeli population had witnessed and had been traumatized by. The entire adult population could still recall the nerve gas war of Nasser, the hero of Arab nationalism against civilians in the Yemen war of the 1960s . Now, who could bear the accusation that Israel was using the same methods against the Palestinians? More ominously, was the world accusing the Jews, all over again, of well-poisoning, that anti-Semitic worn out *cliché* which had blamed the devastating epidemics of plague, pest and smallpox on the perfidy of Jews who had allegedly contaminated the water sources of Europe?. These questions were asked, not because the symptoms of mass poisoning were gradually being passed on from the victims to the suspected culprits; for indeed, it was reported that Israeli girl soldiers, who had accompanied the Palestinian patients to Israeli hospitals, had themselves been attained by the Jenin symptom[87]. AS other reports continued to stream in to the effect that 80 more people residing in the eastern suburbs of Jenin were also hurt by the mysterious disease, which consisted of nausea, drowsiness and respiratory difficulties, two Israeli police border policemen were also hospitalized suffering from the same malaise. The Israeli health authorities, caught in disarray, convened a special conference of the Ministry of Health, the Armed Forces Chief Surgeon's Office and the Civil Administration of the West Bank. And, once again, no substantive reason or explanation were provided for the mass poisoning scenes, in order to review the findings, even though a team of 15 experts was dispatched on the spot that could not find any evidence to hang on to. All the experts were able to come up with was that it was neither water nor food-related poisoning, nor was there any sign of gas or pesticide pollution in sight.[88]

---

[87] Ibid.
[88] *Haaretz*, March 30th, 1983.

For the first time in this unfolding drama, psychology and psychosomatic diseases were brought up in an attempt to unravel the mystery a week after it struck. Israeli psychiatrists and psychologists were quoted as citing precedents of "mass poisoning" occurrences which resembled the Jenin syndrome and which had afflicted women for the most part, but that did not dissipate the embarrassment in Israel, as reports in the local Arab and international media continued to feast on the event unabated, of more victims among the Palestinians, this time augmented by outright accusations against Israel, and by "commentaries" which purported to show the reasons for that "new Israeli conspiracy". In the village of Se'ir, in the Hebron district, three people (one girl and two adults) were admitted in the Hebron Hospital after they had inhaled fumes emanating from a tanker in their courtyard, which contained some suspected substance. On March 29 in the afternoon, 37 more girl students were admitted to the Tul Karem Hospital in Western Samaria, thus making the epidemic universal in the entire West Bank. Now the local Arab doctors in the West Bank revealed that unusually high levels of protein were found in the urine of those "patients", which was "proof" that their reproductive system, especially the process of ovulation had been "intentionally intruded into". The fact that those symptoms persisted and necessitated the repeated hospitalization of the previously released patients "proved that this was a long term and severe matter, premeditated by those who had spread the poison in the first place". Those doctors were quoted as wondering why only girls were hit, not boys,, and precisely those among them about to graduate from high school and eligible for marriage, while younger female students from the same schools were spared. The insinuations were horrible: here are the cunning Israelis attempting, no more and no less, than to tamper with the natural growth of the Palestinian population, as part of their strategy in their demographic confrontation with the Palestinians.[89]

Israel's moral predicament was intensified when the Arab faction in the *Hadash* (former Communist Party) in the Israeli Knesset accused the Israeli government of imposing a state of siege around Jenin, and declared that the civilian population was fleeing the city in panic (which proved false, or at least grossly exaggerated), which of course gave credence to the now widespread reports that some central Israeli government-inspired agency had masterminded and orchestrated this evil design. On that same day, the Secretary General of the Arab League was quoted in the Israeli press as having blasted Israel for "using poison against Palestinian school pupils in order to counter their demonstrations against the occupying troops". The fact that Israeli forces had indeed taken up positions on rooftops in Jenin and in other locations, in anticipation of the Land Day in Israel Proper and not to the mass hysteria in the West Bank,[90] did nothing to allay either the widespread malaise among the Palestinians or the plight of the harshly accused Israelis. Quite the contrary, widespread riots in the territories increased the specter of a new confrontation between Israelis and Palestinians. The distraught Israelis needed and looked up to an outside arbiter of supernational authority, not politicians of soldiers who might have an axe to grind in the affair, but some agency with an impeccable integrity and professional credentials, to guide and enlighten them on the whirlpool of incredulous stories that floated around, all focused on putting Israel in the bad light of the culprit. In the beginning, the Director General of the Israeli Ministry of Health, Professor Baruch Modan, a world renowned epidemiologist, came out publicly in an attempt to dispel doubts and to distil facts from rumors. Being a

---

[89] Ibid.

[90] Land Day has been marked annually since March 30, 1976 by the Palestinian Arabs in Israel, to state their discontent with the land confiscation policy of the government. Often, these annual demonstrations escalated into violent riots which were frequently backed by parallel unrest in the West Bank and Gaza.

doctor of high stature and held in deep respect both professionally and as a public servant, his explanations found resonance in the minds of all reasonable milieus who cared to listen to him. He spent many sleepless nights answering hordes of hard pressing foreign correspondents and local journalists and other inquirers, and he willingly summed up the situation as follows:

It has become necessary to explain to the world that there was here neither poisoning nor a physical disease, nor any obscure scheme against those young women's health. We did everything we could, because in such cases, one does nor spare any time and any effort…At first, when the reports came out of Arrabeh, there was talk of some 40 young women who were poisoned, but in fact 60 were hospitalized. My first impression was, before we had had any opportunity to carry out any field or laboratory tests, that this was a normal epidemiological phenomenon resulting from air, water or food pollution. This area is particularly sensitive, therefore my thoughts have wandered farther afield than would be normally the case. This was so because some time ago, we had stumbled into another case of pollution, this time real, in another village in Samaria, and in order to avoid panic, we tackled it discreetly. Our district doctor had indeed discovered widespread anemia in that village, due to lead poisoning. Our investigation showed that the population used to store flour in lead containers, and that contaminated their bread. WE contacted all the household in the village and convinced them to desist from their custom and not to store any edibles in those utensils. We also made sure that other villages did not espouse the same practice.

As soon as we learned about the Arrabeh affair, we took all the necessary measures: We sent teams of doctors and investigators to the spot and carried out all the epidemiological tests. I thought, at first, that it was perhaps the doing of some hostile provocateurs who would instigate the local population against the Israeli authorities in order to create unrest. In such a sensitive area, you have to think about the possibility that some hostile actors might have poisoned food, water or air. Aware of the possible political ramifications of this affair I did what I would usually refrain from doing on Sabbath days: I called the Minister of Health at home and expressed my concern about the rapid pace of developments: on 21 March in Arrabeh, on 26-7 in Jenin and suburbs, as well as in the village of Matlul on the Nablus Road. On 28 March, the Eve of Passover, another case in Jenin, and the following day in Hebron and Anabta (near Tul Karem). In all, some 800-900 people had been attained by the syndrome, but many more showed up in hospitals, for in some cases victims applied for admission in more than one hospital or were readmitted after their release. There were girls who were readmitted up to four times. As a doctor, I am very wary of mixing politics with medicine, and I have to admit that all the girls involved in the first 3 or 4 occurrences were truly sick and not putting up an act, not in the sense that they were physically contaminated, but they were psychologically discomforted. I do not like the term "mass hysteria" because when you say that, you connote something derogatory. I prefer the term "mass phenomenon", where people feel truly drowsy and sick and have difficulty to move their limbs and to function, although all this has no physiological reason whatsoever, and is but the expression of emotional anxiety. We have to remember that from the victim's viewpoint, she genuinely feels all the symptoms of true poisoning, and when she reports them to the doctor, she is not inventing of feigning them.

All this was true, however, only as regards the first 3-4 incidents. Since last Sunday, we had *prima facie*, and now conclusive, proofs of girls who were hurt neither physically nor psychologically, but were part of a deliberate hoax. Arab doctors in the various hospitals were appraised of the truth, almost at the very outset, not only because there were no findings of any poisoning in all the sophisticated surveys and intricate tests we conducted, but because they realized the truth by themselves. At first, they carried out their duties beyond reproach as they took seriously their patients arriving in the emergency wards under affliction with nausea, drowsiness, and physical pain. But when the fourth cycle began, of new "patients" who were neither physically nor emotionally attained the doctors understood that it was an act, but they could not always react in purely professional terms. They were under pressure by hostile elements not to release the girls and pretend that they were truly poisoned and needed hospitalization. They were also warned under threats to conceal the truth from both Israeli and international media. I have to say that in most cases, the Arab doctors admitted to the truth when talking to us, but also explained their fears to go public. We could see how those doctors were torn between their professional obligation to say the truth and their acute concern that they might be harmed if they were to do so. It was not difficult to see the hoax building up. The hospitalized girls from the fourth wave on signaled to foreign reporters, and not only to them, their V signs in celebration of their "victory. I myself took picture of those sights. In one instance I saw a girl yelling from pain in my presence, and took pictures of her, but when I came back to that hospital from a field visit, a short while later, I saw the same girl standing outside the ward, all basking in smiles and radiating in in good health. I took another picture of her, this time without her noticing, and it is greatly puzzling to me to realize that those were two photos of the same person taken at a short interval between them.

As an epidemiologist myself, I took many precautions and carried out all the necessary tests, and beyond, before I could appear before the world media and state categorically that there was no poisoning.. For one thing, I know of no pollution epidemic which affects almost exclusively adolescent girls. During our thorough investigations, we found in the rural areas surrounding the scenes of the incidents, various empty or full vessels containing suspicious materials that we took to our laboratories to verify whether they were, even remotely connected to the incident... But while the tests revealed no findings, any collection of such suspicious objects created a factory of rumors and "proofs" that something had been found, or stealthily removed from the scene... Every "finding" of that sort, of course produced another cycle of fake "contaminations" and real hospitalizations. But we do assume that the very first cases, in Arrabeh and thereafter, were caused by real environmental irritation, not poisoning, . For example, our mobile laboratory did detect strong odors of rotten eggs, which is a sign of sulfuric hydrogen in the air, or perhaps leaks from the local sewer system... I was present myself when we opened the gutters in Arrabeh in order to test them and we could not stand the stench. None of these can cause poisoning. But the combination of the two can cause the discomfort experienced in this mass phenomenon. Girls are more sensitive to these smells than other parties, in turn creating new anxieties and new female victims. Why girls, I do not want to drag you into a feminist argument. I have a wife and three daughters at home. Usually, more men than women are exposed to epidemics and diseases in general. But these mass phenomena are the exception. An American female journalist has given me her explanation for this: In traditional societies women had less opportunity of self-expression than men, and therefore their mass-hysteria was their way to call attention to the fact that they existed, as if to declare"" I am sick so I exist". I know not whether this is the trues answer, or whether any other would account for the difference between the genders, but the fact is indisputable: more women than men are afflicted by this syndrome.

What is clear is that these phenomena, whatever their source and interpretations, were exploited politically by hostile parties to bash Israel. This is a sort of psychological warfare that is waged on two levels: first, by using biological symptoms, namely while the first Arrabeh occurrence was spontaneous and generated by objectively detectable stenches, some hostile parties did not hesitate to spread the feeling of discomfort to other places where no environmental irritation existed to justify them. In Hebron, for example, an Arab was seized diffusing some nauseating substance in order to create anxiety. This is a population predisposed to believe any story about Israel's ill-will, and to link between the Sabra-Shatilla massacre in Lebanon (perpetrated by the Christians against the Palestinians) and Israel's conspiracy to "harm the reproductive capacity of these adolescent Palestinian girls". It can even be persuaded that this is the modern version of the "Jewish Passover sacrifice", which has been the basis for the infamous blood libel accusation against the Jews throughout the generations. Realizing the international repercussions of this affair, we have set up a coordinating committee of all health agencies in the country to deal with this aspect too. We have contacted the largest and most important epidemiological research center in the world, in Atlanta (Georgia), and we asked for a delegation to lead an independent investigation. Two doctors have arrived, a man and a woman, and they have been busy in their endeavor. They are very sensitive to their independence and want no assistance or contact on our part. They are being coached by the American Embassy, and also by the American Consulate General in Jerusalem. They have even refused to stay in Israeli territory and they have opted for a hotel in East Jerusalem. Realizing the political pressures to which they are exposed, they have refused any contact with the press. I cannot say anything about their findings because I do not want to seem as exerting pressure on them. The Director General of The World Health Organization (WHO) has also contacted me and I proposed to him to send his own team to verify all the tests and findings. They too arrived and launched their own investigation. A representative of the Red Cross was also here and he accepted our findings that there was no intoxication and that there was no physiological cause for the mass phenomena we have witnessed[91].

No sooner had Modan's forceful, authoritative and morally-

---

[91] The entire text was included in a dispatch by the Israeli MInistry of Foreign Affairs to all Israeli missions worldwide., on April 17, 1983.

soothing statements come to the open, than Israeli columnists, politicians, psychologists, journalists, intellectuals, panelists, publicists and men in the street, burst into an extraordinary eruption of anger and vindictiveness. For not only had Modan's analysis completely exonerated Israel from any wrong doing, but he had also addressed the worst fears of Israelis lest, here and now again, the Jewish people are exposed to calumnies and machinations of the most dreadful type. And while they had not expected the Arabs to behave any better due to their psychological war to demean Israel, the Israelis were shaken to their bones by the abysmal realization, that Europe, the mother and cradle of anti-Semitism, seemed, once again, to savor the anti-Semitic *bouillon* that the Arabs had concocted. They were dismayed to comprehend that even America, the closest friend of Israel, looked indifferent in the face of the campaign of condemnation and libelous accusations that were picking up momentum against the Jews in the international arena. Though Palestinian, Arab and Islamic hostile exploitation of the incident to bash Israel was to be expected, the world's complicity or indifference was disappointing, and the world media's un-professionalism was outrageous, cynical and vindictive, and all amounting to a clear statement that politics and rating took precedence over justice, truth and decency. Differentiation has to be made be made, though, between international bodies who were UN-affiliated, such as WHO, or expected to be impartial, like the International Red Cross, and others such as the Arab League, The Islamic Conference Organization (OIC), the Organization of African Unity (OAU), or even the UN Security Council, not justice or impartiality, dictated the bias their intervention would take. On another level, distinction has to be made between organizations which could deliver practically by taking measures of investigation and relief, and others which were confined to statements and words. Yet another way to differentiate between the multifarious witnesses of the events in the poison affair, were the Various shades of opinion, and the nuances in the positions of various governments towards the crisis. Predictably, the entire Islamic and Arab worlds, closely, blindly and in fine details that they could not even verify, were followed by the entire Soviet Bloc at the height of the Cold War, and much of the third world, threw their lot in with the Palestinian accusations, and duplicated verbatim extracts of the Arab claims and statements regarding the mass poisoning.

In the latter category of countries and governments, one could not expect independent views to be voiced, much less investigative reporting. Those systems at the time were all tightly controlled by the governments in place, the press and the electronic media were either government-owned or, at the very least, government -controlled, and all statements, commentaries, critiques and "reports" had to toe the party line. What was more complex and far from uniform, were the media in the Western world where a great variety of reports, some live from the scene of the events, commentaries and opinions were aired. But there too, the left-wing media usually supported, almost without questioning, the Palestinian reports and claims, especially in the initial stages of the crisis, when only flimsy and contradictory reports, rumors and accusations were available from both sides of the aisle. In that situation, every medium relied either on its political predisposition, and backed the views and claims that suited its own. Or speculated on rather hazardous grounds in that same vein. In that regard, all those views seemed to be the various aspects of a Rashomon story., assuming of course, that no ill-will or vicious bias was hiding, at that point, behind their inclinations. So it goes for the automatic supporters of the Arabs, listed above, who presumably adopted the Palestinian accusations lock, stock and barrel, out of the belief that they were right or at least worthy of support. Quite another matter were the independent liberal media in those Western countries. While none of them conducted a serious investigative reporting, though they owed their readership a fair and subjective analysis of those events, many of them, especially the French, embraced an inexplicably anti-Israeli bias which made them look and sound happy to jump on the occasion to bash Israel and "show its true face". The fact is that even when the reports of the pre-meditated mass-poisoning by Israel were debunked when proved false, none of them had the decency to retract or apologize for their earlier condemnations and accusations. There were far-reaching consequences to their irresponsible writings[92]:

a. The image of Israel was perhaps irretrievably (and unjustly in that context) tarnished, as most media in Europe seemed to gang up against the Jewish state in order to show its culpability, briefly following the Israeli incursion into Lebanon a year earlier in order to disband the PLO bases in that country which Arafat used to harass the Israeli settlements in the Galilee;

b. Anti-Semitism in Europe got a boost. Which together with the rise of the extreme right, encouraged the revisionist historians to question the veracity of the Holocaust and to relativize it as "a detail of history" of W W II[93]. For, if what had been done to the Jews by the Nazis is now allegedly done by Israel to Palestinians, this indeed banalizes the Holocaust and makes it a recurrent theme in history.

c. The Jewish communities in Europe, not only in Israel, began to think seriously about the insecurity of their existence on that continent, if at the end of the 20th Century,

---

[92] For a detailed survey of the press of Western countries for the coverage of the Poison Affair in March-May 2983, see the relevant chapters of R. Israeli, *Poison,* op. cit.

[93] The Israeli branch of that trend, encouraged by foreign scholars, began to question the very legitimacy of the birth of Israel, and it became connected in people's minds with the idea of revisionism(see R. Israeli, *Old Historians, New Historians, No Historians,* Wipf and Stock, Eugene, 2016).

blood libel of that scale can still be allowed to be reported as fact in the liberal press of those countries.

d. The reports of the liberal media, which usually enjoy widespread audiences, readerships and credibility, had unwittingly encouraged the mass hysteria to last beyond its natural span. Many cases were indeed recounted in the Israeli press of "cynical exploitation of the Western media" in order to stage mass hysteria on the ground when foreign reporters were around handing for sensations". Those news report, especially televised ones, were assiduously studied by their instigators, who also learned how to improve on them and prolong the anti-Israeli campaign as much as possible.

This blatant travesty of justice and truth was not evident only in the opinion-making European, and to a lesser extent in other Western media, but in the official statements of countries, organizations and international bodies[94], which not only seemed to accept it as a fact of life, but even to legitimize it as a desirable standard of behavior. In view of the violence of accusations and counter-accusations which accompanied the poison affair since its inception, and the confusion occasioned by the exhibited Palestinian outrage, on the one hand, and the Israeli disarray of the other, everyone involved was crying for international support and for outside arbiters to put things straight. It was the Palestinians who, from the outset asked the Arab League and then the UN to intervene in order to stop the poisoning epidemic, before the whole affair turned into political recriminations in the face of what was presented as a "genocidal attempt" by Israel against Palestinian victims. It was the Israelis who, almost from the outbreak of the crisis, appealed to international bodies to execute an independent inquiry in order to exonerate it from the blames that were hurled against it. As the malaise

---

[94] See details in R. Israeli, *Poison*, op. cit. Chp 3.

spread, and was widely publicized (and almost universally con-demned) by the world press, usually giving more credence to the Palestine version while denigrating Israel's line of defense, the neces-sity for such an inquiry became all the more urgent. Naturally, the Palestinians, with the international press backing, expected an unqualified condemnation of Israel, while the latter was confident that its position of total innocence would be vindicated. It is no coincidence that the Palestinians turned to the Arab League, The Islamic Conference and the Soviet Bloc, the Third World and the UN organization where they commanded an automatic majority, and their grievances were assured of a rapid, uncompromising and overwhelmingly supportive treatment, in view of the one-sided biased political nature of those states and organizations and of the tyranny of their regimes and of the automatic vote they guarantee to any cause they deem fit. It is also no coincidence that Israel resisted the UN treatment, whose main executive tool she bitterly dubbed the "Insecurity Council", preferring to turn to independent professional bodies. The reliable and authoritative *Le Monde* pro-vided the best explanation for these measures, when even Jean Kirk-patrick, the American Ambassador to the UN, who was usually one of the most supportive American diplomats of Israel ever, made as the President of the Security Council what was seen by Israel as a hostile declaration (something quite unusual):

> Israel rejected the declaration made by Jean Kirkpatrick, the American President of the Security Council, calling upon the Secretary General of the UN to launch an inde-pendent inquiry of the West Bank poisonings… The Israeli representative at the UN, Yehuda Blum, termed that declaration unjustified because it referred to the investigation of something that had left no trace, and also called into question the professional competence of the medical teams of the International Red Cross, the

World Health Organization (WHO) and the American Center of Epidemiology, which were already investigating the Affair... On the other hand, Yasser Arafat sent a letter to the Secretary General of the UN, denouncing the "new criminal campaign triggered since March 20 by the Israeli occupation authorities, of war crimes and crimes against humanity, because this poisoning caused the sterilization and death of the victims.

The hostile to Israel *Le Monde,* did not lag much behind the other Western media in interpreting the events its own way. Taking the Islamic hoax as a credible base he helped the idea of commercializing by demeaning and discrediting the Jews and their culture when writing:

In facilitating all these investigations, the Israeli government seeks, of course, to deny the rumors circulating in the occupied territories that the wave of poisoning was calculated to encourage the Palestinians to emigrate in order to ensure more colonization and annexation of territory, and to attenuate the echoes that this affair had caused worldwide. The Israeli government released a communique calling the accusations and suspicions a "campaign of calumniation which is directed against the entire Jewish people". In their editorial of April 5th the independent *Haaretz* lends credence to the theory of the military officials in the territories that the most recent numerous hospitalizations, mainly in the Hebron area, had been "organized" by "hostile elements" in order to trigger riots. In Nablus, the Israeli authorities have called up the doctors and the medical personnel of the hospital and reprimanded them for collaborating with the "staging" the malaise in order to let American television teams take pictures…, but many Arab doctors continue to contest the official Israeli view, and put in question the current investigations. They particularly pointed out that the Red Cross investigator did not consult with them sufficiently. According to them, the tests run for 76 students at the Bethlehem Hospital show signs of "anomalies" in the blood composition, and other signs[95].

Two major Swiss media, *La Tribune de Geneve* and *La Tribune Dimanche de Lausanne*, carried the plea of a Swiss citizen, Mr David Littman, who was active in an NGO within the Commission for Human Rights of the UN and summarized his impressions of the affair which alarmed him, four full months after the event, when the world realized the nature of the hoax and its libelous effect on European Jewry, auguring ill on the coming events::

Once the emissary goat was designated, it became automatically guilty of all the troubles which afflict, or could afflict the community at large. The Jews had played that role in Christian Europe for a millennium. They were accused of poisoning water wells, of the responsibility for the pest of 1348… and for the ritual murder of a Christian child every at Passover. The latter calumny has been current until the 20th Century in Czarist Russia, Eastern Europe and the Eastern Mediterranean, including the Arab World, [and championed almost exclusively by the latter ever since]…Since 1948, Israel has become the emissary goat *par excellence*…The Conference on Palestine, prepared by the UN and due to be held in Geneva 29 August-7 September, 1983, will not be other than a campaign of calumnies against Israel, and in no case will

---

[95] *Le Monde*, 6 April, 1983.

it be conducive to negotiations towards a just and durable peace in the Middle East…Arafat himself has declared that he would personally lead the Palestinian delegation. Let us remember that on April 4th Mr Arafat, in a letter addressed to the Secretary General of the UN, regarding the "poisoning" in the West Bank, has accused Israel of "war crimes and crimes against humanity, because those poisoning caused the sterilization and death of the victims, and were part of the policy of genocide against the Palestinian people"(Le *Monde, 5 April, 1983)*. Then, the stakes went higher during the regional Preparatory Meeting for South America, which was organize by the UN in Managua, Nicaragua, (12-15 April, 1983) to precede the Conference, where the PLO Ambassador… repeated the same accusations, this time referring to "1,500 poisoned schoolgirls". The same accusations were repeated, in an even more abusive language by MY Faruk Kaddumi, the Head of Foreign Affairs of the PLO, at the parallel Regional Preparatory Meeting for Asia, held in Kuala Lumpur Malaysia (3-6 May, 1983).

Besides the well taken care by the UN to propagate this Arab propaganda in the regional "preparatory work " of its institutions for the incoming Palestine Conference of September, while there was no substantive evidence to hang on to; and in addition to the exposure to the world of the abysmal "failure' of Israel to implement its genocidal conspiracy against its Palestinian victims, this decent Swiss investigator, who was horrified by the UN procedure of scapegoating which had no other purpose than to blame, condemn and calumniate Israel and to exhibit thereby its standard of justice, added for the education of Swiss readership:

The General Assembly of the UN had asked WHO to

investigate this affair…. Those specialists… have informed the Assembly on May 11 that after having investigated in full freedom, and without any hitch, have found "nothing abnormal, except for one case of anemia and no fatalities" (*Le Monde*, 13 May, 1983). One can therefore wonder why would the UN choose to ignore an investigation conducted by WHO and whose findings were revealed to an audience of the world's health ministers, especially that the investigation had been commissioned by the UN itself?

This defamatory exploitation of the "poisoning affair" demonstrates that Palestinian propaganda has drawn its inspiration from Hitler's right- hand aide, Josef Goebbels, who said that the bigger the lie the easier is to make it credible. The accusation of well poisoning had already been launched against Israel in 1948 by certain Arab leaders. How can one fail to become alarmed in view of the upcoming Conference on Palestine at the *Palais des Nations* in Geneva on the coming 29 of August?[96]

Interestingly enough, this Poison Affair which reverberated across Europe and the US and resuscitated old memories, also brought together groups of decent Christians who thought it was their business to sound the alarm, probably reminiscing the old anti-Nazi parable that "evil unfolds when decent people elect to keep quiet". One of those groups published in their *Rencontres Chretiens et Juifs,* a wide report on the affair under the heading: "A Psychosis of Calumniations: Israelis are accused of Poisoning Arab populations", in an attempt to check the new anti-Semitic wave, to learn its significance and to alleviate Jewish anguish[97].

---

[96] David Littman, *Tribune de Geneve,* 20-21 August 1983.
[97] Renee Neher—Bernheim, in *Rencontre Chretiens et Juifs,* Paris,, 2nd Semester, 1983, pp. 31-4.

These are excerpts of how the official UN Yearbook summed up the horrible calumnies of that year, which tried to circumvent the Organization's embarrassment and dismay at the contradictions and travesties it encountered in its dealings with the Poison affair. Not all calumnies were the fruit of Islamic commercialization, but the heavy impact of the Muslim bloc in the UN and the arm twisting that it spawned were unmistakable:

> On 29 of March Jordan transmitted to the President of the Security Council a letter from the PLO alleging that more than 1,000 Palestinian schoolgirls in the West Bank had been poisoned as part of a new phase in Israel's campaign against the Palestinians, and calling upon the UN to form an international medical committee to investigate, document and report on the poisoning.
>
> On March 30, the Chairman of the Committee on Palestinian Rights stated that local residents believed the illness had been induced by some kind of poison, perhaps gas, in the girls' classrooms. Pending results of the investigations, the Red Cross and the UN and others, the Chairman urged the Secretary General to exercise his office to ascertain the full extent, cause and perpetrators of that event [the suspicion in the meantime became a fact that had to be investigated]
>
> On March 31, Iraq's representative, the Head of the Arab group in the UN requested an urgent Security Council meeting to discuss the situation [as if there were anything to discuss before there were any findings pending results of the investigations].
>
> On April 3, Israel rejected the charges by Iraq and Jordan as unfounded, asserting that extensive clinical, laboratory and environmental tests by competent Israeli medical teams, which have yielded no traces of poisoning.

It added that the Israeli Ministry of Health had additionally requested international health authorities, among them WHO, to assess independently the causes of the phenomenon [these specialist remarks were put in equal consideration as the charges by Arab diplomats].

On April 4 the President of the Security Council asked the Secretary General to inquire into the problem and report on the findings [as if there were any substance to investigate], following which WHO conducted an independent investigation. On the same day, the President made a statement on behalf of all members of the Council to the effect that they had met and discussed "cases of mass poisoning in the occupied Arab territory of the West Bank, as referred to in Document S/15673. The members requested the Secretary General to conduct independent inquiries "concerning the causes and effects of the serious problem of the reported cases of poisoning and urgently report on the findings" [this is the exact wording of Arab charges, but no trace of the Israeli expert refutation].

On 5 April, Israel refuted by letter the Council's statement, asserting that it did not take into account the investigations by Israeli medical authorities and other medical teams, and that it contained an unwarranted reference to cases of mass poisoning effects of the serious [exactly the wording used in the Arab demand, implying that there was a justification for the inquiry] while the request of the Secretary General was totally unjustified.

On May 10, the Secretary General submitted his report indicating that the independent inquiry was carried out by WHO, whose Director came to the conclusion that he could not "indicate any specific cause of the reported health emergency". However, he emphasized that the initial medical records and interviews with cases of the first outbreak, and with local health and other authorities suggested that an environmental agent could have provoked at least some cases. WHO, after having admitted to the Israelis that they found no trace of any poisoning, now changed their taste and discovered a mysterious "agent" in an environment controlled by Israel, which makes them the suspects of the malaise. This outrageous bias was further augmented by the "recommendation" of the Director General that "in view of the anxiety under which the population lived in the occupied territories, and given the susceptibility of girls during adolescence, Who should take measures to deal with any likelihood of any suspected recrudescence", thus leaving in the hands of the Palestinians to complain against Israel at any time in the future, at their whim, again ignoring the fact that much of the affair had been a manufactured hoax in the first place.[98]

This convoluted report of the Director General of WHO, that was backed by the UN Secretary General and whitewashed in the UN official Report, speaks for itself. There was no trace of the rejection of the calumny hurled at Israel, which prompted the investigation in the first place, no castigation of the calumniators, nor a demand that they should apologize and retract their libel from the UN records, only an admission that WHO, unlike other teams of experts, were "unable to indicate any specific cause of the reported health emergency". The significance is far-reaching: that there was an emergency, whose cause WHO was unable to determine, and therefore the putative culprits remained to blame, for somebody must have caused the emergency and take the responsibility for it.

---

[98] *Yearbook of the UN*, NY, 1987, pp. 332-3.

Moreover, the "victims" were to be afforded open channels to charge any complaint they wish against Israel, whenever they felt or imagined they were in a "state of anxiety", which would always have to apologize and defend itself, like that decent person whose charged that his sister was a whore, and it was left to him to prove that he had no sister in the first place. Like in the classic anti-Semitic blood libels, the victims of calumny and libel became responsible for it, and the calumniators got rewarded by having their victim constantly placed on the culprit's bench. The lack of moral spine, and of courage to stand up to defamation in the heart of the UN, and the complicity of silence shown at the highest level of the organization, have naturally not only eroded its image, but also opened the gates for other calumnies and libels to be diffused and upheld in other UN agencies. When in 1991, the General Assembly abolished its own 1975 resolution to condemn Zionism, there remained enough of Israel's detractors to oppose the abolition, mainly Arab, Islamic and Third World regimes who elected their commitment to defamation and injustice over justice and truth. Aided by the UN and most countries' silence after the findings became clear, they felt to urge to withdraw their initial accusations against Israel, which had proved patently false, and occasionally even chose to whip them up whenever they felt like it.

A sad exemplification of this failure of the UN procedures and of the strength of the promoters of fallacies there has to be reported in the context of a new accusation of March 1983, decried by the Palestinian Representative at the Human Rights Commission in Geneva in 1997, claiming that Israel had injected 300 Palestinian children with AIDS virus. In the context of the UN that meant that the Palestinians could play the same trick as in 1983 once the Poison hoax had been swallowed by the world with impunity. On that reprehensible occasion too, no representative from any country, in that august body of the UN, which was supposed to safeguard the rights of all nations to be free from defamation, stood up against that abominable defamation. In fact, only following the protest lodged by the representative of the Christian Solidarity International, an NGO, not a member, did Mr Miroslav Somol, the decent Czech representative who also chaired the 53rd Session of the Commission, send a letter to the Ambassador of Israel, which was then circulated as an official document of the UN, stating:

> I share your feeling about such a serious allegation made without evidence, on the basis of a newspaper article. From the context of the situation and information generally available, I assume that the speaker should be aware of the fact that these allegations have proved completely false.
>
> This unfortunate case reminds me of a very similar accusation made towards your country in 1991 in the Commission on Human Rights. Already at that time, my predecessor... expressed the conviction that declarations provoking racist discriminatory sentiments must not be tolerated in the Commission...[99]

But the story did not end there. The Arab group, incensed by the unexpected breach of the traditional pattern which had allowed them to calumniate and condemn Israel without refutation, demanded to meet the Chairman of the Commission, and made their reservations about this out-of-order outburst of fairness and decency. He had to apologize [probably under threats of losing his job] for his "infraction", in a letter to Ambassador Nabil [ironically meaning "noble"] Ramlawi the Palestinian Ambassador, author of the defamation, to wit:

I should like to refer to the meeting I had with a delegation of

---

[99] Document E/CN/4/1997/122, letter addressed by the Chair of the Commission to the Ambassador of Israel.

distinguished Arab Ambassadors headed by the Chairman of the group, regarding my reply to the letter of the Israeli Ambassador concerning parts of the statement you made in the Commission[of course, the libelous parts are not cited]on March 11, 1997.

> I am personally very sorry for any harm this may have caused to you. It was certainly not my intention to do so.
>
> Although I consider it my prerogative as Chairman to react to the letter of the Ambassador of Israel, I did not realize that it would have been better to consult with the Bureau before undertaking such [a terribly decent] action. I will bear this in mind in the future.
>
> Please be assured, Mr Ambassador, of my firm intention and duty to continue to be an impartial[i.e. partial, biased and docile] Chairman of the UN Commission on Human Rights
>
> With the Highest consideration…[100]

So much for UN and international justice and decency. But just to come full circles and comprehend how the Poison Affair was silenced/terminated/ never unresolved, since almost no one of the calumniators repented or apologized. It was no coincidence that the Palestinians turned first to the Arab League, the Islamic Conference, the Soviet Bloc, the Third World and the UN, all renowned for their commitment to "justice", where they were assured of quick, unchallenged, uncompromising and overwhelmingly supportive treatment, in view of the biased political nature of those states and organizations and the automatic vote they provide as a guaranteed shield to their fellow-calumniators and liars, even if they should table a resolution that the earth is flat. It was also no coin-

---

[100] Letter by Ambassador Miroslav Somol, to Ambassador Nabil Ramlawi, the Observer of Palestine at the Human Rights Commission, 3 April, 1997. The Letter was circulated by Ramlawi upon reception.

cidence that Israel resisted the UN treatment and preferred to turn to professional independent bodies. The interpretations accorded to the world press were also unprofessional and unfair, and served either their national interests and suspicions or the prevailing politically correct mood of the time. At any rate, they produced more heat than light. Two other inquiries instigated by Israel, may throw some more objective light when no specific political interests are there to be obeyed and served: The International Red Cross and the Atlanta Center for the Prevention of Disease.

The International Committee of the Red Cross(ICRC)

On 7 April, 1983, the IRC released in Geneva a communique which essentially said:

> The Committee sent to the spot Dr Franz Altherr, a general practitioner, namely less qualified than the toxicologists and epidemiologists, some of them world famous, who preceded him investigating on the ground, though he had in the past accomplished various evaluation missions for ICRC. He met during his 5 day mission with Israeli doctors who treated the first cases and visited various hospitals in the West Bank in order to examine the patients and talk to the Arab doctors who treated them. The conclusion was that in view of the uncertainties, it recommended that a body acceptable to the parties and recognized as competent, should proceed at the earliest and carry out thorough tests over a long period of time to find out the causes of the malaise[101].

What is troubling, however, is that the press communique cited above was not the report written by Dr Altherr. According to the

---

[101] Press Communique, No 1461, 7 April, 1983, Geneva.

Israeli press, during the days following his visit to the territories, (end of March-beginning of April)he appears to have intimidated to the Israeli authorities that there was no poisoning and that the whole affair was mass hysteria, exactly as Israel had declared since the second week of the crisis.[102] But these exonerating news to the Israelis came together with the disturbing reports from the UN that the Security Council had acceded to the Ab demands to discuss the "mass-poisoning of more than 1,000 girls in the West Bank". For the council does not tackle *a priori* theoretical matters, and if it decided to take up the issue there must have been some substance to it. The Palestinian demand was to investigate the "mass poisoning" as a forgone fact, not to examine the controversial malaise in order to establish the truth. What was more, the American Ambassador, Jane Kirkpatrick, who had usually been a staunch supporter of Israel, now joined the cacophony of demands by reading at the Council, in her capacity as the President for April 1983, the unanimous call to all members to appoint the Secretary General of the UN to run the investigation. The terms of the discussion and the resolution were bitterly by Israeli Ambassador, Yehuda Blum, a recognized authority on International law, who decried the procedure due to the "groundless accusations of poisoning"[103]. Thus, the terms of reference of the investigation set up by the UN turned out to be grounded on false assumptions. Hence the lukewarm nature of the WHO Report cited above, which it had found "no trace of poisoning", but shifted the attention of the world from the false accusation which could not be substantiated, to the "need to protect the population" which was beyond its mandate to investigate and recommend. In other words, instead of responding to the Iraqi and Palestinian claims at the UN by categorically rejecting their claims, based on the early investigations (by Israel and WHO), the Report

---

[102] *Yedioth Aharonot*, Tel Aviv, 5 April, 1983, chief headline on front page.
[103] Ibid, column 3.

left Israel on the culprit's bench, assuming that if it was not found guilty today, it would tomorrow, under the UN axiom that Israel is always assumed guilty unless proved otherwise. It appears that never in the annals of the UN was any member-state treated in such malevolent fashion. In that international climate, which later forced the US Trump Administration to cut its subsidies to UNRWA and to withdraw from UNESCO, where Israel stood alone as a pariah, with its best friends distancing themselves from it, one can understand why the Red Cross also joined the negative "neutrality" posture and did not acknowledge publicly its exoneration of Israel.

Following the Arab/Muslim success at the UN, which had come to recognize in fact the legitimacy of their libel against Israel, a delegation of Arab ambassadors in Geneva met again with the President of the ICRC, Alexander Hay and discussed with him the "poisoning affair"[104]. To some extent this explains the backtracking that the ICRC took in spite of the fact that their delegate doctor knew the facts and reported them to his superiors. When questioned on the matter, the Spokesman of the organization in Geneva reportedly replied that the ICRC Emissary was not entrusted with the task of "verifying whether or not there was poisoning", and that his mission was to "ensure adequate treatment of the patients". Again, instead of refuting the accusation that he knew was false, he shifted it to caring about the patients[105] . A decade later, this author inquired with the Red Cross about any report it may have compiled and published since about the affair, the answer was no less puzzling:

> Your letter requires a slight correction: the ICRC did not publish any report in March-April, 1983 following the mysterious hospitalization of hundreds of persons in the

---

[104] *Haaretz,* 6 April, 1983.
[105] *Yedioth Aharonoth,* 6 April, 1983.

> occupied West Bank. There one only one Report of Mission, which remained confidential and it was written by a doctor of the Red Cross who had been assigned the task of evaluating the situation…The Red Cross had released a press communique on April 7 and we enclose a copy of it herewith, as well as some press clips of the time…[106]

So, the Red Cross knew the facts but it preferred to keep them under wraps, a strange procedure for an international body which purports to be impartial and in whose findings all parties would have been interested, except if they wished to hide their refutations of the Arab claims. Exonerating Israel publicly in the face of virulent Arab accusations would not have been exactly politically correct in the atmosphere of those days. What one can deduce from all this is that Dr Altherr had apparently agreed with the Israeli findings of mass hysteria and he probably included that remark in his report, otherwise why were they kept confidential ?. It is certain than incriminating findings against Israel would have been published immediately and enthusiastically. For the Red Cross never refuted Prof Modan's allegation about mass hysteria; what seemed to incense them was the "breach of confidentiality". A press article in Lausanne [107] even raised the stakes in its comment about the ICRC communique when it introduced some broad insinuations like:

> The ICRC has been considered a master of diplomatic communiques which have to be read between the lines. The one on the "mass poisoning" in the West Bank, is one of this genre. On the basis of the report of its

---

[106] , Letter by Claude Voilat, the Press Attache for the Middle East of the ICRC, addressed to P. GIniewski, 5 May, 1992 .

[107] *La tribune de Lausanne*, 8 April, 1983.

delegate, Dr Altherr, e general practitioner, who has specialized in missions of "evaluation", in the Arab territories occupied by Israel, it recommends an "acceptable mechanism to proceed to thorough and prolonged investigations etc...". In other words, the Red Cross, while keeping silent ion the source of this affair, which could erupt into violence, still considers the matter serious enough to necessitate an extraordinary recommendation to invest a body that would be acceptable to all including the PLO, and whose results would be irrefutable., to lead an investigation... This statement of position of the ICRC happens while two experts of WHO... and two American experts from Atlanta... have been conducting their investigations ... [The ICRC} did not launch an investigation of its own... It simply performed an "evaluation" of the situation in the territories by a man who had a ten year experience in the field and is well known by the local population...His recommendation, though not explicitly stated, adopts exactly the reverse version of the Israeli authorities which have claimed no responsibility. If one were to believe Israeli General Ilia, the mysterious epidemic which has sent to date more than 1,000 persons to hospital... amounts to an "enormous political hoax concocted by Palestinian student organizations which have been abusing of the good faith of international media...

But the Red Cross... did not want to nourish the current polemics on the origin of the malaise, namely whether it was a mass hysteria, a premeditated act or an attempt to deliberate genocide according to Arafat. The mystery remains total, it is inexplicable.... The current investigation by General Ilia... has resulted in the arrest of dozens of Palestinian suspects who are accused of having incited the population to fake poisoning.... According to Prof. Modan, himself an epidemiologist, this epidemic is about a new form of "psychobiological warfare" which generates, at will, new cases all the time... The enigma is there to be resolved, the reports of the various experts will not perhaps produce satisfactory answers due to political reasons. Therefore we should dare to provide one ourselves: the "poisonings" are but a clinical phenomenon of a population under occupation, subjected to relentless repression over the years, which has become intolerable.[108]

The author of this article, which has been embraced as a document to be diffused by the Red Cross, also incorporated a revulsive cartoon featuring a hideous Jew in the worst ant-Semitic tradition, exclaiming to a patient (presumably Palestinian) who is rushed on a stretcher toward a medical installation (symbolically bearing a Red Cross mark): "This is what happens when you do not eat Kosher!"[109]. However, the writer of the article, unlike the Red Cross which borrowed his piece to promote its version, did not hide the truth: he spoke about the concealment of the Red Cross findings, but he accepted it; he obliquely referred to the competence of the general practitioner sent by ICRC, as contrasted with the expertise of Prof Modan, but he yielded to it; he implicitly criticized the political nature of the political investigations, and therefore he had to volunteer his own guess; he acknowledged that the Palestinians wish to steer away from Israeli hospitals for fear that their bluff might be revealed, but he still maintained the suspicions toward Israel; and finally, he accepted the assumption that there were no clinical traces of poisoning, but he still blamed Israel

---

[108] Ibid.
[109] Ibid.

(for occupation, not for poisoning). All this was correct and legitimate, except that the Red cross did not dispatch its emissary to check the "intolerable state of repression" in the West Bank, but to answer the specific accusation of poisoning. And when he crowns his article with that heinous caricature of Jews and Israel, and his entire package of "neutrality" is adopted lock, stock and barrel by the Red Cross, one wonders about the validity of the entire report.

The Atlanta Center for Disease Control

Fortunately for the prestige of the medical profession, especially for the individuals and organizations who see no wrong with mixing politics with their medical profession in spite of their pledge as professionals to refrain from so doing, there are some decent doctors and some centers of medical decency and fairness, in Israel, Atlanta and hopefully in other parts of the world where neither UN nor ICRC, certainly not Arab and Islamic politics are involved, who still cling to the truth and regard it as their paramount commitment to their profession. The Atlanta Center's report published on April 29, 1983[110], stated *inter-alia*:

a. In the village of Arrabeh, site of the initial outbreaks, 95% of the affected adults participated in the study; 64% of the 88 affected girls… participated… all reported having noted an unusual odor before onset of illness;

b. Detailed general and neurological examinations after onset of illness with persistent symptoms showed no demonstrable abnormalities or cerebral dysfunctions.

c. Electromyography was performed on severely symptomatic, and was within normal limits in all cases

---

[110] *Morbidity and Mortality, Weekly Reports* 29 April, 1983, Vol 32, Nom 16.

d. Environmental studies found low concentrations of H2S in an outdoor latrine adjacent to the schoolgirl's school in Arrabeh… No toxins were detected in any of the samples;

e. The epidemic was triggered either by psychological factors, or, more probably, by the odor of low sub-toxic concentrations of H2S gas escaping from the latrine…

f. Subsequent propagation of the outbreak was mediated by psychological factors occurred against a background of anxiety and stress, facilitated by press and radio reports suggesting strongly that a toxic gas was the cause.

g. The epidemic was terminated by the closing of the West Bank schools[111].

This report put the clinical matter to rest, having answered all the hard questions that were raised during the crisis; but the injustice, the libel and accusations, with their related damage to Israel's reputation was irreparably done, especially, no press media (except an inner page minor notice in the NYT), nor a government, organization, politician or world organization either repented or apologized for the defamation they were all part of against Jews and Israel, something that contributed markedly to the rise of anti-Semitism in the world, Arab and Muslim hatred toward Israel and the transfiguration of anti-Semitism into the more acceptable anti-Zionism around the world. But most of all, it demonstrated the situation of justice, fairness, equity, decency, concern for human rights in the UN and other international organizations that were created to cultivate those lofty ideas, but instead proved to nourish libel, hatred, discrimination, indecency, fraud, hypocrisy, sycophancy and mistrust. When we realize that this thinking and these anti-humanitarian resolutions do not remain the exclusive domain of the Islamic word(which is bad enough in itself)but are embraced universally by

---

[111] MMWR report, op. cit. p.p.. 205-8.

world organizations, that does not only lend to them global authority and credibility, but makes Muslims more credulous in their mythical power to shape the world to their tune, but not only determining the hierarchies between their own centers and peripheries, but by occupying the high ground to enable them to become the center of the world. When Secretary General Kofi Annan established the High Level Group (HLG), ostensibly for addressing and solving the clash of civilizations, it submitted its report in November 2006 which adopted the Islamic view of history and put the blame on the West and Israel for the current conflicts that it claimed had started with European colonialism and Zionism, without any regard for the vast campaign of Islamic conquests since the 7th Century. Bat Ye'or, who researched Islamo-European relations, emphasized:

> It is difficult to imagine a more simplistic and shallow text, replete with sleights of hand, than this report drawn by an organization which adorns itself with the grand-sounding title "Alliance of Civilizations". How does it present the 20th Century? For many, the last century brought unprecedented progress, prosperity and freedom. For others it marked an era of subjugation, humiliation and dispossession". The domination of totalitarian systems across Europe, Asia and Africa; the genocide of the Armenians, Greeks and Assyrians in the Ottoman Empire, the Caucasus, Balkans, Iraq, Syria from 1914-1933; two world wars with over 20 million killed in the first and 40 million in the second; the unparalleled horror of the genocide of European Jewry, followed by the ethnic cleansing of Jews from Arab lands accompanied by pogroms, killings rape, expropriations, arbitrary imprisonment expulsion are all insignificant, as were the tens of millions massacred in the Soviet Union, Cambo-

dia, Rwanda, Sudan and elsewhere. All these cataclysms of human barbarity vanished, replaced by the doctrine of OIC "subjugation, humiliation and dispossession", alluding probably to Palestinian Arabs, with no reference to the Jewish population of Judea, Samaria and Jerusalem who were expelled after the Arab League's war against Israel in 1948, with the invasion of five Arab armies and the active participation of the Palestinian Arabs. That is the HlG'a wisdom on the unequaled high point of the great human tragedies of the 20th Century[112]

---

[112] Bat Ye'or, *Europe, Globalization, and the Coming Universal Caliphate,* Fairleigh Dickinson University Press, Madison, 2011, p. 94.

Summary

The Hamas Rampage

There is little doubt that the most earth-shattering event that has impacted the thought, politics, society, and conduct of the Muslim world in recent times has been the collapse of the Soviet Bloc, and with it of Communism as a competing alternative to Western capitalism. The ramifications of those developments were multifaceted among the Islamic countries. Internally, their old inborn Communist parties simply shrank into insignificance once it was shown that their promise had been a thin veneer of pretense, which waned away under the burden of its own inefficacy and helplessness in the face of the contemporary world's requirements. In view of Islam's traditional dislike toward the old Western rival, which had been reinforced by Muslim radical thinkers since Hassan al-Banna and Sayyid Qut'b, the great luminaries of the Muslim Brothers who had accused the Western colonizers of oppression, exploitation, and penchant for laxity in social behavior that corrupted the Muslim youth, it was no surprise that the West was shunned by the Islamic world, at least in theory. In those years, the Soviet Union, the loyal ally who had never failed its Muslim clients, seemed the alternative to counter the Western threat. Indeed, many promising young people in the Muslim world were invited or sent to Moscow to pursue their studies-cum-political indoctrination. They enrolled in professions like medicine and engineering or underwent other training courses that prepared them for community or political work in their countries. They learned Russian, and the elite among them took advanced degrees, such as PhDs in Marxist theory, Marxist economics, and Marxist history as viewed and analyzed from the Communist point of view. The case in point was Mahmoud Abbas, otherwise known as Abu Mazen, then a senior PLO official and after Yasser Arafat's death the president of the Palestinian Authority (PA). He chose a topic for his dissertation that suited both his dedication to fight Zionism and Israel and his hosts' propaganda line, which promoted anti-Semitism, masquerading as "anti-Zionism." His thesis, later published as a book, claimed a collaboration between Zionism and Nazism and diminished the Holocaust by cutting down the number of victims from six to less than one million. In other words, the import of those studies was not to discover historical truth but to serve the propaganda campaign of both his organization and his hosts. The world has changed since, and Moscow reoriented itself toward a more correct relationship with the Jewish people, the Zionist movement and Israel, but Abu Mazen showed little propensity to "change his spots"[113]when upon his visit to Germany's Chancellor Olaf Scholz in August, 2022, he charged Israel of having "Committed 50 Holocausts to Palestinians", though no evidence was cited of the existence of death camps or crematoria, or other modes of mass annihilation were ever claimed to exist, except for the mass killing of Palestinians by Jordan in the "Black September", 1970 uprising against King Hussein, or during the Lebanese and Syrian onslaughts on Palestinian refugee camps during the civil wars there. What Abu Mazen neglected to mention was his predecessor in the leadership of the Palestinian movement, Haj Amin al-Husseini, who had collaborated with the Nazis and the Muslim Brothers during the 1930s and 1940s in the extermination of the Jews in the framework of the "final solution", that the Germans committed to perpetrate it in Europe and

---

[113] Allusion is made, of course to Jeremiah 13/23 where a skeptic question was asked: "Can the leopard change his spots?".

the Muslims in the Middle East which was one of the targets of the Nazi conquests[114].

After the Denazification of Europe, Islam took over the banner of virulent anti-Semitism, which signifies, according to Sartre: "To ensure that the Jews are dead". Muslims have engaged in a battle to the death against the Jewish people, launching their bloody lust for killing Jews as a continuation of their millennial persecution of the dhimmis under their rule, on Palestinian land in the riots of 1921 and then at the Wailing Wall in 1929, which they appropriated as the "parking lot" of the mythical al Burak, the mysterious stallion on which their Prophet had allegedly flown from Mecca to Jerusalem. Then, they attempted to scuttle Jewish independence in 1948, and they launched more wars on the Jewish state in 1956, 1967, 1973, 1982, 2006 etc., each time vowing not only to defeat Zionism on the battle field, but also to annihilate the Jewish people from existence. Islamic religion, which since its inception was "commercialized" so as to accommodate this wish, has always aimed at either humiliating the Jews under their rule, or eliminating them when they could not control them. To this day, Iran declares openly and repeatedly its goal to erase Israel and its Jews off the map, and it is encouraged to reiterate that vow by the fact that no other nation or international organization has stood up against that commitment. In December, 1987, when the first Palestinian Intifadah was launched, its initiator, Sheikh Ahmed Yassin from Gaza also helped formulate the Charter of the Hamas which dared to put in precise words and then in articulate deeds the notion of killing Jews as a sacred mission. That was the inception of the Hamas Movement which won the hearts of the Palestinians in the general elections of 2007 and won the majority in the Palestinian Legislative Council. But since the PLO Abu Mazen was the President of the PA, and he accepted to negotiate with Israel,

---

[114] R. Israeli, *The Death Camps of Croatia: Visions and Revisions: 1941-5*, Transaction, NJ, 2013.

the Hamas took over the Gaza Strip, which Israel had relinquished unilaterally in 2005, believing it left it in PLO hands, and inaugurated its separate (though never recognized) state, which ran independent of the PLO PA and in rivalry to it.

Since it grew independent, the Hamas managed the Gaza area, populated by ca two million Palestinians (roughly equal to the West Bank managed by the PLO) and gradually built up its support among the Palestinians of the PA, based on its reputation as the firm opponent of Israel, rejecting the Oslo Accords, which failed in any case, and refusing to negotiate with Israel or deal with it. In 2006 Hamas troops kidnapped an Israeli soldier on the border and it was not before 2011 that they released him in exchange for one thousand heavily sentenced Hamas prisoners who had been incarcerated in Israeli jails for grave security contraventions. It so happened that the main leadership of Gaza these days is made up of many of those released life prisoners. That new and fresh leadership reorganized Gaza and with the support and technical and financial aid of Iran and Hizbullah in Lebanon, notwithstanding it Sunnite /Muslim Brother conviction and their Shi'ite identity, they manufactured rockets and missiles and maintained a strict and severe Islamic rejectionist regime. They tested Israeli state of alert from time to time and built on their battle experience during those rounds of war to harden their training and toughen their rejectionist position. Following the May 2021 round of war when those war rounds peaked, the Hamas was beaten so severely that successive Israeli governments were fooled to believe that it was finally reconciled to the reality that it needed to adapt to Israel as a neighbor, which it needed to survive, despite its negative stance. Not that Abu Mazen was much better, because he persisted in paying salaries to the families of the PLO operatives who were killed or imprisoned in their clashes with Israel. That meant that in fact he, like the Hamas, paid those who killed Jews, while he was sermonizing Israelis about his desire for peace.

When the Hamas leadership, abroad and at home, became persuaded, with Iran and Hizbullah prodding, that inner dissent and factional division in Israel had brought the country to the threshold of chaos and ungovernability, during the long months of mass demonstrations and anti-government sentiment, it started to plan and train to implement secretly its vision of removing the Jews out of their way, while soothing Israel successfully with ambiguous statements of accommodation. So, while Israel was sound asleep (literally) and unsuspecting, a couple of thousand Hamas members, with their Islamic Jihad associates, mounted on pick up cars like ISIS fighters, and on motorcycles, that were loaded with automatic weapons, explosives and implements of destruction, accompanied by other killers and robbers of the Palestinian Gazan community, eager to kill Jews, rob their property and take revenge on their superior standard of living and abundance by burning their housing facilities, breaking their furniture and house implements to smithereens, wrecking to pieces every installation and devastating anything alive or growing back into the stone age. The human rampage and desecration was even more outrageous: houses were broken into while people were in bed, entire families were shot while parents and their babies were embracing in horror; young girls were abused and then murdered, elderly were beaten, humiliated and them killed or herded into exile to Gaza as hostage. All in all, some 3,000 armed Hamas members broke the separating fence and penetrated into 22 Israeli peaceful Kibbutzim and villages and slaughtered an equal number of innocent Israeli civilians and kidnapped upward of 200 more. A thoughtful Australian Anglican Priest and Islamic scholar from Melbourne, Mark Durie, wrote under the title "After the Hamas Deluge"[115]

---

[115] Mark Durie, "After the Hamas Deluge", 15 October, 2023. This article first appeared in the Australian edition of the Spectator. Mark Durie is the founding director of the Institute for Spiritual Awareness, a Writing Fellow at the Middle East Forum, and a Senior Research Fellow of the Arthur Jeffery Centre for the Study of Islam at the Melbourne School of Theology.

On 7 October Hamas jihadis launched Operation Al-Aqsa Deluge, entering Israel to kill over 1,500 people, and take more than a hundred captives, many of them women and children, as well as an unknown number of male IDF soldiers. In scenes reminiscent of ISIS atrocities, one video shows a room full of young Jewish women being held captive. Another displays the semi-naked body of a young woman – a German citizen, identified from her tattoos by her relatives – being paraded through the streets of Gaza, and spat upon by passers-by, to cries of 'Allahu Akbar'. Another video shows a young Jewish boy, around five years old, who had been taken captive to Gaza, being tormented by Muslim children. Israeli soldiers have reported horrific scenes in the villages where the attacks took place; young families slaughtered, babies beheaded and mutilated corpses. Hamas has called on Muslims all over the world to come out in support, and in the light of all this horror, it is disturbing just how many voices have been raised in support of the 7 October attacks, including in Australia.

Support can take many forms, ranging from direct praise, through to indirect assertions of Palestinians' right to 'resistance', and objections that too much is being made of Jewish victimhood. Al-Azhar University in Cairo is considered the premier Sunni center of learning in the world. Its head, Sheikh Al-Tayyeb, was quick to issue a statement to celebrate the attacks: 'The honorable Al-Azhar salutes with utmost pride the resistance efforts of the Palestinian people.'

At a Muslim street rally held in western Sydney on Sunday night after the attacks, Imam Ibrahim Dadoun, a prominent Australian-born preacher affiliated with the United Muslims of Australia, was shouting with joy, his phrases punctuated by roars of 'Allahu Akbar' from the enthusiastic crowd around him: 'I'm smiling and I'm happy. I'm elated. It's a day of courage. It's a day of happiness. It's a day of pride. It's a day of victory! This is the day we've been waiting for!' The following day in Sydney a large crowd of protestors gathered near the Town Hall and made their way to the Opera House, chanting 'Free, Free Palestine' interspersed with chants in Arabic of: 'There is no God but Allah' and 'Allah is Greater'. Attending in solidarity were supporters from the Greens. One protestor held up a sign which stated, 'When there is apartheid, resistance is justified,' implying that the massacre was indeed justified. Another protestor explained to a journalist that, 'decolonialisation is not an easy process… it is messy'. When the rally reached the Opera House, Israeli flags were burnt, while the crowd aggressively chanted 'Gas the Jews' and 'F–k the Jews'.

The NSW police have come under criticism for permitting this rally. Sydney Jews had been advised by the police, for their own safety, to stay away from the Opera House, which was to be lit up with the colours of Israel's flag in sympathy for the massacre victims. A lone Jewish man who was present outside the Town Hall, holding an Israeli flag, was arrested by the police for 'disturbing the peace' – later the police explained it was for his own safety – but none of the pro-Palestinian protestors were arrested. It seems the police made a decision to allow what was in fact an illegal protest to take place in order to prevent the violence that could have erupted if they had attempted to stop it.

Comments in support of Israel by Australia's leaders have angered local Muslim organisations. The Lebanese Muslim Association strongly objected to any statement that Israel has a right to defend itself. The Australian National Imams Council declared that it 'supports the Palestinian people's right of self determination' and complained about expressions of concern for the lives of Israeli Jews, stating that: people should 'avoid one-sided statements of support which ignore the Palestinian people'.

In contrast to all this, Australia's Prime Minister Anthony Albanese and its Foreign Minister, Penny Wong, have both expressed abhorrence at the attacks in Israel and upheld Israel's right to defend itself. Penny Wong, however, appalled many by urging 'restraint' on the part of the Israelis. Both also condemned the Sydney pro-Palestine rallies, as have many other Australian leaders, but notably Chris Bowen and Tony Burke, the two MPs whose electorates include high Arab populations, have remained silent. (Hamas has been classed as a terrorist organisation in Australia since 2001.)

The 7 October massacre has demonstrated to the world that Israel is engaged in an existential struggle. The international expressions of support for the Operation Al-Aqsa Deluge massacre have only served to underscore the urgency of this crucial point. But what does it really mean to have the right to defend against an existential threat? First, this is not a struggle against all Muslims. It would be a grave mistake to conclude from the exuberant joy of some Muslims this past week that all followers of Islam support Hamas. On the contrary, the obvious repeated failures of radical Islam in our time have caused a great many Muslims to distance themselves from radical expressions of Islam. Today the majority of Iranians resent their government having made jihad Iran's top export; polls have shown that there are many in Gaza who dislike Hamas' iron rule; and in the aftermath of the Hamas massacre, many Muslims across the Middle East have taken to social media to condemn what Hamas has done.

Second, as long as Hamas holds the reins in Gaza, a negotiated peace will be impossible. This, the biggest massacre in one day of Jewish civilians since the Holocaust, has made that crystal clear. No amount of diplomacy can overcome this fact. The Hamas military commander, Mohammad Deif, declared, on announcing Operation Al-Aqsa Deluge, 'I say to our pure mujahideen: This is the day that you make this criminal enemy understand that its time is up. Kill them wherever you may find them'. (His last phrase was quoted from the Qur'an's Verse of the Sword, Surah 9:5). In a similar vein, Hamas leader Isma'il Haiyeh declared on the Al-Jazeera Network (Qatar), 'We are on the verge of victory… Get out of our Jerusalem and our Al-Aqsa Mosque… This land is ours, Jerusalem is ours, everything is ours.' Such overweening confidence is supported by a fallacy, derived from the Qur'an, that Jews love life while Muslims love death (Surah 2:94-96, 62:6). Hamas does not believe Israelis will have the courage to defeat it.

The intention of Hamas is that, confronted by the horror, Israel will be forced to meekly accept that 'its time is up'. This is not going to happen. Instead, what lies ahead is a hard, bitter war. This is not a war which can be resolved through a negotiated settlement. Hamas has shown the world, in its own bloody way, that this is a war to destroy Israel together with its people. This logic is not to be reasoned with. Israel does have the right to defend itself. It now has no choice but to make this a war to completely uproot and destroy Hamas.

The Arab/Muslim students who dwelt in Moscow in the

thousands, as part of the large body of invited cadres from all non-aligned nations, were not necessarily committed Communists but had a vested interest in training for careers without incurring any cost. They not only learned what was needed for their training but were also indoctrinated with the idea that the Soviet Paradise, which promoted exemplary models of economic and social development, was also the international hub of world peace and fraternity between nations. After the devastating Muslim defeat in the War of 1967 against Israel, it was the Soviet Union who helped rehabilitate the routed Muslim nations, replace their destroyed military equipment, and encourage native models of "socialism" that resembled the structure of the strict authoritarian and hierarchic Soviet Union itself, and of the Soviet Communist Party in their organization, centralism, and conduct. It seemed then that the Islamic world, save for the very conservative monarchical regimes of the Gulf, was comfortably placed in the bosom of the Soviets and well disposed to enjoy that position indefinitely. But 1967 also generated a countercurrent of religious revival throughout that Islamic world, especially following the October 1968 Cairo Islamic Conference, which convened chief clerics and scholars covering the entire span of the Muslim world, from Morocco to Indonesia[116]. In the painful soul-searching deliberations, which attempted to ponder the reasons for that unprecedented "glorious Muslim defeat" in modern times, they came to the conclusion that, while Islam had reached its climax close to the time of the Prophet and thereafter, when it was upright and ruled by the standards set by the Messenger of Allah, it was the Western corrupting influence on Islam that had caused its demise. The lesson was inescapable: only a return to Islam and its ancient norms could rescue it from oblivion. In other words, while Western utopia for progress and improvement lay sometime in the future

---

[116] D.F. Green, *Arab Theologians on Jews and Israel: The Fourth Conference of the Academy of Islamic Research*, Editions de l'Avenir, Geneva, 1974.

and may be attained gradually by determined social, political, and intellectual measures; Islamic utopia was projected into the time of the Prophet in the past, and all that was needed was to strive to approximate the achievements of the Prophet's generation by studying and applying them in the real world. Hence the spread of many Salafi movements, connoting a return to the era of the *aslaf,* that is the ancients.

The Islamic movements, which emerged under various appellations, were not at ease with the Soviet alliance that had been thrust upon them as a matter of convenience. Therefore, as soon as the Soviet Union collapsed and the Communist parties in the Arab world withered away for want of commitment to the idea of Communism, a giant vacuum was created that needed to be filled urgently. In Israel, for example, one of the few places in the Middle East where a Communist Party was legal, an Islamic movement emerged where local politics had been previously dominated by the Communists (later converted to Rakah and then Hadash Parties that connoted "new democracy and equality"). So those who remained within the Communist Party and had brandished the names of Brezhnev and Ceaucescu as the epitomes of ideal democracy, had to change their name, as other Communists in the rest of the world had done, as if they were beginning something new, and started lecturing Israel on democracy. The wedding of convenience between Islam and Communism had come to an end in any case. Russia, who inherited the Soviet Union, became a close ally to the least mainstream (i.e. Sunnite) Islamic regimes in the Islamic world, that is the Alawites of Syria, and the Shi'ites of Iran in an attempt to regain what it had lost on the way to rehabilitating the dissolved Empire. But the defeat of the Soviets in Afghanistan in 1989, which put an end to their ten-year, "Vietnam-like" venture, only precipitated Soviet prestige to its lowest ebb. For the world of Islam, the Soviet demise in Afghanistan meant more than that. It meant that Muslim *mujahideen* were able, by their primitive weaponry but with the aid of other Muslims, namely the Muslim volunteers who flocked in from the entire Islamic world, to beat one of the two superpowers and force her to retreat. The conclusion was swift and clear: the other superpower (the United States) could not be far behind, an assumption that was not off the mark in view of the upcoming retreat of the United States and the takeover by the Taliban in Afghanistan when foreign intervention ebbed in 2015 and drew to its end in 2021. Moreover, the very intervention of the Soviets on Christmas 1979 had been motivated by their fear, lest the Islamic upheaval that began with the Iranian Revolution one year earlier might seep into its five Islamic republics of Central Asia, which were adjacent to Iran (Tajikistan, Turkmenistan, Kyrgyzstan, Uzbekistan, and Kazakhstan), and to the Islamic Republic of the Caucasus—Azerbaijan—which borders Iran. The Soviets had hoped to stem that danger by demonstrating that the Iranian Revolution had been a paper tiger, but they eventually failed, much to the delight of Muslim radicals worldwide, who seized the opportunity to organize their forces and launch their onslaught on the West and the Jews. The end result was that those six Muslims republics were freed from the Soviet yoke and became independent once the Soviet Federation crumbled. It was tempting for Muslims across the world to conclude that it was *their* mujahideen who were to be credited for that achievement and that thanks to other Muslims, not foreign powers, their brethren were liberated, increasing the number of Muslim countries to 57, almost one third of the world count in those days, when membership of the United Nations amounted to 180. The Muslim mood in the world was upbeat, not only due to the numbers of believers approaching the billion mark, billing their creed as "one quarter of humanity," but also boasting Muslim identity and promoting its international success. Indeed, the Organization of Islamic Cooperation (OIC), which had made its debut in 1968 as a result of the arson of the al-Aqsa Mosque in Jerusalem, when Muslims across the world rushed to falsely indict Israel of its premeditation, was a manifestation of that newfound pride. The first Rabat Summit Conference of Islamic countries in 1968, under the pretext that it was urgent to "come to the rescue of Jerusalem," was concluded with a unanimous decision to establish a Jerusalem Committee, headed by the host of the conference, King Hassan, who hastened to call the central square in Fez, the ancient Royal Capital (the Kyoto of Morocco), "the Jerusalem Plaza," to evince his loyalty to Islam, for he had been much maligned by many Muslim radicals for "selling off" to the United States, France, and Western values and for maintaining secret contact with the Israelis, all unforgivable sins in Islamic politics. Since 1968, membership in the OIC continued to grow in leaps and bounds, and in 1976 the incredible happened: Turkey, which under her civil governments jealously guarded her secular nature, and avoided any official involvement with religion, suddenly yielded to the public mood and agreed not only to join the OIC but also to host that year's conference in Istanbul. The symbolism could not be missed: what used to be the splendid capital of the Muslim Ottoman Empire and the seat of its glamorous Sultan, who was also the caliph of all Muslims, unexpectedly admitted to her Islamic past and present Islamic identity and joined that great association of modern Muslim states. Not since the disappearance of the Caliphate after World War One, when the Ottoman Empire was dismantled, had Muslims across the world experienced that feeling of great Muslim power converging together—as if the gathered heads of states of the Islamic world represented the corporate caliphate that was no more. Since the Istanbul encounter, the membership of OIC grew to include such countries as Uganda, who was not exactly Muslim but was ruled by a Muslim tyrant, Idi Amin Dada, and that was enough for him to draw his country into the fray. Naturally, since the rise to power of the Islamic Party of Tayyip Erdogan in Ankara in 2002, the feeling of exhilaration with growing Muslim power has heightened, as it did in the 1970s when Pakistan revealed its "Islamic bomb" and as the Muslim world is bound to boast again when Iran achieves its own. Admittedly, the Iranian Revolution of 1978 has caused unease in some quarters of the Sunnite majority, which fears the aggression of the Shi'ite Crescent, constituted by Iran, Iraq, Syria, and Lebanon, to the point that some Sunnite clerics have dubbed the Shi'ites as "worse than the Jews," a compliment not easily disbursed to a rival in the Islamic world. But, beyond these divisions, which pit Iran and its satellites against Saudi Arabia and its cohorts, there is agreement between the two parties that the victory of Islam takes no less precedence than the theological differences between Shi'a and Sunna, as long as Iranian power is kept at bay and does not threaten the relatively moderate Muslim countries like the Gulf States, Morocco, Tunisia and Jordan. For example, the acts of terror, which were invented originally by Shi'ites (and were wrongly dubbed "suicide bombings"), have become a favorite modus operandi of many Sunnite groups, such as Hamas, some PLO factions, such as the al-Aqsa Brigades, some terrorists in Iraq and in Afghanistan, and others. Hamas in Gaza has been relying on aid from Iran, and many Muslim terrorists convene for their annual meetings in Tehran, regardless of their Sunnite affiliation.

Those years that followed the Soviet debacle in Afghanistan also saw the rise of the Afghani phenomenon in the Islamic world. Tens of thousands of Muslim mujahideen had indeed been recruited by American encouragement and Saudi financing from all over the Islamic world to flock to Afghanistan and to fight against the hated Communist superpower until its capitulation. Those Moroccan, Saudi, Jordanian, Iraqi, Chechnyan, Bosnian, European, and other volunteers had gathered in Afghani camps financed by the CIA, and they kept the stream of reinforcements from drying up in that demanding ten-year fight against the Soviet Russians. But when dwindling Russia capitulated and the war was officially terminated, those Afghani outsiders returned home and began to pose a local problem for their governments. In 1989 and thereafter, those repatriated fighters, who had now become a roving international jihadist camp, ready to go where they were needed for the cause of Islam, soon became one major issue for their governments[117]. They went to Iraq to fight the Americans, returned to Afghanistan to face their former American allies who had assisted them against the Soviets, and then became the major component of the Syrian rebels against the Assad regime, al-Qa'ida, and the ISIS movement in Iraq and Syria. One of their founders and leaders, probably the most renowned and the most influential, was Osama bin Laden. Bin Laden contributed more than any Muslim at that time to debunk the myth that Muslim terrorism was due to poverty and disaffection. The South American favelas, those makeshift slums that surround all major cities in that continent, provide daily proof that material misery does not necessarily produce indiscriminate terrorism against innocent people. But bin Laden's personal wealth had attested to the contrary. He could have led an easy life, like his peers in Saudi Arabia, in the opulence of his palaces, but he elected to fight for his ideas in the mountains of Tora Bora in Afghanistan, pursued by American aircraft and Special Forces attempting to eliminate him for a decade or more before he was gunned down in his secret abode in the garrison city of Abbottabad in Pakistan in 2012. It also happens that the two most fundamentalist Muslim countries—Saudi Arabia and Iran—are also the richest, so that poverty could not have been the reason for their radicalism. While Iran continues to serve as the international hub of Muslim terrorism, it has been the massive participation of individual Saudi donors in the world jihadi effort that had first allowed thousands of Saudi volunteers to fight in Afghanistan against the Soviets, then for the 9/11 events to happen, and for the continued bloodletting in the Syrian civil war and in ISIS's onslaughts in Syria and Iraq. Under the Ira-

---

[117] R. Israeli, *Itinerant Jihadis:Arab and Muslim War Volunteers,* Strategic Books, TX, 2011.

nian nuclear threat, and the resulting discreet and half-hearted Saudi adhesion to the Abrahamic Treaty which brought moderate Arab countries to terms with Israel outwardly, and to adopt moderate policies domestically to protect their own regimes from the take over by Islamic parties, as had happened in Egypt, Tunisia, Libya and Sudan, the changing mood in the mainstream world of Islam came to full bloom. Even radicalized Turkey under Erdogan, has shown signs of balancing out its enthusiastic support for Palestinian terrorism by a more compromising attitude towards Israel, taking account of its commitment to NATO which does not officially condone acts of terrorism in its areas of jurisdiction.

In Afghanistan Bin Laden had met the militant Muslim scholar Abdullah Azzam, of Palestinian origin, who devoted his latter years to posing the ideological fundaments of the universal jihad that radical Islam had launched against the United States and the Jews. He was, like others of his conviction, thoroughly influenced by the Imam's knowledge, his political and theological acumen, his total devotion to the cause of Islam, that he was swayed to the point of foregoing his family life and his initially positive economic activity, which had made him wealthy. Upon returning to Saudi Arabia as an "Afghani," who had been hardened by his battlefield experience as a *mujahid,* bin Laden became restless and fanatically determined to overthrow the corrupt and elitist royal regime under which he had grown in Riyadh. But soon he was singled out for the danger he posed to his peers in the kingdom, was stripped of his Saudi citizenship, which had caused much embarrassment to the relations between his country and the United States, and expelled from the country. He was on the road from then on, together with his nuclear family, on the lookout for a land of shelter that was Islamic enough to accept and protect him, poor enough to vie for the funds he could provide in return, and deserted and inaccessible enough for foreign powers to remain unable to locate him or to dislodge him from there. That land would serve as the physical base for his new organization, al-Qa'ida (literally, "the Base"), and as the metaphoric base of the world jihadi movement he was determined to found, lead, and fund by his own means.

The organization spoke about confronting "American arrogance" and world Jewry (not Israel or Zionism, as others who wish to dissimulate their anti-Semitism pretend), which were seen as close allies with Jews at the lead. They were accused of providing the ideological underpinnings for "controlling the world" under the well-known and widely diffused "world Jewish conspiracy", and other conspiracy theories that jihadi Islam, like Hamas and the Muslim Brothers, had liberally borrowed from the *Protocols of the Elders of Zion*. Powerful America, it was claimed, was the financial and military arm that was manipulated by world Jewry to achieve its goals. That was the reason that on September 11, al-Qa'ida attacked the Twin Towers and the Pentagon, the symbols of American economic and military power, and all over the Muslim world there was great jubilation. However, some Muslim quarters were so embarrassed by the scope of that horror that they tried to impute it to the CIA or Mossad, claiming that Jews were in any case involved in it. After he was ejected from his homeland, bin Laden sought and found shelter in Sudan, which in 1989 came under the rule of General Omar al-Bashir, who later became involved in the Darfur massacre and was indicted by the International Criminal Court for crimes against humanity. That poor country was hungry for bin Laden's foreign currency and was itself too involved in horrific mass murdering to resent bin Laden's terrorist schemes. For that reason, bin Laden settled there until the 1998 al-Qa'ida's terrorist acts against the American embassies in Kenya and Tanzania, resulting in hundreds of fatalities, both American and African, raised the wrath of the United States. The Clinton administration retaliated with a few bombings of the Sudan and threatened the host country with more unless bin Laden and his group were expelled from the country. In his search for a new asylum, bin Laden identified Afghanistan as such a target. Since 1996, the Taliban had taken over the rule in Kabul and established such a strict Islamic rule there under Mullah Omar as to make Saudi Arabia and Iran look like bastions of democracy and liberalism. The mullah was an unknown cleric who had gained spiritual control of his Taliban during the Afghani civil war. Once bin Laden was introduced to him in Kandahar, they became close friends, and the determined Afghani mullah guaranteed asylum to his guest, whatever the price he would have to pay.

It is often claimed that this strict interpretation of Islam with its abuses, including a blatant anti-Semitism, is only the lot of "fanatic," "radical," "fundamentalist," or "Islamist" Muslims, usually quantified as some 15 percent of the 1.5 billion world Muslims, as if that were a different faith embracing different principles than those followed by the rank-and-file Muslims. In fact, even if that were true, we are talking about 200 million individuals, spread among all nations—from the Boko Haram in Nigeria to the Lashkar-e-Taiba in Pakistan—whose numbers are large enough to cause trouble for the entire world. In reality, all 1.5 billion Muslims belong to one creed, who uphold Sharia law to various degrees but champion the same tenets, though those who do not follow them to the letter are not adepts of another alternative faith known as "moderate Islam," which is sometimes dubbed by ignorant politicians as "a religion of peace" to distinguish from the violent and aggressive conduct of the "extremists." In reality, no such separate Islam exists, though there are certainly many truly moderate Muslims who have broken off from the bloody path of Sharia law, especially some of those dwelling in the West, who can from a safe distance criticize the recurring killings of "apostates," "traitors," the phenomenon of the Islamikaze bombers against Westerners and Israelis, the culture of death that is groomed in many Islamic lands, and indeed the unbridled anti-Semitic calumnies that are rife in their environments. But "moderate Muslims" have yet to produce an alternative doctrine and worldview that could rival official Islam or posit a creed and a set of rules to persuade Muslims to relinquish the Shari'a and embrace another way, thus excluding themselves from the community of the believers in the eyes of established Islam. Moderate Muslims often accuse the radicals, who are in fact Muslims who behave in accordance with the accepted rules of the Shari'a, of having "hijacked Islam" or distorted its real meanings, or misinterpreted it, and they in turn are condemned by their rivals for having abandoned the path of Allah or for having themselves been corrupted by Western ideologies. But, for better or for worse, it is the standards of the radicals that prevail in the Islamic world for the most part. One can watch the mass demonstrations in the streets of Gaza, Quetta, Casablanca, Durban, and Jakarta, or in the Muslim neighborhoods of Paris, London, Sydney, Amsterdam, and Toronto to realize how alive, universal, and popular are the Muslim mantras that are uttered, along with the rampages that are performed daily by men, women, and children, including leaders and clerics. Are they all Islamists? No, they are simply Muslims, and the common denominator that links them in their hatred of the West and the Jews is Islam, standard Islam, under the justification of the Sharia, which is promoted by their imams. While some moderate and courageous Muslim individuals will be there to save the honor of their faith when they raise their lone voices against the abuses perpetrated in the name of their creed, mainstream Muslims, including Westernized and modern professionals, intellectuals, and students, will also always be there to glorify in the executions of Westerners and Jews by Muslim terrorists, to write or broadcast in favor of the Islamikaze, and to distribute sweets in the streets to celebrate the deaths of Americans and Jews. The champions of the spurious distinction between the so-called Islamist minority and the peaceful Muslim majority—who became entrapped in their reluctance from a carpet condemnation of Islam lest they be accused of Islamophobia or racism (as if Islam were a race and not a multiracial and multicultural creed) if they are non-Muslims and of treason if they are—are also enslaved by another distinction of their own making, which has equally no leg to stand on.

Throughout the Muslim world, the legitimacy of Israel has been challenged, and the Holocaust is denied systematically, as evidenced by the popularity of such Holocaust deniers as Robert Faurisson, Roger Garaudy, or David Irving. Those countries also prohibited *Schindler's List* from their screens and condoned the violent declarations of the Iranian president on both scores. This is a common denominator among most Muslims, and just like the anti-Jewish stereotypes, nothing differentiates between radicals and moderates. That is the reason why we find Muslims contradicting themselves on the Shoah, denying it on the one hand and wishing Hitler had brought his annihilation plan to completion on the other; they also urge a "scholarly, free, and objective" research of the Holocaust, but only in order to prove that it never was. Similarly, the belief in and the spread of the *Protocols of the Elders of Zion,* the blood libel, the poisoning of wells by Jews, and conspiracy theories concerning the Jews are recurring themes in Palestinian (not only Hamas) as well as mainstream Egyptian, Jordanian, Saudi, Pakistani, and others' writings, systems of beliefs, and propaganda. Genocidal threats against the Jews have abounded not only in bin Laden's statements and in Ahmadinejad's delusions, but also in columns of Egyptian, Saudi, Palestinian, and other mainstream newspapers. Is this Judeophobia of the moderates or plain anti-Semitism of the Islamists? Words have a significance, and it is imperative to streamline our vocabulary; otherwise we are under the permanent threat of losing our ability to express what we mean or to comprehend what we are told. Matters are further complicated by the paranoia and conspiracy theories that are widespread in the Muslim world among Islamists and others, whether modern and Western-educated or traditionalist and obscurantist. Those theories that are rampant even among Muslims living in the West would insist that world leaders who support Israel are Jewish (like presidents Reagan and

Bush), that the United Nations, of all places, is the mastermind of the Jews, who utilize it as the tool for their world dominion, and that the major violent acts that have shaken the world, such as the World Wars, world revolutions, and September 11, are all the fruit of Jewish imagination and execution. Their minds are so permeated with these nonsense theories that they have become impervious to logical, rational debate. Therefore, the difficulty of dealing with Muslim minds consists not only in removing the mountains of pure delusion that choke their thinking, but also in persuading them that the very attempt to counter those untruths is not necessarily part of the world conspiracy that is being woven against them. It is possible to explain their imaginary picture of the world by their need to project on their enemies the analytical shortcomings that bewitch them, but it is impossible to move them out of the illusory scenarios that they have constructed around themselves, and then they cling to them with a tenacity that defies and contradicts Western standards of logic. The result is that even when Muslims initiate and launch an act of violence, they accuse the West or Israel of an act of aggression against them, of which they are the victims and which requires their retaliation or vengeance. This maze of global developments, where Muslims in general and Palestinians specifically regard themselves as victims to world discrimination and conspiracy, has increased after the Russian invasion of the Ukraine which has pitted the entire wealthy and dominant West against the Russian- Iranian-Syrian alliance which are all threatened and exhibit signs of wokeism-inspired rhetoric.

Some insightful criticism of these upside down invention of history were published by Attorney Maurice Hirsch in the Palestinian Media Watch (PMW)[118], which shows how repetitive and adamant are these views among the Arabs:

---

[118] Maurice Hirsch, "When you lack any history, just invent one ", PMW, Sep 4, 2022.

According to the Palestinian Authority, Jews have no historical connection to the Land of Israel. To support the assertion, the PA argues that archaeological artifacts that unequivocally prove this connection are fake. The Palestinians on the other hand, so claims the PA, are actually a 4,500 year-old people who are descendants of the Canaanites. There is no honest way to deny the Jewish connection to the Land of Israel. Tens of thousands (if not more) of archaeological artifacts prove that connection. When the international community allocated the whole of Israel, in 1922, for the reconstitution of the Jewish homeland, they recognized that historical connection. When the Supreme Muslim Council wanted to describe the Temple Mount, it noted that "This site is one of the oldest in the world. Its sanctity dates from the earliest (perhaps from pre-historic) times. Its identity with the site of Solomon's Temple is beyond dispute. In order to explain away and negate the historical Jewish connection to Israel, the PA has invented an entire alternative reality. In the PA reality, Jews/Israelis have no history, and therefore they try to "steal" the Palestinian identity. The Jews, according to the PA, try to steal Palestinian foods and clothes, and even plant historical Jewish coins at excavation sites in order to invent a false history.

A series of quotes from contemporary Arab press were cited by Attorney Hirsch to back up his claims, and confirm the fact that part of wokeism is to reverse historical events into narratives to fit in with their whims, wishful thinking fertile imagination, among others:

Official PA TV host: They are attempting to market the

Palestinian people's heritage and the Palestinian garb as if it were part of the Israeli heritage and that they have a place here in this land. Even in the excavations under the Al-Aqsa Mosque and everywhere, they try to place some coins, as if [to say]: 'Here, we found coins, and this land is ours.' These are ongoing attempts at falsification.

Faiqa Al-Sous (a writer, retorted): They lie. They know they're lying and the world knows they're lying… Look at the evil world, we whose narrative is reliable must not publish it, while they spread the false narrative, the false narrative of the occupation.[119]

The goal behind the false PA narrative is to convince the Palestinians that Jews are merely colonizers who came to inhabit a land to which they have no historical connection. This claim enables the PA to persuade the Palestinians that the Jews are simply thieves who stole "Palestinian land". However, for the PA narrative to be effective, it not only needs to negate the Jewish connection to Israel, but it also needs to invent the "Palestinian" historical connection that dates back thousands of years and provides the Palestinians with a history older than that of the Jews. To do so, the PA has even established the "Palestinian Clothing Day" to celebrate the Palestinian national dress, which it claims proves the Palestinian presence in the area going "back to the Canaanite period". In their words:

The Palestinians mark Palestinian Clothing Day every year on July 25, in accordance with [PA] President Mahmoud Abbas' decision on Aug. 1, 2018… Clothing Day was established to preserve the ancestors' history and protect it from theft and the Judaization that the Israeli

---

[119] Official PA TV, *Returning*, July 16, 2022.

occupation is carrying out... Palestinian clothing is one of the main supporting pillars that shape the Palestinian cultural identity, and it is witness to the Palestinian presence whose roots on this land go back to the Canaanite period. According to the historians, some of the shapes and images that were woven into the Canaanite royal garments (the queen's garb) [parentheses in source] are the same ones that exist today [in the Palestinian women's clothing]. Something that draws attention in most of the Palestinian women's clothing is the octagonal star. This is a Canaanite star whose roots go back to 4500 BCE. This star represented 'the goddess of fertility' among our Canaanite ancestors.[120]When the PA refers to the "historians," claims Hirsch, it is clearly not referring to Palestinian Historian Abd Al-Ghani Salameh, who explained that even as late as 1917 he said those same words as in the same official Palestinian TV, verbatim:

> Before the Balfour Pledge (i.e., Declaration) when the Ottoman rule ended (1517-1917), Palestine's political borders as we know them today did not exist, and there was nothing called a Palestinian people with a political identity as we know today, since Palestine's lines of administrative division stretched from east to west and included Jordan and southern Lebanon, and like all peoples of the region [the Palestinians] were liberated from the Turkish rule and immediately moved to colonial rule, without forming a Palestinian

---

[120] Official PA daily *Al-Hayat Al-Jadida,* July 26, 2022.

people's political identity.[121]

The fact of the matter, concludes Attorney Hirsch, is that the Palestinians have no history prior to the modern period and no connection to the Canaanites. Had this ancient Palestinian-Canaanite people actually existed, it would certainly have been able to show centuries of history and culture. It would certainly have been mentioned in historical documents and would have certainly appeared in contemporary documents such as the 1922 League of Nations Mandate for Palestine, the 1947 UN Partition Plan and even UN Security Council Resolution 242 which the Palestinians often refer to as the basis for their false claim that Israel is occupying "Palestinian territory." The fact that none of the above mentioned documents make any reference to a "Palestinian people", let alone a 4,500 year-old Palestinian people, does not bother the PA. For the PA, in the absence of any real history, all you have to do is make it up. The bothersome aspect of all this fabricated history, is that no known decent Arab, Palestinian or Muslim scholars (and there are many of them, mainly living in the West and educated to scholarly accuracy and intellectual righteousness), has ever debunked those masses of lies and delusionary fabrications. This reversal of facts which amounts to manipulation of Islamic history (or "commercialization" in order to obtain a certain stance in political debate is what characterizes the behavior of Muslim terrorists who seek refuge in the West, for the most part while on the run from their home regimes that they tried unsuccessfully to topple. Since they are persuaded that they fight for the path of Allah, they certainly do not regard themselves as terrorists, and, when they are arrested for terrorist activities within their host countries, which had generously, naively, and self-defeatingly given them shelter and provided for their needs, they accuse their benefactors and condemn their

---

[121] Ibid, November 1, 2017.

"barbaric behavior." This mechanism of denial, which posits Western democracy as a milking cow that owes them sustenance while they owe it nothing, allows them to deny the good and the protection they get and to even mount subversive cells that are liable to act in the heart of their countries of refuge. Their denial allows them to wreak havoc, death, destruction, and terror upon the nations that took them in, in spite of their repeated promises to the authorities that they will refrain from political or subversive activity as a condition of being accorded the status of refugees[122]. A sort of political denial is also adopted in the Western chanceries as well, under the belief that if they meant well for the Muslim refugees they would encounter exemplary behavior on their part in return. Even the al-Qaida entrenchment in the United States and Europe and their illicit activities were not enough to stir suspicions and to instigate the slumbering Western governments to take measures of self-defense until the Muslim radicals struck, first in the United States then in Europe. The new Muslim terrorists put the blame on the West for rescuing them from their own corrupt regimes, and therefore the host countries that have tried to fight terrorism are accused of racism, Islamophobia, an anti-Islamic drive, inhumanity, and the like. The democratic countries of shelter that have absorbed these streams of refugees, who have arrived uninvited, now become the oppressors of the poor and peaceful Muslims, like their original oppressive countries of Saudi Arabia, Egypt, Morocco, Yemen, Libya, and all the rest.[123]

Muslim diasporas in the West, which have vastly expanded since the 1990s and have acquired political power through sheer numbers of their coreligionists, have attempted to dislodge the older and more established, though far less numerous, Jewish communities from their advantageous positions. By doing so, they wish to elim-

---

[122] *Executive Intelligence Review,* September 4, 1998 .
[123] *Al-Ahram Weekly,* October 1, 2001.

inate the Jewish influence on the local governments and thereby shift the traditional political sympathies of the West from Jews and Israel to the Arabs and the Palestinians. This is why Islamic protests in Western societies almost invariably go hand in hand with anti-Semitic eruptions of violence. Again, this would seem an acceptable and legitimate way of political lobbying in any liberal political system, except that Muslim populations most often do not fulfill the two conditions that accompany political protest in the democratic West: they do not act in the interest of their host countries but rather against it, and they do not refrain from violence and the breaking of the law. For Muslim immigrants do not seem to have internalized these restrictions at the same pace that they have mastered the benefits they can extract from their countries of shelter. Many naturalized Muslims—for example some of the perpetrators of 9/11 and then the London attacks of July 2005—did not hesitate to act against their hosts, who had showered them with benefits; and many other Muslims who have sought shelter in Europe, Canada, and Australia devote their time not to assimilating into new environments but to cultivating their separate identities and building enclaves of Islam in their host countries. For example, far from accepting their host countries' Middle Eastern policies or their anti-terrorist struggles, they protest against them, often violently. The second count of using violence, which is usually shunned in Western societies, raises even more concern, because it ultimately hurts public order and value systems in host cultures. Since the outbreak of the Palestinian al-Aqsa Intifada in late 2000, thousands of violent demonstrations by Muslim immigrant populations have unfolded from Montreal to Sydney, from Sao Paulo to Durban (South Africa), from Oslo to Rome—apart from the usual anti-Israel and anti-Jewish demonstrations that have exploded throughout the Arab and Muslim world. Anti-Israeli demonstrations are certainly legitimate, but when they involve bouts of rage, the burning down of foreign embassies and flags, the pelting of rocks against houses of prayer, and sometimes murdering of innocent civilians or when effigies of American and Israeli leaders, who are often personal friends and certainly political allies of the local leaders are burnt and abuses hurled at them, this is the limit that the rule of law can permit, of which Muslim immigrants often seem to be unaware. Indeed, few Westerners participate in these acts of violence, and conversely no Jews have responded by committing the same acts against Western or Muslim countries with which the host society maintains relations. What is more, although Jewish communities worldwide have rallied around Israel, they have done so with dignity and full respect for the law and have not allowed harm to be committed against their home countries or against the violent crowds of Muslims and their supporters.

The most distressing aspects of these outbursts of violence have been that Western countries have been turned by their Muslim communities into violent arenas where the Middle Eastern conflict has been exported. Not content with attacking American and Israeli symbols in Western capitals, these hooligans who terrorize the downtown areas of their countries of residence turned to brutal onslaughts of the local Jewish communities in France, Britain, Germany, Belgium, and others, thus signaling to the world that Jews and Israel were to be equated and that anti-Semitism meant also anti-Zionism, or even pure and simple anti-Israeli outbursts. The worst hit were the Jewish communities in those countries, where hundreds of Jewish synagogues, cemeteries, schools, and other institutions were torched or otherwise desecrated; Jewish adults were attacked on their way to and from prayer; and children on their way to and from school. All this has happened under the eyes of the local police, who have not dared to intervene forcefully for fear of the politically correct politicians. One can only imagine what would have happened if a mosque or a church were likewise burned, or non-Jewish worshippers or children attacked and harmed. Other places have also experienced the full extent of this pogrom, which in many Jewish circles was reminiscent of the infamous Kristall-nacht of 1938. In most, though not all, cases, these horrific anti-Semitic attacks were orchestrated by the Muslim communities of Europe, at times in conjunction with local inveterate anti-Semites. The outcome of all this is that the Muslim communities in the Western democracies have shown since the 1990s that they can act in unison to undermine public order, to pose a serious threat to national security, and to harm their fellow citizens, Jewish and otherwise. This means that they can organize and demonstrate in the same fashion in their host countries when they judge an issue important enough or when local authorities are too lenient or reluctant to confront them. Polls organized in the United States after 9/11 found that Americans overwhelmingly tied Islam and Muslims to those horrific events: 68 percent of them approved of randomly stopping people who might fit the profile of suspected terrorists, 83 percent of Americans favored stricter controls on Muslims entering the country, 58 percent wanted tighter controls on Muslims traveling on planes and trains, 35 percent of New Yorkers favored establishing internment camps for individuals who the authorities identified as sympathetic to terrorist causes, and 31 percent of all Americans favored detention camps for Arab Americans as a way of preventing terrorist attacks in the United States.[124] This means that the threatened population found itself ahead of their authorities, which were more cautious in limiting civil rights, and the general public was prepared to a great extent to replay the unfortunate experience of the internment of Japanese Americans in World War II. It was to be expected then that if and when more major acts of terror unfolded in the West, the West would find itself compelled to curtail civil liberties and take radical measures against the Muslim minority in its midst. Only in this light did the very moderate

---

[124] See Daniel Pipes, "Fighting Militant Islam, Without Bias," *City Journal*, Autumn 2001. http://www.city-journal.org/htm/41/fightingmilitant.html.

measures taken by Israel against its demonstratively hostile Muslim minority, which had come under scathing criticism from the pre-9/11 world, look incredibly generous and even border at times on neglect. All these developments, which have swept through both Islamic countries and Muslim communities in the West, have created a mood that has evolved since 1989 creating awe, and often outright fear, in the West from militant Islam and from the chaos it can create if not addressed. The 2006 Cartoon Affair, in which Denmark and other European nations shamefully capitulated to the violent and murderous attacks against them, are a case in point. Instead of defending the liberal ideas of the West, including the hallowed freedom of expression, as they were being dramatically and violently challenged, the Danes, the European foreign minister, and the United Nations elected to placate the hooligans and their supportive Arab governments, particularly Saudi Arabia, who threatened economic boycott of Danish dairy products. That show of muscular force, which ended up intimidating Europe, could not help but boost self-confidence in the Islamic world that their economic power could easily bring Europe to its knees, not only on the cartoon issue but on any policy that displeased them. How much more concerning when it involved the Arab-Israeli conflict, where unless the European Union took a clear-cut anti-Israeli position, the Muslim world would act, by force if necessary, to impose its views. And what has happened to Western ideas of fairness and support for freedom and democracy? Who cares? No one of consequence talks about that any more, and no one acts to stop the Western drift toward submitting to tyranny. So much so that Europeans have come to accept the Muslim thesis that the honor of the Prophet of Islam was more important than the lives of innocent people who were killed during the Muslim rampage as a result of the Cartoon Affair, or the material losses that were sustained by the boycotted countries.

If we look at all this, as it is customary today, from the vantage point of Human Rights, just like humans themselves, are native of places and of ideas which evolved in certain locations and under certain circumstances. So, humanity prides itself not only of its great thinkers, but also of the great homelands which gave birth to the idea of human rights. Chief among those are America and France, where their national revolutions, unfolding within 13 years of each other (1776 and 1789 respectively) and were nourished from the same sources, have become the world revolutions that came closest to implement that lofty idea. But Americans, while focusing on the affinities of their thoughts with their European roots, and believing that if they meant well, then the entire span of humanity would behave likewise, did not relent on their delusions, like most recently under the Obama Administration (2008-16) about the "significant common ground linking America and the Muslim world, which offered a real promise that working together ["engaging"] with other leading international players [specifically Muslims] to improve the human condition across the world in general, including the Muslim world, was possible and vital". Improving the human condition is what America's ideals have been all about, for "life, liberty and the pursuit of happiness" are not just hollow words; they embody the ideals that lay at the foundation of America's aspirations, not only for itself but for citizens around the world. Thus, they embraced the notion that human development has broad and highly relevant significance for humanity in general and for the functioning of harmonious international relations. Human development is a concept that embraces enhancing the quality of life for the whole world; it encompasses the key dimensions of economics, health, education, human and civil rights, democracy and freedom, all protected by an independent judiciary, and sustained by a high quality of life. But in practice, if America ever had any "common ground" with the Islamic world, it was based on economic and strategic interests (mainly petroleum and military positions during the Cold War, and mainly strategic common grounds presently, as its dependence on foreign oil has dramatically plummeted), never on shared values of democracy, freedom and human rights that radical Islam, and even less radical Westernized Muslim individuals have declared as alien and "hated" in and by their societies. And when the US tried at an exorbitant human and material price to enforce those ideas in Afghanistan and Iraq, it finally realized that its dismal failure to enforce and promote them reflected precisely the lack of such a common ground. Numerous have been the manifestations of this alienation between the Western world of Human Rights as described above, and the Muslim interpretation and application of its ideas, as amply sampled in the above text. On 9 and 10 November, 1998, the Office of the High Commissioner for Human Rights at the UN, under Mary Robinson, in cooperation with the Islamic Cooperation Conference (OIC), organized at the UN Office in Geneva a seminar, entitled: "Enriching the Universality of Human Rights, Islamic Perspectives on the Universal Declaration of Human Rights", to mark the 50th Anniversary of the Universal Declaration of Human Rights, ostensibly "to promote respect among peoples and a better understanding of the significance of cultural and religious backgrounds in the context of the Universal Declaration. As we explained above, twenty experts in Islamic Law and Human Rights were selected by the High Commissioner, in consultation with the OIC, though no final resolutions or conclusions were expected from that august gathering, due to its "academic character". Thus, all the High Commissioner could conclude was that "it had opened a channel of communication and indicated her intention of publishing the proceedings of the seminar", which was finally, done in a shortened version owing to "lack of resources".[125] The three themes that were discussed (namely preached by the Muslim participants), were the principle of non-discrimination, civil and political rights, and

---

[125] HR/IP/SEM/1999/1 (Part I), 15 March, 1999.

economic, social and economic rights in Islam. But, due to Robinson's effort to preserve the "scholarly objective" nature of the speeches, the discussion was limited only to the invited experts (Muslims). In her ignorance of Islam and her extreme desire to please within the rules of political correctness, she defied the totally contradictory statements of those experts and rendered a disservice to the cause of human rights by legitimizing the revolting Islamic version of "human rights" as a worthy topic of discussion on the international state. Did not she not hear, or understand, the repeated statements of Iranian officials, including at the UN, of their wish to wipe Israel from map? Did not she see the murderous horrors that the radicals of al-Qaida committed all across the world? Did not she identify the cruelty and oppression that many Islamic regimes were practicing against their own civilians while she was praising the greatness, tolerance and contributions to humanity? Bat Ye'or's numerous books on the enslaved Christians and Jews under Islam[126] . If she had persisted in her job until 2022 she would have had to resign in disgrace when she took cognizance of the new specific studies of Human rights in Islam[127].The other attempt of the Obama Administration at engagement with a Muslim power was done when it thought that an agreed deal with Iran, to limit and supervise its nuclearization program, would contain, or at least slow down its pace, has proven futile, unwittingly aided by President Trump's (2016-20) determination to scuttle that deal and better rely on harsh, and growingly harsher, economic sanctions. Both of them ignored or simply were ignorant of, the ideological foundations of the regime of the Ayatullahs which hates, despises and is committed to resist any Westernization ("Westoxication" in their parlance) or reform which would obviate or weaken their "Death

---

[126] *The Dhimmi, the Decline of Eastern Christianism under Islam, Eurabia, Islam and Dhimmitude* are only a few samples.
[127] Raphael Israeli's, *The Rebellion of the Dhimmis, Human Rights and Human development in Islam,* both published by Strategic Books, TX, in 2022.

to America (and Israel)" slogan which seemed to endure as the most solid base of their rule. Both strategies were a priori doomed to failure due to the Shi'ite doctrine of the Hidden Imam which governs that regime, and came to its most brutal expression during the eight years of President Ahmadinejad, who came to see and present it not only as an apocalyptic vision or traditional belief in the end of times when the Hidden Imam will appear and bring justice and plenty to all humanity (under whom, who would need human rights?), but as an imminent divine program of action to be implemented under our very eyes. As a former Mayor of Tehran, that president, who had no clerical pretentions himself, seemed to be in constant expectation of fulfilling that prophecy in his own days, as the "pangs of the Messiah" indicated to his delusioned mind, namely that the more pressing and worsening earthly conditions in the world, the nearer the realization of that day of relief and redemption for the Shi'ite world. According to that logic, bad or disastrous events are the surest signs of messianic days, hence the vanity of the logic behind the great powers' balance of power, which was at the base of MAD (Mutually Assured Destruction) which alone prevented a new world war, each power being deterred from attacking or threatening the other by reason of their mutual capacity to annihilate the other in case of a nuclear conflict. Therefore, under the spell of that theory, owning nuclear power or being threatened by it, far from deterring the Ayatullahs in Tehran, on the contrary augmented their creed in the imminence of apocalyptic days, which under that scheme would invalidate MAD and make it obsolete and unnecessary. He and his coreligionists are firm in their belief that it was precisely that threat of annihilation which augured the return if the Imam, i.e. that the worse was the best, the darkest was the most promising.

As far as Israel is concerned, she is becoming more than ever, despite her domestic upheaval in which the judicial elites that took over the supreme rule of the country since the 1990s, with the support of liberal left, now refuse, in the wake of the overwhelming victory of the popular-conservative Right in November 2022, to validate the rules of the democratic game respect for the majority in both the ballot and the Knesset. They have clearly opted for the "tyranny of the minority" over the much condemned by them of the feared "tyranny of the majority", which would have shifted the supreme power back again from the judicial elite to the political majority as it was practiced until the judicial revolution of Aharon Barak which was enforced by minority votes of an unaware political elite of its long term confrontational consequences. The issue is fateful for Israel, because decision must be finally determined on what component of the existing shaky construct of "democratic and Jewish state" should Israel orient itself: the democratic or Jewish. Naturally, the liberals stress the democratic, but they never confronted the dilemma of what they would do if the Arabs gain their demographic dominance and the Jewish state is gone which they are working hard to achieve. Nor have the Haredi partners of government resolved who is to defend their Halachic state if they were in charge of it. Its Jewish character would certainly gain priority over democracy, but only temporarily. Because there are no Haredi pilots who will fly in the air to repulse an Arab-Iranian attack, nor troops on the ground to defend Israel's cities and villages from any such combined onslaught against the Jewish date. Its defenders will be all studying Torah in the yeshivot, to prove the impotence of God to come to the rescue, the Third Destruction will be ushered in, demonstrating that the Jewish people may be smart, resourceful and ingenuous, but is not fit for self-governance.

Melanie Philips gave her sharp twist to Wokeism and governance in her review of Richard Landes' seminal volume on this vogue which was launched in America, like many other fashionable styles of conduct, and in the same vein converged with world globalism to become a universally emulated pattern of conduct, which did take long to land in our shores, dwelling on the Muhammad al-Dura hoax of May 2013 as the trigger for his thoughtful book, and querying: how has the West simply lost its mind over the issue of the Palestinian Arabs, and fell in for a series of abominable blood-libels against the Jews and Israel that no one has hitherto got the courage to confront and correct ? She wrote inter alia, in February, 2023:

> …Appallingly, the Israelis were described at the time as the new Nazis. But the malice that was unleashed was even worse… As Landes writes: "It was mostly about being freed from a sense of obligation to the Jews, a chance to take up again the Jew-baiting so long denied Europeans by a politically correct post-Holocaust sobriety." Landes quotes a poisonous comment made by a member of the House of Lords and reported in the Spectator: "Well, the Jews have been asking for it, and now, thank God, we can say what we think at last." During that time, I was told something horrifyingly similar to my face…This lethal western mindset among liberals and progressives goes beyond bigotry against Israel. It has also fuelled the west's failure to identify and deal with the jihadi war of conquest being waged against Western civilisation. ..Liberals, writes Landes, have enforced the primary law of submission[128]: do not offend Muslims. The inevitable cognitive and moral dissonance has produced a "politics of outrage" that has left a radically disoriented West defenseless before the jihadist attack…
>
> Western politicians maintained after 9/11 that Muslims around the world were outraged by the atrocity because Islam was a "religion of peace". They did so even though Muslims were celebrating across the world and

---

[128] *Soumission* was incidentally, the title of the French writer Michel Houellebecq, in January 2015 by Flammarion in Paris, became instantly a best-seller and was translated into several European languages.

some 90 per cent of them, according to various commentators, thought America "had it coming". When an Islamist named Ahmad al Aliwi Alissa murdered ten people in Boulder, Colorado in March 2021, many identified him on Twitter as a "white Christian supremacist". Ayaan Hirsi Ali[129], a Somali-born woman who fled Islam to become one of its most forceful accusers and lives under a *fatwa* commanding her murder, was denounced by feminists and disinvited by Brandeis University in Boston, in 2014 as an Islamophobe.

…This critical blindness is rooted in half a century of the West being blamed for its "original sins" of colonialism and imperialism. This cultural self-loathing has spawned the identity politics of race and gender. "Human rights" NGOs excoriating Israel and the US for racism and slavery have adopted the jihadi apocalyptic narrative that holds that the US and Israel are the Big and the Little Satan. This has led to what Landes terms: "The Alice in Wonderland mindset: when jihadis attack a democracy, blame the democracy". So while jihadi anti-semitism is sanitised as resistance against the oppressor, criticism of Islam or the Palestinians has been denounced as "hate speech".

As Landes writes, in this poisonous mix a new anti-semitism has taken hold in progressive circles around the world. It is a stupefying alchemy of inverted narratives, which Landes describes as a pre-emptive surrender to Islamist attack. The result, he writes, is that "when the worst Jew-haters in the planet act out their Jew-hatred in the most revolting fashion, supporting them has become the litmus test for radical credentials". And the most

---

[129] Repeatedly cited above for her linking wokeism with Islam.

tragic aspect of all is that so many progressive Jews have gone along with this madness. So how can we fight it? In the only way we know how: with facts, evidence and reason. But we should be in no doubt that we are not just fighting to establish the truth about Israel and push antisemitism back underneath its stone. We are fighting to rescue a Western world that has simply lost its collective.

The total war declared by Israel to eradicate the Hamas was triggered on October 7, 2023, in response to the latter's surprise outrage launched the same day at dawn, which occasioned the murder of 1,300 innocent Israelis in 22, border villages who were still in their beds or in their war shelters or assembled in a nightly music festival of youth in the open. The included entire families, elderly, youth , children, even babies . Those were the "fortunate" who lay dead, and when their mutilated corpses were discovered in their ruined and burned houses or in their incinerated cares, their relatives and the authorities became aware of their cruel and tragic fate. But the 200 of all ages, from the old to the babies, who were taken hostages and force-led into exile and captivity as hostages to Gaza have gone in the most enervating doubt, for now one is sure or whether they killed, they are alive, wounded or maimed, and those barbars who kidnapped them won't yield any details on their number, identity or any sign that may indicate their status of bring relief to their unknowing families, so obtuse to their captives and their parents have been their captors. This heartless and uncivilized act brought to its summum, openly backed by Muslims from the Iranian axis who celebrated by distribution of sweets and dances of popular joy among the Muslim populace in many of the 57 Muslim-majority countries and in the Muslim diasporas in the West, even in such "moderate and pro-American" Muslim countries such as Egypt, Jordan and Morocco, who have made peace with Israel, the peak of joviality and mass merry in their streets, not so much for the "heroic exploit" of their mass murderers as for the disaster , the pain and the humiliation (in their eyes) they caused the hated Jews, and for the forthcoming pleasure of watching the Zionists suffering and licking their wounds.

The sharp universal disapproval by the civilized world, even among moderate countries "friends of Islam and its allies", was a worthwhile trade-off   to exhibit Islamic unity of sentiment and action, in mass murder and vengeance, which provides a sterling example of commercialization of religion at its worst, for which lies are manufactured and repeated so profusely that their inventors and accusers become themselves their most vocal devotees. On 17 of October, the 11th day of the war, Islamic Jihad in Gazah blindly misfired a misguided rocket intended for some Israeli urban center which fell, like 450 others during this war into Gazan territory, which caused never acknowledged self-inflicted fatalities and damage. This time it exploded over one on this unfortunate city's hospitals causing hundreds of casualties. But instead of apologizing to their crowds, they found the opportunity too tempting to miss the pretext of the war and accuse Israel of the horror. Once again, the Muslim world was in effusion celebrating the occasion to blame the Jewish state of barbarity unanimously and to mount furious popular demonstrations against it, with some Western media and capitals, rushing to join the condemnation or to or to put Israel on a par in terms of cruelty and barbarity with the Hamas. Israel was the lone voice trying to claim innocence in view of its history of having never targeted a hospital, citing the many occasions when an air attack had been often scuttle on an Arab /Muslim target when it became evident of the presence of children, women, elderly or other innocent persons in the close proximity. Only after Israel provided technical and circumstantial evidence to the world of its innocence and of Islamic Jihad culpability, that was consequently confirmed by the Pentagon's own intelligence sources, did a few reasonable

Muslim sources begin to express doubt on their previous conviction, though no one dared to commit the blaspheme of exonerating Israel and return to blame to Islamic Jihad. Never can a Muslim do wrong and always the evil Jews are the eternal practitioners of evil. That is the supreme law of commercialization of Islam and they would let no fact to prove the contrary.

BIBLIOGRAPHY

Foundational Documents

The Holy Bible

The Holy Qur'an

Hamas Charter

Abingdon Dictionary of Living Religions, Nashville, 1981, p.802.

The entire text of Professor Baruch Modan, Director General of the
Ministry of Health of Israel was included in a dispatch by the Israeli
Ministry of Foreign Affairs to all Israeli missions worldwide., on
April 17, 1983.

A detailed survey of the press of Western countries for the coverage of
the Poison Affair in March-May 1983, see the relevant chapters of
R. Israeli, *Poison (Bibliography)*

Yearbook of the UN, NY, 1987, pp. 332-3

Document E/CN/4/1997/122, letter addressed by the Chair of the
Commission to the Ambassador of Israel.

Letter by Ambassador Miroslav Somol, to Ambassador Nabil Ramlawi,
the Observer of Palestine at the Human Rights Commission, 3
April, 1997. The Letter was circulated by Ramlawi upon reception
among the members of the Council.

Press Communique, No 1461, of the International Red Cross, 7 April,
1983, Geneva

Letter by Claude Voilat, the Press Attache for the Middle East of the

ICRC, addressed to P. GIniewski, 5 May, 1992

Written and Broadcast Media and Journals
Al-Ahram Weekly, October 1, 2001.
Al-Hayat Al-Jadida, Sept. 5, 2023
Al-sharq Al-Awsat
Al Watan, Saudi Arabia
City Journal
Dagbladet, Norway
Executive Intelligence Review
Foreign Affairs
The Guardian
Haaretz
Iran
Israeli TV
Ma'an, independent Palestinian news
Ma'ariv
MEMRI
Le Monde
Morbidity and Mortality, Weekly Reports(Atlanta)
Muslim World
PMW (Palestinian Media Watch
Rencontres des Chretiens et Juifs (Paris)
Reuters, Berlin
The Spectator(Australia)
The Voice of Israel Radio
The Wall Street Journal
Tribune de Geneve
Tribune de Lausanne
Yedioth Aharonot

Books
Bat Ye'or, *The Dhimmi,* Fairleigh Dickinson University Press, Madison,

1985, translated into several languages.

Bat Ye'or, *Europe, Globalization, and the Coming Universal Caliphate,* Fairleigh Dickinson University Press, Madison, 2011, p. 94

Bostom, Andrew, *The Legacy of Jihad,* Prometheus Books, Amherst, 2005, p. 31.

Dufourcq, .Charles, *La Vie Quotidienne and l'Europe Medievale sous Domination Arabe,* Hachette, Paris 1978, p. 20. Cited by Bostom, p. 40.

Fenton, Paul and David Littman, *Exile in the Maghreb: 10th to 20th Centuries,* Fairleigh Dickinson Univ Press, Madison, 2012. (also a French and Hebrew version).

Dostoievski, Fyodor, *The Brothers Karamazov (*In French translation), Editions MInerve, Paris, Traduction Nouvelle, p. 83.

Fernandez-Morera, Dario. *The myth of the Andalusian Paradise,* ISIS Books, Wylmington, 2015.

Green, D.F., *Arab Theologians on Jews and Israel: The Fourth Conference of the Academy of Islamic Research*, Editions de l'Avenir, Geneva, 1974.

Houellebecq, Michel, *Soumission,* January 2015 by Flammarion in Paris.

Israeli, Raphael, *Poison:Modern Manifestations of a Blood Libel,*Lexington, Lanham. 2002.

Israeli, Raphael, *Islamikaze: Manifestations of Islamic Martyrology*, Frank Cass, London. 2003.

Israeli, Raphael, *Back to Nowhere: Moroccan Jews in Dream and Reality,* Lampert Press, Germany, 2008.

Israeli, Raphael, *The Templars of Islam: Ra'id Salah and the Islamic Radicalism and Political Violence,*

Vallentine and Mitchell, 2008, London.

Israeli, Raphael, *Muslim Minorities in the Modern States,* Transaction, NJ, 2009.

Israeli, Raphael, *Itinerant Jihadis:Arab and Muslim War Volunteers,* Strategic Books, TX, 2011.

Israeli, Raphael, *The Blood Libel and its Derivatives*, Transaction, NJ, 2012.

Israeli, Raphael, *The Death Camps of Croatia: Visions and Revisions: 1941-5*, Transaction, NJ, 2013 .

Israeli, Raphael, *Hatred, Lies and Violence in the Islamic World*, Transaction, NJ, 2013 .

Israeli, Raphael, *Pisces out of Morocco: the Saga of the Clandestine Jewish Emigration*, Strategic Books, TX, 2016.

Israeli, Raphael, *Old Historians, New Historians, No Historians*, Wipf and Stock, Eugene, 2016).

Israeli, Raphael, *Retreating from the Mirage of Multi-Culturalism?*, Strategic Books, TX, 2018 .

Israeli, Raphael, *Suicidal Democracy (2019) ; Expedient Identity (2020)*, both by Strategic Books, TX.

Israeli, Raphael, *The Rebellion of the Dhimmis* Strategic Books, TX, in 2022.

Israeli, Raphael, *Human Rights and Human development in Islam*, Strategic Books, TX, 2022.

Israeli, Raphael, *The Vanity of Conversion Therapy:, The Delusion of Metastasizing Israeli Arabs*, Strategic Books, TX, 2022.

Israeli, Raphael, *Helene Cazes Ben Attar: The Saga of how Moroccan Jewry Shelter Jewish Refugees from the Nazis*, Strategic Books, TX, 2022.

Israeli, Raphael,: *Justice, for whom?*, Lambert Academic Publishing, Germany, 2022.

Israeli, Raphael, *Perception, Conviction, Action*, Strategic Books, TX, 2023.

Levtzion, Nehemia, *Conversion to Islam*, Holmes and Meier, London, 1979., pp. 1-23.

Sha'ban, M. *Islamic History (600-75)*, Cambridge, 1971, cited in M. Sh Sha'ban, M."Conversion to Early Islam", in N. Levtzion, op. cit., pp. 24- 29.

Schechtman, joseph, *Postwar Population Transfers in Europe 1945-1955*,

Oxford, 1946.

Stillman, Norman, *The Jews of Arab Lands, Jewish Publication Society,* 1979, Philadelphia, p. 159.

Yang, . C.K, *Religion in Chinese Society,* University of California, Berkeley, 1967.

Articles

Ali, Aayan Hirshi, "What Islamists and Wokeists Have in Common, *The Wall Street Journal,* September 10, 2020.

al-Amari, Tarad, "Interview with Sheikh Abd al-Aziz about September 11", *al Watan,* Saudi Arabia,, 22 November, 2001, cited by MEMRI, Terror in America, No 44 (Hebrew).

Baily, Clinton, "A Note on the Bedouin Image of *'adl* as Justice", *Muslim World,* Vol 66, No 2, 1966.

Bulliet, Richard, "Naw Bahar and the Survival of Iranian Buddhism", in *Iran, 14 (1976),* . Cited by Levtzion, p. 9.

Durie, "Mark After the Hamas Deluge", 15 October, 2023.Henley, John,"Inside Story," *The Guardian,* November 4, 2004.

Hirsch, Maurice, Adv., PMW, Nov 7, 2022.

Hirsch, Maurice, "When you lack any history, just invent one ", PMW, Sep 4, 2022.

Israeli, Raphael, "Islamization and Sinicization in Chinese Islam", in Levztion (ed) op cit, pp. 159-176.

Krekar, Sheikh, "Interview". *Dagbladet,* 13 March, 2006.

Lawrence, Bruce "Waqf", In Keith Crim, *Abingdon Dictionary of Living Religions,* Nashville, 1981, p. 802.

Leiken, Robert, "Europe's Angry Muslims ", *Foreign Affairs,* July/August 2005.

Littman, David, "l'Affaire des Poisons ", *Tribune de Geneve,* 20-21August 1983.

Maistrovoy, Alexander, "Revolution of Tanks'? Having Lost in Israel, Globalists Face a Dangerous Precedent: With the Stakes so High, will the Globalists turn to Violent Extremes?, *Times of Israel,* Blogs,

February 13, 2023.

Neher—Bernheim, Renee, "The Poison Affair" in *Rencontre Chretiens et Juifs*, Paris,, 2nd Semester, 1983, pp. 31-

Pidd, Helen, *Reuters* Berlin, *Mon 28 Feb 2011 10.39 GMT.*

Pipes, Daniel, "Fighting Militant Islam, Without Bias," *City Journal*, Autumn 2001. http://www.city-journal.org/htm/41/ fightingmilitant.html.

Zilberdik, Nan Jacques, PMW, Nov 9, 2022.

INDEX

Names, Places, Events and Terms